Exploring the Boundaries of Big Data

The Netherlands Scientific Council for Government Policy (WRR) is an independent think tank that provides the Dutch government and parliament with advice both on request and of its own accord, from a long-term perspective. The topics are cross-sectoral and cover societal issues with which the government may need to deal in the future.

THE NETHERLANDS SCIENTIFIC COUNCIL FOR GOVERNMENT POLICY

Exploring the Boundaries of Big Data

Bart van der Sloot, Dennis Broeders & Erik Schrijvers (eds.)

LONDON AND NEW YORK

First published in 2016 by Amsterdam University Press Ltd.

Published 2025 by Routledge
4 Park Square, Milton Park, Abingdon, Oxon OX14 4RN
605 Third Avenue, New York, NY 10158

Routledge is an imprint of the Taylor & Francis Group, an informa business

© WWR / Taylor & Francis Group 2016

Views and opinions expressed in this publication are those of the authors.

Cover design: cimon communicatie, The Hague

ISBN: 9789462983588 (pbk)
ISBN: 9781003695202 (ebk)
NUR   740

For Product Safety Concerns and Information please contact our EU representative:
GPSR@taylorandfrancis.com
Taylor & Francis Verlag GmbH, Kaufingerstraße 24, 80331 München, Germany

CONTENTS

PART III   LEGAL PERSPECTIVES ON BIG DATA

Paul De Hert & Hans Lammerant

PART IV   REGULATORY PERSPECTIVES ON BIG DATA

Bart van der Sloot

Colin J. Bennett & Robin M. Bayley

PREFACE

This study on the boundaries of Big Data brings together a number of leading academics to describe, analyse and theorize upon issues involved in Big Data from a wide variety of perspectives. As the exact nature and delineation of Big Data is still unclear, the authors explore the boundaries of Big Data rather than go to the core of this new phenomenon. They help us understand the relation of Big Data to areas such as cryptology, predictive policing, profiling, privacy, and regimes of data protection in the United States, Europe, the Netherlands and Germany, and outline some new challenges that lie ahead of us.

Big Data will have an enormous impact on our daily lives. Many businesses are applying Big Data analytics to find patterns and statistical correlations in order to optimize their services, target their customers, and personalize their content. Governments are applying new data technologies to predict, prevent, and detect crime, to develop profiles of potential terrorists, and to make better informed policy choices in the social and economic domains, the domain of security and justice, the healthcare sector, and the fields of mobility and infrastructure. What everyone appears to agree on is that Big Data may have a hugely positive effect on the world we live in, by promoting efficiency, justice, customer service, and security, but that it might also result in discrimination, privacy violations, and chilling effects.

This study, therefore, is aiming to build a framework that will help to promote and facilitate the beneficial uses of Big Data while preventing or sanctioning its negative effects. It serves as a background study for the advisory report *Big Data in a Free and Secure Society* (Big Data in een vrije en veilige samenleving), which the Netherlands Scientific Council for Government Policy (WRR) has been invited to produce by the Dutch Government. It has been edited by our staff members LLM. MPhil. Bart van der Sloot, prof. dr. Dennis Broeders (project coordinator), and dr. Erik Schrijvers, and brings together insights from international experts on a range of disciplines. The Council is grateful to the authors for their contributions.

Prof. dr. J. A. Knottnerus   Dr. F. W. A. Brom
Chairman WRR   Secretary WRR

1   INTRODUCTION: EXPLORING THE BOUNDARIES OF BIG DATA

Bart van der Sloot, Dennis Broeders & Erik Schrijvers

This book deals with issues involved in Big Data from a technological, economic, empirical, legal, and regulatory perspective. Big Data is a buzzword used frequently in both the private and the public sector, the press, and online media. Large amounts of money are being invested to make companies Big Data-proof, and governmental institutions are eager to experiment with Big Data applications in the fields of crime prevention, intelligence, and fraud, to name but a few areas. Still, an exact and uniform definition of Big Data is hard to come by. Most definitions roughly regard three states of processing: data collection, as Big Data concerns collecting large amounts of data, from varied and often unstructured sources; data analyses, as Big Data revolves around the speed of the analyses and the use of certain instruments such as algorithms, machine learning, and statistic correlations; and use of data, as the results are often predictive in nature and are formulated at a general or group level.

Though the exact nature and delineation of Big Data is still unclear, it seems likely that Big Data will have an enormous impact on our daily lives. Many businesses are applying Big Data analytics to find patterns and statistical correlations in order to optimize their services, to target their customers, and to personalize their content. Governments are applying new data technologies to predict and prevent crime, to develop profiles of potential terrorists, and to make better informed policy choices in the social and economic domains, the legal and the healthcare sectors, and the fields of mobility and infrastructure. What everyone appears to agree on is that Big Data may have a huge positive effect on the world we live in, by promoting efficiency, justice, customer service, and security, but that it might also result in discrimination, privacy violations, and chilling effects. The hope is that an adequate framework will ensure that the beneficial uses of Big Data are promoted and facilitated, while the negative effects are prevented or sanctioned. This book provides building blocks for developing such a framework.

1.1   BACKGROUND OF THIS BOOK

On behalf of the Dutch government, the Minister for Security and Justice has asked the Netherlands Scientific Council for Government Policy (WRR) to write a report on the use of Big Data, especially in relation to national security, including its effect on the right to privacy. The Netherlands Scientific Council for Government Policy is an independent advisory body with the role of informing and advising the government and parliament on issues of significant importance for society. The opinions of the WRR are cross-sectoral, cross-departmental, and multi-disciplinary. They concern the course of government policy in the longer term.

In his request, the Minister formulated four main questions. The first main question was whether a stronger distinction should be made between access to and use of information in Big Data processes, a question that was partly inspired by the transnational nature of many data processing activities. In particular, the Minister asked whether the mere collection and storage of personal data, without the data being analysed or used, should be limited by data protection legislation, pointing to the fact that it cannot be ruled out in Big Data processes that non-identifying data may become personal data at a later stage. In connection with this, the question was how big the role of the state should be, in the Big Data era, in ensuring that the use of Big Data for the promotion of security meets the standards of purpose limitation and data minimization, amongst other things. The Minister also wanted to know whether these principles can be maintained, and if so how.

The second key question concerned the use of Big Data processes and of techniques such as profiling and data mining. In particular, the Minister wished to be informed about how these techniques can be used in a transparent manner and how adequate checks and balances can be formulated to allow these techniques to be used safely and proportionately.

Thirdly, the Minister referred to the emergence of quantum computing and asked whether encryption and anonymity can still be guaranteed in the future. Finally, the Minister wanted to know how the autonomy of citizens can be ensured in Big Data processes. This relates to the question of whether a focus on informed consent is still tenable, what possibilities citizens have for effective control over their data, what responsibility citizens have to contribute to the quality of data in databases, and more in general, how maintaining quality of information can be guaranteed.

Because Big Data processes are relatively new and could be studied from many different perspectives and scientific disciplines, the WRR decided, in preparation of its advice to the government, to invite several scholars to write a contribution to this book. These studies and insights gained from them were used by the WRR as background materials in writing its advice to the government. Because the book serves as preparatory work for the WRR's advice to the government, the intention of this study is to present a wide range of different perspectives on, approaches to, and applications of Big Data.

Rather than going to the core of Big Data, it explores the boundaries of Big Data. What should be called Big Data in a technical sense, and how should it be distinguished from other techniques and applications? How are Big Data processes used in practice, by whom, and to what purposes? What positive and negative effects may follow from Big Data analytics? What legal principles apply to Big Data techniques, and on which points does the current regulatory framework need an overhaul? These are but a few of the questions this book undertakes to answer. The fact that the book explores the boundaries of Big Data is also necessitated by the fact that it is still largely unclear what Big Data precisely is. It is a notion that is still in transition, and its nature and potential implications are still evolving. Consequently, it is still too early to define Big Data with great precision but an opportune moment to outline what new questions and challenges follow from this phenomenon.

1.2   CONTENTS OF THIS BOOK

This book is divided into five parts, each part engaging with a different perspective on Big Data: the technical, empirical, legal, regulatory, and international perspective. It is important to stress that the chapters contained in this volume were mostly written in early 2015, when the exact content of the General Data Protection Regulation was still under discussion, and the Schrems case had not been delivered by the European Court of Justice. The General Data Protection Regulation will replace the current European data protection framework, the Data Protection Directive from 1995. Leaving the core principles mostly intact, the Regulation invests heavily in the compliance and enforcement of those rules, with broader powers for DPAs, wider obligations for data controllers, and higher penalties violators. The (non-)enforcement of the data protection principles is currently considered the biggest problem of data protection instruments. Moreover, a Regulation, as opposed to a Directive, has direct effect at EU level, smoothing out the differences that currently exist between different EU-countries in their interpretation and application of the data protection principles in their respective countries.

The Schrems case was about the protection of personal data of European citizens. The Data Protection Directive holds that personal data may only be transferred to a third country if that country ensures an adequate level of protection. The European Commission had issued a decision, in which it held that the United States had an adequate level of protection. In the Schrems case, however, the European Court of Justice invalidated this decision. Although there are now transatlantic negotiations going on to design an ameliorated agreement that provides more protection to European citizens, it is still unsure at the moment of finalizing this introduction what rules this agreement will contain and whether they will hold before the European Court of Justice. Some of the contributions anticipate these two developments, while others have tried to take a step back and signal general trends and focus on the underlying principles of the regulatory framework.

Part I of this book centres on the technological perspective on Big Data and contains chapter 2, entitled 'Sustainable Harvesting of the Big Data Potential', by Sander Klous and chapter 3, named 'Cryptology and Privacy in the Context of Big Data', by Seda Gürses and Bart Preneel. Part II engages with empirical perspectives on Big Data. It contains Gemma Galdon Clavell's chapter entitled 'Policing, Big Data and the Commodification of Security' and Rosamunde van Brakel's chapter 'Pre-emptive Big Data Surveillance and its (Dis)Empowering Consequences: the Case of Predictive Policing'. Part III investigates specific legal doctrines, as opposed to the general regulatory framework (whether legal or not) analysed in part IV. Chapter 6, entitled 'Predictive Profiling and its Legal Limits: Effectiveness Gone Forever?', is written by Paul De Hert and Hans Lammerant and is the only chapter in this section. Part IV contains regulatory perspectives on Big Data, asking how this new phenomenon should be regulated in the future. It contains two chapters, namely chapter 7 entitled 'The Individual in the Big Data Era: Moving towards an Agent-Based Privacy Paradigm' by Bart van der Sloot and 'Privacy Protection in the Era of 'Big Data': Regulatory Challenges and Social Assessments', chapter 8, written by Colin Bennet and Robin Bayley. Finally, for Part V, the WRR invited two contributions providing the reader with international and comparative research on Big Data. Because Big Data processes are almost by definition transnational, the lessons learned in other jurisdictions may have an important value for the European and Dutch regulator. The contributors to this section are Joris van Hoboken, 'From Collection to Use in Privacy Regulation? A Forward-Looking Comparison of European and US Frameworks for Personal Data Processing', and Alexander Roßnagel and Philipp Richter, 'Big Data and Informational Self-Determination. Regulative Approaches in Germany: the Case of Police and Intelligence Agencies'.

From the chapter by Sander Klous, we may conclude that Big Data is hard to define. Klous first provides the standard definition of Big Data, using the three Vs of Volume, Variety, and Velocity, with Volume referring to the vast amounts of data that are being generated, Variety referring to the different types of data and data sources, and Velocity referring to both the increasing rate of data collection and the increasing demand to get real-time insights and responses. Klous adds one more technical 'V', namely Veracity. Veracity refers to the correctness and accuracy of information. Most importantly, however, Klous argues, these four Vs only symbolize the technical side of Big Data, while one of the most distinguishing features of Big Data compared to other data-related subjects is that it is a topic primarily driven by business, not by technology. Hence, he argues that the most interesting V is a fifth one, namely Value. Moreover, there are several subtleties that need to be addressed to get a better understanding of what Big Data is supposed to mean. First of all, the word 'big' in Big Data can be slightly misleading because these processes are often simply about the smart combination of limited amounts of data for personalization. Second, there are several developments closely related to Big Data, such as cloud computing and the Internet of Things, that act as enablers.

Sometimes these developments are confused with Big Data: cloud computing, for example, aims at transforming the IT architecture, whereas Big Data aims at transforming the decision-making process. Third and finally, Big Data plays an essential role in recent developments that may not immediately spring to mind when considering Big Data, such as the renewed interest in 'technological singularity', i.e. the moment in time when intelligent systems will exceed human intellectual capacity, or the block chain, the mechanism behind bitcoins, allowing trusted transactions without a third party.

Seda Gürses and Bart Preneel signal a number of challenges that Big Data poses to cryptology and privacy. First, services are organized to do computations on the server side, meaning that all data generated in using the services flows to the service providers. This could lead to an erosion of confidentiality. Furthermore, providers often require user authentication as a prerequisite to service use, and user tracking is central to their business models. In addition, the number of entities with access to user data is increasing while transparency is decreasing, and service providers increasingly limit users' ability to view or control what services are actually doing on their devices or their servers. Because data analytics is still a nascent field, finally, its application to daily matters in order to optimize organizational interests amplifies concerns about discrimination, unfair treatment, social sorting, and human experimentation. In relation to these challenges, they suggest that cryptographic techniques can be helpful in protecting data from unintended use and unauthorized access, that they can help to increase the accountability of cloud services and data analytics algorithms, and that applying privacy enhancing technologies is minimum but not sufficient requirement for protecting privacy.

Gemma Galdon Clavell signals several fundamental trends, the most important one being the hybridization of domains by blurring the lines between defence policy, crime prevention, and intelligence, especially in urban environments. Equally important is the move towards prevention, in which the idea of anticipatory action is embraced. While focusing on maintaining order, looking after the physical environment, and caring about some people's 'quality of life' spells care and proximity and can be seen as an attempt to build more democratic and representative police forces, this same rhetoric is underpinning harsh 'zero-tolerance' and 'three-strikes' sentencing approaches. Then there is informationalization: the trend to focus more and more on gathering and processing data. Similarly, reference can be made to the increased interconnectivity between offline and online sources, ensuring that sources can be combined to enhance investigation results. For instance, fingerprints obtained at a crime scene may lead to an official name and date of birth; this name can be linked to numerous additional records, such as credit card utilization, telecommunications, travelling routines, or online social network activities. As a final example of an important trend currently taking place, reference can be made to privatization. According to Galdon Clavell, the global recession intensified pressures on budgets, increasing the need for security agencies to 'do more with less'. The shift to private-supported security often comes with the development of new consumption trends and social phenomena: new residential and shopping areas, or entertainment complexes, for example, which provide the illusion of being public spaces while being subject to private regulations and private security.

Rosamunde van Brakel has studied the use of Big Data in relation to predictive policing. She signals both potentially disempowering and empowering effects that the use of Big Data may have on citizens. With regard to the disempowering effects, she suggests that it is possible that in the future, it will no longer be a human who makes the assessments and decisions, but a computer, or rather the technology, which has serious consequences for questions of accountability.

Moreover, these types of algorithms and computer programs are often not transparent, which may have a disempowering effect on the position of citizens. The use of algorithms may also lead to algorithmic discrimination if the algorithms or the data on which they are based are biased. Furthermore, there is also the danger of both false positives and false negatives, which may lead to stigmatization and may have serious consequences for citizens' well-being and life chances.

The cumulative surveillance effect signals that predictive policing and Big Data may have a cumulative disadvantage effect, and groups such as Amish, Roma, and Luddites may be socially excluded. Van Brakel concludes by suggesting that Big Data may also have an empowering effect on citizens, but that Big Data is rarely applied in such a way at present. Still, Big Data could potentially be used to give more and more detailed information to citizens, about crime rates, for example, so they are in a better position to protect themselves against crime, or to use profiling to provide more protection to the weak.

Paul De Hert and Hans Lammerant investigate the use of profiling in relation to Big Data. They have analysed the standard literature on Knowledge Discovery in Databases, pattern discovery, group profiling, and predictive profiling. They argue that three groups of people may be affected by the use of profiling: the people whose data are used to create the profile, the people to whom the profiles refer, and the people who are subjected to decision-making based on the profile.

They also see three risks following from the use of profiling. Firstly, there is a heightened risk of more intrusive privacy interferences due to heightened surveillance. Secondly, there is the risk associated with social sorting – or sorting people into categories assigning worth or risk – and stereotyping. Thirdly, there are the risks related to opaque decision-making, which plays at two distinct levels: the application of a profile and the decision based on its results. They suggest that there are three general guarantees against the dangers of profiling that can be distilled from the current legal framework. A first safeguard can be found in the legality principle, which substantiates the idea of the rule of law and the need to limit state powers by linking them to competences and purposes. A second safeguard is the proportionality principle, which provides that decisions may not negatively affect people disproportionally in relation to the purpose of the decision and that supervisory and investigative competences may only be used if needed. A third category of safeguards concerns procedural safeguards given to the individual involved in state procedures, obliging the administration to establish and review all the relevant factual and legal elements of a case with due care. The authors conclude, however, that, although these are valuable safeguards, the legal regime needs an overhaul to adequately protect citizens' interests in the age of Big Data.

Bart van der Sloot suggests that privacy and data protection regulation did originally not focus on individual rights and individual interests, or only to a limited extent. The current regime, however, almost exclusively focuses on individuals, their rights, and their interests. He argues that this focus is untenable in the age of Big Data because Big Data processes do not specifically concern individuals but rather large groups of unidentified subjects. The individual interest in these types of processes is often difficult to demonstrate, and they rather they affect group or societal interests.

Likewise, it is increasingly difficult for individuals to invoke their subjective rights because they are often unaware of their personal data being gathered: data processing is so widespread in the Big Data era that it will be undoable for an individual to keep track of every data processing activity that includes (or might include) his or her data, to assess whether the data controller abides by the legal standards applicable, and if not, to file a legal complaint. And if an individual does go to court to defend his or her rights, he or she has to demonstrate a personal interest, i.e., personal harm, which is a particularly problematic notion in Big Data processes: what concrete harm, for example, has the NSA data gathering done to an ordinary American or European citizen? This also shows the fundamental tension between the traditional legal and philosophical discourse and the new technological reality; whereas the traditional discourse focuses on individual rights and individual interests, data processing often affects a structural and societal interest and, in many ways, transcends the individual. This is why Van der Sloot suggests complementing the current regulatory framework, focusing on legal principles, black letter law, and individual rights, with a model that focuses on the agent of the privacy violations, either a state, a company, or an individual.

The core of the framework's attention, then, should not be on the potential harm a particular act may do to a specific individual, but the on the question whether power is used in a good and adequate manner. That means that there must be not only safeguards against abuse of power, but also positive obligations to use power for the good of all.

Colin Bennett and Robin Bayley also signal that many of the current Big Data practices affect not only individuals, but also a set of more general interests. They discuss three types of assessments that may help to ameliorate the current privacy paradigm. First, there are the Privacy Impact Assessments (PIAs) that are proposed in the upcoming General Data Protection Regulation. PIAs can be used to assess the impact a certain project or technique might have on the privacy of individuals before such a programme or technique is applied in practice. Furthermore, the concept of 'Surveillance Impact Assessments' (SIAs) has been introduced to respond to the critique that PIAs are too narrowly focused on individual privacy. A fairly broad definition of surveillance is adopted to include the systematic capture of personal data beyond that collected through visual means. Four nested concentric circles have been proposed to make up an SIA: in the innermost circle is the conventional PIA, focusing on individual privacy. The second layer adds other impacts on an individual's relationships, positions, and freedoms, with the third layer adding the impact on groups and categories. The fourth and outermost ring of the circle adds the broader impacts on society and the political system. The model is intended to be cumulative. Finally, Bennett and Bayley analyse Ethical Impact Assessments (EIAs). Unlike PIAs and SIAs, these assessments are explicitly motivated by the question how Big Data processes should be analysed ethically. Four integrated steps have been conceived: a Unified Ethical Frame, an Interrogation Framework, an Enforcement Discussion, and Industry Interrogation Models, with only drafts of the first two steps being currently available for comment. The idea is that the implementation of such EIAs will begin with an analysis of the larger ethical considerations and progressively drill down to more practical guidance for industry.

Joris van Hoboken has compared EU and US regulation, paying specific attention to the question whether the current focus on regulating the collection of personal data is still tenable in the Big Data era or whether it should be replaced by a focus on the use of data. He signals that the classic self-determination rationale for information privacy regulation entails that the collection of personal data enables the exercise of power and may have chilling effects on individual freedom and behaviour, effects that should be assessed not only in terms of their impact on spe-cific individuals, but also in view of the values of pluralism and democratic self-governance.

According to Van Hoboken, this rationale is widely accepted in European data pri-vacy jurisprudence and affirmed in fundamental rights case law. The data protec-tion principles as engrained in the Data Protection Directive are connected to this rationale and place many restrictions on the gathering of personal data, the most important one being the data minimization principle, which entails that data may only be gathered, stored, and used for data processing activities if this is necessary for achieving the goal of the data processing activity. In the US, the focus lies on the notion of notice and choice, which limits the gathering and use of data to the goal originally communicated to the individuals consenting to the collection of their data. American law also provides a number of rules regarding the use of data, which Europe mostly lacks. These differences notwithstanding, the article con-cludes that there are significant hurdles to overcome to refocus data privacy law towards use-based regulation on both sides of the Atlantic. In Europe, the existing fundamental rights framework is one of these hurdles as well as the omnibus approach to data privacy regulation.

In the US, the ideological attachment to notice and choice, a weak form of consent, as well as the third party doctrine, stand in the way of the radical reorientation use-based regulation advocates are proposing. In addition, existing experiences with use-based regulation in the US context can hardly be described as a resound-ing success.

Alexander Roßnagel and Philipp Richter, finally, have examined the German notion of 'Informational Self-Determination'. The right to Informational Self-Determination was concretized by the German Federal Constitutional Court in 1983 from the basic liberties in Art. 2 I and 1 I GG as adequate protection against the risks of modern data processing. According to this right, data subjects themselves may generally decide about the extent of disclosure and processing of their per-sonal information. Along with Freedom of Information and Secrecy of Telecom-munications, Informational Self-determination is the central basic right of the information society. Informational Self-Determination covers the protection of the individual as well as the objective protection of a democratic society.

On the one hand, it enables freedom of decisions, including the possibility to actually act upon these decisions, while, on the other, it makes possible the self-determined development of the individual. Informational Self-Determination is not only an individual right of the data subject, however. It is also the foundation of a free and democratic society. Roßnagel and Richter argue that the classic princi-ples as entailed in the Data Protection Directive, among other things, follow from the principle of Informational Self-Determination, such the required legitimate ground for processing, purpose limitation, data minimization, transparency, rules regarding profiling, etc.

They signal that each of these principles are put under pressure by Big Data and mass surveillance developments. They specify three risks to this basic right, namely individualized surveillance, pattern recognition, and behaviour prediction. With regard to the first, they argue that the new basic rights challenge is that recent principles for the protection of Informational Self-Determination and Secrecy of Telecommunications, such as purpose binding, necessity, and data reduction lose their effect. With regard to the second, they observe that Informational Self-Determination in its recent shape will not suffice as protection against this normative effect of Big Data. Recognition of suspect behaviour patterns can be conducted using anonymous data, to which data protection law does not apply. With regard to the third, they argue that if police and intelligence agencies used Big Data Analytics to predict future individual behaviour, this would raise fundamental rule of law issues, as when investigation is initiated, for example, prior to reasonable suspicion, which would aggravate the focus on preventive security. This may put fundamental principles such as individual guilt, the presumption of innocence, and reasonable suspicion under threat.

1.3   CONCLUSIONS OF THIS BOOK

As we have observed above, this book serves as preparatory work for the Netherlands Scientific Council for Government Policy's advice to the Dutch government, which has asked the Council to address four specific questions regarding Big Data, security, and privacy. This book should provide the Council with the building blocks for its advice and for developing a regulatory approach to Big Data.

Four general points
First of all, the reality of Big Data is constantly evolving, which makes it difficult to define, to delineate, and to approach it from a regulatory point of view. In addition, Big Data is a node, and many different aspects play an important role in studying this phenomenon: not only technical, but also organizational, societal, and legal aspects come into play. From a technological point of view, as pointed out by Klous, technological developments and new applications are intertwined and sometimes confused with Big Data, such as the Internet of Things, cloud computing, profiling, the use of algorithms, machine learning, etc. From a societal perspective, as Galdon Clavell has observed, developments such as securitization, commodification, informationalization, privatization, and an increased focus on prevention are taking place. The legal chapters show that many scholars and regulators are aware of the new threats to the underlying foundations of the current

legal regime and the need for new regulations, such as those provided by the General Data Protection Regulation of the European Union. Consequently, Big Data is not an isolated phenomenon, but in a sense is the umbrella term for all these different developments that are taking place at different levels.

Second, to the question what Big Data really is, no exact answer has been found. Rather, this book has explored the boundaries of this new phenomenon; it has mapped the outskirts of a new-found island, but its inland areas have remained largely unexplored. What has become clear is that it is difficult, perhaps even impossible, to point to one or a few criteria that are the intrinsic elements of this phenomenon. As Klous has pointed out, the relevance of each of the three classic Vs can be disputed, and he suggests that two other Vs should be added. Other authors embrace a host of definitions, thus showing that it is still too early to map out the new territory with any accuracy. Still, all authors feel that it is important to address this new trend, as all believe that it will bring fundamental changes to their field of expertise.

Third, the government is rightly interested in Big Data, for two reasons: Big Data's potentially positive effects, but also its potentially negative effects. The positive effects are pointed out by Klous, who has hinted at Big Data's economic potential and its use in the private sector. De Hert and Lammerant and Van Brakel also refer to the use of Big Data techniques for predictive profiling purposes by the police. This might not only have a beneficial effect on the distribution of resources and the effectiveness of policing activities, but Big Data may also have an empowering effect on citizens, as Van Brakel suggests. Many authors, however, also emphasize the potentially negative effects of Big Data. Roßnagel and Richter point out that almost every classic data protection principle is put under pressure in Big Data processes. The same has been observed with regard to the Fair Information Practices (FIPs) by Bennett and Bayley and with respect to the fundamental right to privacy by Van der Sloot. De Hert and Lammerant and Van Brakel also signal potential problems regarding discrimination and stigmatization, especially when Big Data is used in relation to predictive policing and group profiling. Authors have also pointed to the Kronos effect, the Matthew effect, and other potentially negative effects. In conclusion, Big Data might have added value when used correctly and appropriately, but it might also have negative effects when applied inadequately. New policies and regulations, therefore, may help to guide the use of Big Data in the right direction.

Fourth, most authors signal a duality with respect to the current regulatory framework in the age of Big Data. On the one hand, they feel that the core principles of privacy law, data protection legislation, discrimination law, and the human rights framework are valuable and should be maintained in the Big Data era. On the other, these principles are often fundamentally at odds with the core of Big Data processes. It is suggested, consequently, that the current principles and frameworks should not only be maintained, but that new laws and regulations should also be introduced to tackle the new challenges posed by Big Data, in order to protect the fundamental values of the democratic rule of law.

Building blocks for answering the four questions of the government

The first main question from the Minister to the Netherlands Scientific Council for Government Policy was whether a stronger distinction should be made between access to and use of information in Big Data processes. Joris van Hoboken has analysed the current regulatory framework in both the EU and the US and their underlying foundations. It appears that both EU and US law entail principles that limit the collection and storage of personal data and contain rules on the use of personal data for specific purposes, even though the EU is more prone to regulating the collection of data and the US has several additional rules limiting the use of personal data compared to the EU. Van Hoboken sees the limitations on the gathering of personal data as intrinsically intertwined with the underlying fundamentals of data protection principles, with the notion of informational self-determination in the EU and with the idea of notion and choice, linked to the value of individual autonomy, in the US. It would appear to be unrealistic, therefore, to abandon regulating the gathering of personal data; rather, European law could supplement the current rules on gathering personal data with more and stricter rules on the use of personal data, inspiration for which might be found across the ocean.

The second key question concerned the use of Big Data processes and of techniques such as profiling and data mining. In particular, the Minister wished to ascertain how these techniques can be used in a transparent manner and how adequate checks and balances can be formulated to allow these techniques to be used safely and carefully. The studies by De Hert and Lammerant and Van Brakel show that this will be one of the key challenges for the next decade. Profiling has been used for a long time but will gain new momentum with the rise of Big Data. Not only the risks of discrimination and stigmatization are pointed out, but also potentially Kafkaesque or 'computer-says-no' situations. The fear is that computer programs and algorithms will increasingly lead their own lives and replace human-led decision-making processes. Both contributions suggest that transparency is key here, but that legal obligations curtailing the use of profiling should also be developed. Although such principles are currently already in place in anti-discrimination law, data protection law, human rights law, administrative law, and penal law, De Hert and Lammerant suggest that, in order to properly protect citizens' interests in the Big Data era, they need an overhaul.

Thirdly, the Minister referred to the emergence of quantum computing and asked whether encryption and anonymity can still be guaranteed in the future. Especially Gürses and Preneel have dealt with this point. They suggest that, for the past two decades, researchers have been working on novel cryptographic algorithms that would resist quantum computers. The focus has been on public-key algorithms, but it cannot be excluded that novel quantum algorithms will be discovered that reduce the strength of symmetric cryptographic algorithms beyond the quantum square root attacks known today. For public-key cryptography (both encryption and digital signatures), approaches are being studied that are typically faster than the current schemes, but most of them have much larger keys. For some of them, evaluating the concrete security level is challenging, and it cannot be excluded that novel quantum algorithms will be discovered that may weaken their security. It can be expected that it will take three to five years before these schemes will start appearing in cryptographic standards, and that it will take another two to four years before efficient implementations are widely available. This is a concern for encryption schemes because even in 2016 there is information that should be protected for ten years; this would mean that those schemes should be used today. This is less of an issue for digital signatures, and one could re-sign all documents every three to five years with improved algorithms with larger keys.

Finally, the Minister wanted to know how the autonomy of citizens can be ensured in Big Data processes. This relates to the question whether a focus on informed consent is still tenable, what possibilities citizens have for effective control over their data, what responsibility citizens have to contribute to the quality of the data in databases, and, more in general, how maintaining quality of information can be guaranteed. Both Van der Sloot and Bennett and Bayley have suggested that the current regulatory framework primarily focuses on individuals, their rights, and their interests. The protection of the individual, they feel, is important and should be maintained. Still, it should not be the sole approach in the Big Data era.

First, individuals are often incapable of protecting their own interests through individual rights because they are often unaware of their personal data being gathered and because it will be impossible for them to keep track of every data processing which includes (or might include) their data, to assess whether the data controller abides by the legal standards applicable, and if not, to file a legal complaint. Consequently, individual rights should be supplemented with more general forms of legal protection, such as more and stricter obligations and duties of care for controllers.

Second, the interests involved in Big Data processes often transcend individuals and their interests and affect group and societal interests. Both Van der Sloot and Bennett and Bayley have suggested to focus not only on legal rules but also on ethical evaluations and, hence, to consider using Ethical Impact Assessments in addition to Privacy Impact Assessments.

PART I

TECHNOLOGICAL PERSPECTIVES ON BIG DATA

2   SUSTAINABLE HARVESTING OF THE BIG DATA POTENTIAL

Sander Klous

Big Data is not only hip. It's also happening. We can see radical changes all around us: new business models based on information are emerging in sectors (Libert et al. 2014) such as the travel industry, the music industry and retail sales. These new models are fuelled by a number of technological innovations and strong customer demand. This article examines both of these aspects of the Big Data revolution, elaborating on the technology and showing how Big Data is driven by our desire for more safety, comfort, health or value in other areas.

2.1   THE INEVITABLE RISE OF BIG DATA

New technology is now part of our lives in a way that we couldn't have dreamed of 20 years ago. Technology related to data, data processing, information and communication improves our society in many ways. A new information society is emerging: a world in which everything is measurable and in which people, and almost every device you can think of, is connected 24/7 through the internet (Mayer-Schönberger and Cukier 2013). This network of connections and sensors provides a phenomenal amount of data and offers fascinating new possibilities which, together, are often called Big Data.

For companies and public organizations, Big Data goes beyond launching new products or services: it's about how to be relevant in a totally different world. In macroeconomic terms, there is reason for great optimism. We are in the middle of a classic economic phenomenon: Schumpeter's 'creative destruction' (Schumpeter 1934), meaning that we can only achieve innovation once old models have broken down. This is what is happening in almost all sectors. The music industry was one of the first to be disrupted by iTunes and more recently by Spotify. In recent years we've seen other industries follow suit. Booking.com and AirBnB brought radical changes to the travel industry. Uber is similarly acting as a catalyst for change in the taxi industry. All of these examples show that new companies bring change to markets by adopting new approaches to data (Klous and Wielaard 2014). Take Uber for instance. In essence, this company is *not* in the taxi business. It's in the business of selling customer data to a network of taxi drivers and vice versa, optimizing the taxi network by introducing greater data intelligence. The customer is in fact the product. Accurate predictions about the future in times of large transformations are difficult, but it is our firm belief that every industry is partly based on information and will sooner or later be impacted in comparable ways. Big Data is a catalyst for this trend.

The term Big Data has grown very popular in recent years. It is often described in terms of the 5 V's: Volume, Variety, Velocity, Veracity (NIST calls this Variability) and Value (Big Data Public Working Group 2015).

Volume refers to the vast amount of data being generated. Oceans of data are growing rapidly now that the 'Internet of things' is tying together billions of devices – TVs, refrigerators, security devices, thermostats, smoke detectors – all of which produce and share data. Many data sets have simply become too large to store, process and analyse with traditional database technology. New paradigms such as MapReduce, NoSQL databases, stream and in-memory processing have been introduced to perform optimally on distributed systems (discussed in more detail in section 2.2). These horizontally scalable solutions are able to process more data by adding more commodity components. Economically, this is a much better solution than super computer-type (i.e. shared memory) solutions. But even with these developments, Moore's law (Moore 1965) tells us that while CPU capacity is doubling every 18 months, storage capacity is doubling only every 14 months. As a result, data is becoming exponentially incomputable (De Laat 2014). The only options to meet this challenge are to become smarter about what data to analyse, or to create smarter algorithms.

Variety refers to the different types of data. Big Data is addressing challenges beyond data analysis with clear structures, such as financial figures. All of our chatter on social media, streaming music and videos, our emails and so on have no clear pre-determined structure (often inaccurately referred to as unstructured data). Big Data tools, implementing the aforementioned paradigms, are largely agnostic on specific structures (Dean and Ghemawat 2004), allowing collection and analysis of different types of data such as messages, social media conversations, photos, sensor data, video or voice recordings, etc. Combining insights from these types of data with classical data analysis can result in a more profound understanding of the behaviour of (groups of) people, systems, diseases, processes, etc.

Velocity refers to both the increasing rate of data collection and the increasing demand for real-time insights and responses. These systems come with their own challenges. On the collection side, decisions are made on the spot about what data is kept and what data is thrown away. Wrong selections are irreversible. Systemic errors are harder to detect when only a biased sample of the data is available for further analysis (Klein and Lehner 2009). On the decision side, several examples exist where data analysis was taken out of context, or was simply wrong, and subsequent real-time decisions resulted in serious instabilities in an ecosystem. The most famous example is probably the 6 May 2010 flash crash on Wall Street (Easley et al. 2011) when the Dow Jones index lost 10 percent of its value within minutes, only to recover most of its value shortly thereafter. The crash was attributed to faulty automatic trading algorithms, making real-time decisions without human intervention.

Veracity refers to the correctness and accuracy of information. In the era of Big Data, perceptions here are changing. In the past decade, master data management, data quality and data governance were at the heart of most large organizations' endeavours to get insight into their data (Loshin 2010). Although the quality of data remains an important issue, the pervasiveness of data makes it impossible to manage and control the quality of all sources. This is often already true within larger organizations, but becomes especially relevant when the data of other organizations is included in an analysis. Still, we need to know how reliable datasets are. This can often be achieved by processing an increasing amount of data, following the mantra 'quantity over quality' (Halevy et al. 2009), either by increasing the sample size to reduce statistical errors or by adding independent sources to reduce systemic errors. Although this may sound like a straight-forward solution, advanced statistics and modelling techniques are often required to properly estimate the impact of combining datasets (Hair et al. 2006). Adding datasets also increases complexity; there are limits on the number of sources one can integrate and understand.

The first four V's focus on the technical elements of Big Data. One of the distinguishing features of Big Data is that it is primarily driven by business (Zikopoulos and Eaton 2011), not by technology. Arguably the most interesting 'V' is the *Value* it can bring.

Big Data offers opportunities to all sectors and industries to be organized differently, to offer new products and services and to do things that were until recently impossible. Many people associate the term Big Data with companies that want to sell to customers ever more things by learning everything there is to know about them (Davis 2012). But this is just one side of the coin. There is also societal value in Big Data. We can use it to save human lives by optimizing care pathways (Groves et al. 2013). We can improve maintenance and plan more cost-effectively, for instance by analysing data collected with sensors on bridges and off shore installations (Feblowitz 2013). We can increase agricultural yields based on information obtained from scanning farm land (Kaloxylos et al.), e.g. with satellites or drones. Or we can reduce traffic congestion through intelligent analysis of the movements of smartphones (Amin et al. 2008). All of these examples have already been implemented and are continuously being developed.

As Big Data-based solutions touch the lives of almost everyone, society has become much more involved in discussing them. Although not all applications of Big Data are privacy sensitive, the general public tends to be highly sensitive and critical of how organizations using Big Data benefit our well-being, or even society as a whole. The public demands more from companies than mere compliance with the law (Weij 2013). Companies perceived to have bad intentions – even if their actions remain within the law – risk their brand value and reputation (Jue 2014). Numerous examples, e.g. (KRO / NCRV 2015) or (Hennis-Plasschaert 2011), show that customers, patients and citizens are reluctant to allow additional analysis of their data without enjoying the immediate benefits themselves (either monetary or otherwise), or in some cases experiencing the benefits to society as a whole. Every Big Data strategy should thus begin by defining the value to customers or citizens. Doing so significantly reduces the risks of being perceived as invading privacy and damaging brand reputation.

Reflecting on the 5V's definition of Big Data

Although the 5 V's are the most common definition of Big Data, several alternatives exist. One is from the McKinsey Global Institute in their 2011 market research on Big Data (Chui et al. 2011):

> "Big Data refers to datasets whose size is beyond the ability of typical database software tools to capture, store, manage and analyze. This definition is intentionally subjective and incorporates a moving definition on how big a dataset needs to be in order to be considered Big Data – i.e., we don't define Big Data in terms of being larger than a certain number of terabytes. We assume that, as technology advances over time, the size of datasets that qualify as Big Data will also increase."

With the claim that capabilities are required beyond typically available tools, this definition classifies Big Data as a science rather than engineering. This is in line with how most Big Data practitioners see themselves: as 'data scientists', which according to Thomas Davenport in the *Harvard Business Review*, is the sexiest job of the 21st century (Davenport and Patil 2012).

Alongside the different definitions, several subtleties must be addressed to get a better understanding of what we mean by Big Data.

First of all, the word 'big' in Big Data can be misleading. Many new applications associated with Big Data are not about editing or interpreting enormous amounts of data – the so-called 'big, messy data' – but about the smart combination of limited amounts of data for personalization. Take for example the 'quantified self', a movement to incorporate technology into data acquisition on aspects of a person's daily life (Wolf 2010). Although this movement is often associated with Big Data, only a very limited amount of (mainly) structured data is collected by each individual (Gurrin et al. 2014). The applications associated with 'the quantified self' do not need huge amounts of data, but base their advice on smart algorithms that understand, combine and interpret data from different sources. It appears as if the social implications of 'the quantified self' movement and the association with data are enough to make it qualify as Big Data, even though it does not fit within the 5 V's definition.

Secondly, there are developments closely related to Big Data that act as enablers, such as cloud computing and the Internet of Things (IOT). Sometimes these developments are confused with Big Data, e.g. cloud computing aims to transform the IT architecture (Abadi 2009) whereas Big Data aims to transform the decision-making process. The gain of cloud computing is typically described at the level of technology: of bringing formidable computing and storage resources under concentrated management, which can subsequently be provided at an infrastructure, platform or software level as a fine-grained service to clients. The IOT paradigm describes the enormous increase of network-connected sensors in our society, embedded in all kinds of products, devices and machines to make them 'smart'. One trillion sensors are expected to exist by 2030 and the data they collect will be a dominant part of Big Data (Chen et al. 2014).

Thirdly, Big Data plays an essential role in recent developments that may not immediately be associated with Big Data. Consider the renewed interest in the 'technological singularity' (i.e. the moment when intelligent systems will exceed human intellectual capacity) or the block chain, the mechanism behind bitcoin allowing trusted transactions without a third party. We will elaborate on these developments in section 2.2.

Conclusion

The 5 V's and other definitions notwithstanding, in this article we use Big Data as an umbrella term, one that covers all the new opportunities, possibilities, threats and techniques associated with being able to deal with data in a different way. In other words, Big Data is about the positive and negative sides of the 'datafication' of society, including social elements such as privacy and transparency (Boyd and Crawford 2012). It ranges from the commercial precision-bombing of customers and extensive monitoring of personal behaviour by intelligence agencies to resolving traffic congestion, stopping epidemics and even connecting refrigerators or thermostats to the internet.

Several indications lead us to believe that the growth of the Big Data phenomenon is inevitable. Technological developments tend to arouse higher expectations (Bostrom 2006) and as many of us become addicted to the convenience, comfort and ease of use of new services (Karaiskos et al. 2015), competition will drive further advances in Big Data technology and applications. These technological developments are the subject of section 2.2.

2.2   TECHNOLOGICAL PROGRESS TOWARDS THE SINGULARITY

The increasing popularity of the internet and internet-related products and services is one of the main drivers behind the rise of Big Data. It challenges storage systems, programming models, and data management alike (Chen et al. 2014). Below we elaborate on developments that underpin the emergence of Big Data.

Storage systems

Traditional data management and analysis are based on relational database management systems. These systems typically require data to be entered in a structured way, i.e. filling columns with specific information (Gray and Reuter 1993). The architecture of a relational database management system is not well suited for distribution over multiple machines, necessitating increasingly expensive hardware to handle growing volumes of data or to allow increasingly complex analysis (DeWitt and Gray 1992).

Relational database management systems typically use direct attached storage or network attached storage systems. These systems store data in a single location, meaning updated data can be both consistent (there is only a single instance of the data at any given time) and available (updates can be immediately accessed). Consistency and availability are crucial for the proper operation of a relational database management system, as they allow transactions in real-time (Haerder and Reuter 1983).

Because they are not partitioned (data is only stored in a single location), direct attached storage and network attached storage do not easily scale. On the other hand, a Storage Area Network is a dedicated local area network specifically meant to redundantly store large amounts of data (Barker and Massiglia 2002). These distributed systems are partitioned and as a result cannot simultaneously meet the requirements of consistency and availability as shown by Gilbert and Lynch (2002). Intuitively this can be explained as follows: an update of data in a distributed system takes time to propagate. Although data can be available immediately, it may be inaccurate in case of an update. Or data can be consistent, but will only be available when the update is propagated everywhere.

Big Data storage systems aim to deploy storage area networks on commodity hardware to cost-effectively store and manage large datasets. The system's complexity is reduced as much as possible to reliably make data available for analysis. This is achieved by adopting a 'share nothing' system architecture, proposed as early as the 1980s to cope with increasing data volumes (DeWitt and Gray 1992). In this architecture each node in a cluster has its own processor, storage and disk, requiring as little coordination between the nodes as possible to simplify the parallelization of tasks. Well-known examples include the Google File System (Ghemawat et al. 2003) and the Hadoop Distributed File System (Shvachko et al. 2010).

Parallel database systems based on a 'share nothing' system architecture can be divided into three classes: key-value databases, column-oriented databases, and document databases (Chen et al. 2014). Key-value databases such as Redis or Dynamo use a simple key-value pair data model, are typically highly expandable, and have a shorter query response time than classical database systems. Column-oriented databases such as HBase and Cassandra segment both columns and rows over multiple nodes for scalability and usually support transaction processing. Document databases such as MongoDB and CouchDB typically store their data in a standardized and flexible object format like binary JSON (BSON) to support more complex data forms.

Programming models
Programmers over the past decades have become familiar with the advanced queries of SQL (structured query language) to extract results from a database.
As explained above, distributed storage systems do not simultaneously guarantee consistency and availability, posing challenges for SQL and relational database management systems. Furthermore, traditional parallel programming models, such as Message Passing Interface (MPI), do not work well with network latency (Xu and Hwang 1996). Alternative processing frameworks have thus been developed and deployed for Big Data. These alternatives and the storage systems underlying them, as described in the previous paragraphs, are collectively named NoSQL, as opposed to SQL-compliant database systems (Yi et al. 2010).

The best known alternative programming model for Big Data is MapReduce (Dean and Ghemawat 2004). In MapReduce, there are only two functions, Map and Reduce, which are programmed by users. The Map function processes input key-value pairs and generates intermediate key-value pairs to gather all the intermediate values related to the same key; the Reduce function compresses the value set into a smaller set. Hadoop (Apache 2005) contains an open source implementation of the MapReduce data processing framework and is the most popular Big Data programming model available. Several higher level languages are available to improve programming efficiency, either by making it look more like SQL as Hive does (Thusoo et al. 2009), or by hiding the complications of MapReduce as Pig Latin does (Olston et al. 2008). Besides the complexity of building MapReduce algorithms, another disadvantage of MapReduce is its primary focus on batch processing, which significantly limits its suitability for real-time analytics.

Real-time analytics aims to query and find patterns in massive data streams, and requires a fundamentally different data handling and analysis approach than batch computations (Garofalakis et al. 2002). Resources are limited (in time and capacity) and algorithms run single-pass, i.e. they take an input, calculate a result and make an irreversible decision. Modern stream processing architectures are made scalable by task parallelism with distributed Directed Acyclic Graphs known as topologies, such as with STORM (Toshniwal et al. 2014), or by data parallelism with a micro-batch scheduler and discretized streams, as with Spark (Zaharia et al. 2012). Processing usually takes place in-memory to avoid the latency of writing and reading to a storage device. Note that in-memory processing is more widely applicable than just for stream processing. Spark for example was originally designed for iterative data processing and interactive analysis (Zaharia et al. 2010) while SAP HANA (Färber et al. 2012), a commercial in-memory solution in the SAP ecosystem, aims to bridge the gap of running Big Data analytical workloads on a relational database management system.

Data analytics

In many ways, Big Data analytics is similar to traditional data analysis, as it is based on applying proper statistical methods to extract features or insights from data. Technological advances and the ubiquity of data, however, have given rise to several new or improved techniques of analysis. We begin with some of the traditional data analysis methods (Snijders 2011) applied to Big Data before addressing some of the newer, more advanced methods.

Cluster analysis, i.e. differentiating and classifying objects based on particular features. *Identification of correlations*, i.e. changes in variables are related to each other, either through strict or undetermined dependence relationships. *Regression analysis*, a mathematical method to determine correlations. *A/B testing*, hypothesis testing by applying different conditions to different groups and comparing results. *Monte Carlo simulation*, analysing behaviour of a system by random sampling of predefined probability distributions. Some traditional methods, like *Graph processing*, become more powerful through new programming models. Graphs are structures that model relationships among objects; consisting of nodes and edges, they are typically hard to analyze when they become too large. However, extensions of MapReduce enable analysis of large graphs (Lin and Schatz 2010) to for example determine the shortest path between two nodes or to identify communities in social networks.

More advanced technologies for data mining often include *machine learning algorithms* such as random forest (Breiman 2001) or support vector machines (Cortes and Vapnik 1995). They allow computers to be trained, rather than programmed, either supervised or unsupervised. In case of supervised learning, example inputs are provided together with the desired output, whereas with unsupervised learning, algorithms are expected to identify hidden or unknown patterns in data.

A variation on the theme of machine learning is *cognitive computing*, made famous by IBM when Watson – a supercomputer capable of answering questions posed in natural language – won Jeopardy and subsequently received a medical degree and became a chef (Ferrucci 2012). Although Watson only employs rule-based artificial intelligence (combined with superior information retrieval systems and natural language processing), it shows that the cognitive capabilities of computers can already exceed those of human beings, at least in some respects. Arguably the most advanced form of Big Data analytics is *deep learning* (Hinton et al. 2006), a revival of what used to be called neural networks. One of the main benefits of deep learning is the capacity for unsupervised or semi-supervised learning, allowing automated feature extraction with no or minimal human intervention, which is essential when datasets grow exponentially. Two companies, Vicarious and Numenta (Kurzweil 2012), are making significant progress in replicating the neocortex, the analytical part of the human brain, with deep learning techniques. Google recently bought a company called Deep Mind (Gannes 2014) doing similar research.

The developments above have triggered a renewed interest in 'technological singularity' (Vinge 1993) – the moment in time when intelligent systems will exceed human intellectual capacity. According to this hypothesis, these systems will be able to create even smarter systems, causing a runaway effect, accelerating progress beyond human comprehension and changing civilization in a way that is fundamentally unpredictable from a state before the singularity. Hollywood leads the way in helping us imagine why we may not always be happy with how it turns out (Zimmerman 2008), while dystopian best-sellers fuel public fear (Citron and Pasquale 2014). But real world consequences are apparent as well: Deep Mind demanded an ethics board (Efrati 2014) to place boundaries on the applications of Artificial Intelligence when the company was acquired by Google, while prominent researchers and businessmen have signed an open letter penned by the Future of Life Institute (Russel et al. 2015) warning about the social risks of artificial intelligence.

Data management
The main challenges of working with Big Data include (Chen et al. 2014): data representation (understanding what the data means), redundancy of information (is the data consistent and what does one keep), life cycle management (how reliable is the data and how long does one keep it), distributed processing (how to get a response within a reasonable amount of time), confidentiality (who one can

share the data with), scalability (how to deal with the exponential growth of data) and cooperation (who is responsible for what, who must invest, and how to address risks).

The traditional field addressing these issues is known as master data management, comprising the processes, governance, policies, standards and tools that consistently define and manage the critical data of an organization to provide a single point of reference (Loshin 2010). The main focus of master data management is on the proper integration of data sources and on assuring data quality before analysis.

Master data management can be a time consuming process. With the growing trend towards short delivery cycles, e.g. manifested through methods like agile development (Beck et al. 2001), a complimentary approach is gaining popularity in the world of Big Data. Rather than the upfront definition of standards, data from various sources (sometimes from outside the organization) are brought together without changing their original structure in a so-called 'data lake' (O'Leary 2014). Standardization and data quality-related activities are postponed to the analysis stage. The benefits of this approach are ease of implementation (standardization and data quality issues are not holistically addressed) and flexibility, as standards and quality requirements may differ from one analysis to the other. The disadvantages include the need to revisit data definitions and data quality for each analysis, which can lead to double work and confusion. Hybrid models will most likely appear, where a data lake contains one or several standardization and data quality layers, combining the strengths of classical master data management with the flexibility of a Big Data approach.

Besides this evolutionary shift from the traditional master data management approach, Big Data is also driving unorthodox data management solutions. The popularization of these solutions began with the BitTorrent protocol (Cohen 2003), which has become massively popular for downloading music and movies. The system operates without central computers or intermediary partners. Downloading data with a torrent boils down to getting the pieces from hundreds of other users in the network. The redundancy and incentives provided by these peer to peer networks allows them to operate reliably, even when the reliability of each individual data provider is limited.

Transaction handling has recently undergone a similar transformation with the introduction of Bitcoin (Nakamoto 2008). Trust no longer needs to be provided by an intermediary, such as a bank or notary, but can be provided by a mathematical solution that ensures trust from within the network itself. In its simplest form, all participants in the network have a ledger of all the transactions of all other participants on their system: the so-called block chain. The block chain is updated on every transaction, allowing trustworthy transactions even when there are unreliable partners in the network. In other words, the network is the trusted party that oversees and audits the proper completion of transactions.

The way torrent networks and the block chain have changed the handling of data has resulted in and continues to result in fundamental changes to applications and business models. They are in a sense the foundation of the Big Data revolution, which touches all information-based industries. But they are also only the beginning; new developments are already on the way to mainstream adoption. Ethereum is to provide a system for running a decentralized application platform (Buterin 2015). As each element in this system is fully dynamic, it is not tied to a specific physical space; it therefore cannot be managed as a physical object (with e.g. a location, a presence, or an owner). Ethereum brings us very close to the original idealist view of the internet. To quote the libertarian John Perry Barlow in early internet history (Barlow 2000):

"Governments of the Industrial World, you weary giants of flesh and steel, I come from Cyberspace, the new home of Mind. On behalf of the future, I ask you of the past to leave us alone. You are not welcome among us. You have no sovereignty where we gather."

Interestingly enough, Ethereum brings real-world challenges to cyberspace, such as where does one pay taxes for this service, and under what jurisdiction does it fall? BitCoin trading has already shown how difficult it is for 'real world' authorities to gain control over dynamic distributed systems. The potential impact of Ethereum on applications and business models is even more fundamental, which could lead to a new chapter in the Big Data revolution.

Conclusion

Combining all Big Data-related developments in data storage, analytics and management may still be a long way ahead of us. We would end up with a hyper-intelligent system that does not conform to current standards of civilization, existing autonomously in cyberspace, unconstrained by the rules and regulations of the physical world. Summing it up suggests why such system autonomy lies beyond our current comfort zone, and reveals the source of unease among the signatories of the Future of Life Institute's open letter. With this in mind, we need to be careful not to equate Big Data with mere number crunching.

New ecosystems are required to be able to deal with such a new reality. Ensuring the responsible application of Big Data analytics begins with transparency and privacy by design, and by encouraging quality based on peer review and certification (Klous 2015). The result should be a new foundation based on platform thinking (Choudary 2013), enabling partners in the value chain to intensify the way they work together, in such a way that participants can easily plug in and out. A new ecosystem where parties (governments, companies, programmers, data scientists, social groups, lawyers, users, etc.) can work together, creating good Big Data applications, generating responsible insights and bringing them to the market in the right way. section 2.3 addresses the opportunities and challenges that arise with these new ecosystems.

2.3   THE ECONOMIC IMPACT OF BIG DATA

Transforming business models

We now return to the reality of today, where Big Data has been coined the 'New Oil'. Although Big Data offers significant potential for enhancing sales and rendering processes more efficient (Chui et al. 2011),[1] we focus mainly on opportunities for creating value with new business concepts, leading to a diversity of applications. The automotive industry is moving towards connected cars with advantages for driver security and comfort, and in the longer run towards driverless cars (Silberg 2012), while service industries may soon rely on sensors in installations and buildings that monitor and predict maintenance patterns (Abowd and Sterbenz 2000). One example is the Dutch start-up Algoritmica, which has developed software to predict the maintenance needs of wind turbines (Harte 2014). Another example is the transformation of the agricultural industry into a precision-based endeavour, with Big Data Analytics offering farmers the potential to optimize yields. New industrial ecosystems and business models are being formed in this sector, where e.g. the Climate Corporation offers farmers an insurance based on results from machine-learning algorithms and massive data analysis (Lakshmanan et al. 2015). The insurance company also advises farmers on how to maximize yields, thereby mitigating claims.

We appear to be at the forefront of big changes in the medical world as well. Chances are it is only a matter of time before cancer is transformed from a killer into a chronic disease (Bettegowda et al. 2014). One of the main ingredients in these developments is the mapping and analysis of DNA, where quantum leaps have been made: after pouring hundreds of millions into research and computing power, scientists were able to unravel a full human DNA in 2001 (Ventor 2001). Commercial companies today offer this service online for less than a few hundred dollars, e.g. 23 and me (2015). To stimulate research in this area, the American National Cancer Institute has begun sharing data in the cloud (Goldsmith 2014). This is merely one example of how scientists and companies are striving to offer precision approaches in care and cure. The combination of personal medical data with lifestyle and other parameters offers unparalleled opportunities for healthcare to become more predictive and tailored to individual treatment (Wolf 2010).

Today's world is becoming ever more measurable. Several locations have already become living labs, or urban labs, where society is studied and optimized in a live setting. The Mobile Territorial Lab in Trento run by MIT professor Alex 'Sandy'

Pentland is a famous example (Moise et al. 2012). We often no longer have to ask what people do (as we do in surveys). We can simply measure it, sometimes with surgical precision. The greatest challenge for companies in such environments is to build data-driven strategies that combine value for their customers or for society as a whole – in terms of comfort, safety, etc. – with commercial value. In other words, Michael Porter's ideas on striving for Shared Value should be put into action in every data-driven strategy (Porter and Kramer 2011). In the past years we have seen several major companies struggle to find the right combination, or at least to explain it properly. Telecom companies have tried to constrain internet messaging applications like WhatsApp to avoid revenue drops for their text messaging services (Layton 2013). The financial sector has difficulty explaining to clients how better understanding their spending behaviour helps improve services (Jue 2014). Retailers still find it difficult to be transparent about how they are trying to profile their customers and why (Schellevis 2014). As a result, the general public often responds with frustration. The discussion must mature to be able to work constructively towards responsible ways of generating value out of data.

We must realize that in our current society, software and hardware increasingly determine our behaviour, probably much more so than laws and regulations (Morozov 2012). Google's algorithm that determines which items are relevant to individuals; the software and hardware of the smartcard system that determines how one uses public transport – 'the system' is becoming increasingly dominant in determining our behaviour. Some claim it is even limiting our democracy, as it fundamentally affects our decision-making. As Lawrence Lessig claimed: "Code is law" (Lessig 1999). This in itself is no bad thing as we can change the code, i.e. our systems, to our liking if we wish. But when a system becomes the equivalent of the law, the system developer becomes the legislator, heralding a new power balance (Hildebrandt 2014). System design can thus be misaligned with what we want as a society (Calo 2014). The principles we value in society – for example in the areas of privacy, transparency, 'the right to be forgotten' – are not the priority of system developers, who are trained to focus on system robustness and efficiency.
Such misalignments can lead to abuse of power by companies, for instance the big internet powerhouses, that deploy the systems and have access to huge amounts of data.

In his book *The Master Switch*, Harvard professor Tim Wu speaks of the Kronos Effect (Wu and Vietor 2011). Wu is referring to the mythical figure Kronos who, for the ancient Greeks, was the ultimate boss of the universe. Kronos was warned by the Oracle of Delphi that one of his children would overthrow him at some point in the future. With this in mind, he decided to eat the children that his wife kept giving birth to. This turned out to be Kronos' downfall: his wife fed him a stone wrapped in swaddling to save their child, and he was finally defeated by his son Zeus, who he thought he had eaten. Kronos represents the large companies in the information and communications industry, which historically have often become monopolists. There comes a time when they are more concerned with defending their own positions than developing better products and services, leading to the destruction of better products produced by competitors or the 'eating' of these competitors by simply buying them.

What does the Kronos Effect mean for today's internet industry? Players such as Google, Facebook, Amazon, Apple and other internet giants have powerful positions. Google in particular is often cited as an example of a company with too much influence over everything we do. This not only reflects the size of the company, but also the wide portfolio of its products and services (Fast FT 2014). Well-known services such as Gmail, Google Maps and YouTube, but also relative newcomers to the broadcasting family, such as Nest (smart thermostats) and Deep Mind (artificial intelligence) fall under the Google umbrella. Without a doubt, Google will go down in the history of the internet as a company that achieved many great things. The question is whether, in this history, Google will join the list of companies that fell prey to the Kronos Effect. Another striking example is the acquisition of WhatsApp by Facebook in 2013 for the almost unheard of sum of 19 (later corrected to 22) billion dollars (Olson 2014). WhatsApp still lacks a proper revenue model. It seems that Facebook bought the service to protect its own strategy – connecting as many people as possible – against new competitors. This is reminiscent of Kronos eating his new-born to defend his throne.

A good example of how business models related to Big Data can affect government policy is found in recent discussions over net neutrality (Layton 2013). Net neutrality is quite a technical topic; few people are interested or even know about it. Net neutrality means that internet service providers have to treat all internet traffic equally; they are not allowed to prioritize or delay certain types of traffic. Changes in policies here can have a huge financial impact on companies with Big Data-related business models like Netflix, Facebook or Google. While net neutrality has been properly guaranteed in Dutch legislation for several years now, in Europe negotiations are still ongoing. Several amendments are being discussed, opening the door to various commercial offers to provide 'improved quality of service' (European Commission 2015). Note that these additional charges protect established parties by raising entry barriers for new entrants. In essence, reducing net neutrality is like reducing anti-trust legislation, intended to prevent the abuse of power by established parties.

Government has a clear role to play in this discussion – not only to balance commercial interests represented by lobbyists from all sides, but to represent the general public and protect them from the Kronos Effect by raising awareness and by protecting fundamental human rights, even when only few are paying attention. Other issues around data require similar discussion, not least the transparency of large organizations' methods when dealing with (our) data (Boyd and Crawford 2012). Especially in sensitive areas such as healthcare and the financial sector, we would expect codes of good conduct to appear.

In conclusion

In a world where data is rapidly turning into the most valuable asset, opportunities and challenges are appearing at an incredible pace. We don't have the luxury to wait and see where it is leading us, neither from an economic nor from a security and safety perspective. If history has taught us anything, it is that technological developments can be a boon to society when they are controlled, but devastating without such guidance. Over the next few years, it is our obligation to gain control of Big Data and avoid its unethical applications. It could be enormously beneficial for The Netherlands to become a leading contributor to this new ecosystem.

Our country is small enough to be flexible, big enough to be interesting, and digital enough to make advanced initiatives feasible. Let us unite business, government and research to maximize the impact we can make on the fast evolving data-driven society.

REFERENCES

23 and me (2015) 'Genetic Information for You and Your Family', *23 and Me*, available at: www.23andme.com/en-gb.

Abadi, D. (2009) 'Data Management in the Cloud: Limitations and Opportunities', *IEEE Bulletin of the Technical Committee on Data Engineering* 32, 1: 3-12.

Abowd, G. and J. Sterbenz, (2000) 'Final Report on the Inter-Agency Workshop on Research Issues for Smart Environments', *IEEE Personal Communications* 7, 5: 36-40.

Akyildiz, I. et al. (2002) 'Wireless Sensor Networks: a Survey', *Computer Networks* 38, 4: 393-422.

Amin, S. et al. (2008) 'Mobile Century Using GPS Mobile Phones as Traffic Sensors: a Field Experiment', pp. 16-20 in *World Congress on Intelligent Transportation Systems*.

Apache (2005) 'Welcome to Apache Hadoop', *Hadoop*, available at: http://hadoop. apache.org.

Barker, R. and P. Massiglia (2002) *Storage Area Network Essentials: a Complete Guide to Understanding and Implementing SANs*, New York: John Wiley and Sons.

Barlow, J. (2000) 'Déclaration d'indépendance du cyberespace', pp. 47-54 in *Libres Enfants du Savoir Numérique,* Paris: Editions de l'Éclat.

Beck, K. et al. (2001) 'Manifesto for Agile Software Development', *Agile Manifesto*, available at: http://agilemanifesto.org.

Bettegowda, C. et al. (2014) 'Detection of Circulating Tumor DNA in Early- and Late-Stage Human Malignancies', *Science Translational Medicine* 6, 224.

Big Data Public Working Group (2015) *Big Data Interoperability Framework 1, Definitions,* Gaithersburg, MD: NIST.

Bostrom, N. (2006) 'Welcome to a World of Exponential Change', pp. 40-50 in P. Miller, J. Wilsdon (eds.) *Better Humans? The Politics of Human Enhancement and Life Extension*, London: Demos.

Boyd, D. and K. Crawford (2012) 'Critical Questions for Big Data: Provocations for a Cultural, Technological and Scholarly Phenomenon', *Information, Communication & Society* 15, 5: 662-679.

Breiman, L. (2001) 'Random Forests', *Machine Learning* 45, 1: 5-32.

Buterin, V. (2015) 'A Next-Generation Smart Contract and Decentralized Application Platform', *Ethereum* / wiki, available at: https://github.com/ethereum/wiki/ wiki/White-Paper.

Calo, R. (2014) 'Code, Nudge, or Notice', *Iowa Law Review* 99, 773: 773-802.

Chen, M., S. Mao and Y. Liu (2014) 'Big Data: a Survey', *Mobile Networks and Applications* 19, 2: 171-209.

Chui, M. et al. (2011) *Big Data: The Next Frontier for Innovation, Competition and Productivity*, McKinsey Global Institute.

Citron, D. and F. Pasquale (2014) 'The Scored Society: Due Process for Automated Predictions', *Washington Law Review* 89: 1.

Cohen, B. (2003) 'Incentives Build Robustness in BitTorrent', *Workshop on Economics of Peer-to-Peer Systems:* 68-72.

Cortes, C. and V. Vapnik (1995) 'Support-Vector Networks', *Machine Learning* 20: 273-97.

Davenport, T. and D. Patil (2012) 'Data Scientist: the Sexiest Job of the 21st Century', *Harvard Business Review:* October.

Davis, K. (2012) *Ethics of Big Data: Balancing Risk and Innovation,* O'Reilly Media.

De Laat, C. (2014) 'Smart Cyber Infrastructure for Big Data Processing', PIRE *and* RDA, available at: www.osapublishing.org/abstract.cfm?uri=ofc-2014-Tu3I.3.

Dean, J. and S. Ghemawat (2004) 'MapReduce: Simplified Data Processing on Large Clusters', OSDI, available at: http://static.googleusercontent.com/media/research.google.com/nl//archive/mapreduce-osdi04.pdf.

DeWitt, D. and J. Gray (1992) 'Parallel Database Systems: the Future of High Performance Database Systems', *Communications of the* ACM 35, 6: 85-98.

Easley, D., M. Lopez de Prado and M. O'Hara (2011) 'Microstructure of the 'Flash Crash': Flow Toxicity, Liquidity Crashes and the Probability of Informed Trading', *Journal of Portfolio Management* 37, 2: 118-28.

Efrati, M. (2014) 'Google Beat Facebook for DeepMind, Creates Ethics Board', *The Information*, available at: www.theinformation.com/Google-beat-Facebook-For-DeepMind-Creates-Ethics-Board.

European Commission (2015) 'Roaming Charges and Open Internet: Questions and Answers', *Press Release Database*, available at: http://europa.eu/rapid/press-release_MEMO-15-5275_en.htm.

Färber, F. et al. (2012) 'The SAP HANA Database - an Architecture Overview', *Data Engineering Bulletin.* IEEE 35, 1: 28-33.

Fast FT. (2014) 'European Parliament Votes for Google Split Idea', *Financial Times*, available at: www.ft.com/fastft/242562/european-parliament-votes-google-split.

Feblowitz, J. (2013) 'Analytics in Oil and Gas: the Big Deal about Big Data', *Digital Energy Conference*, Society of Petroleum Engineers.

Ferrucci, D. (2012) 'Introduction to 'This is Watson'', IBM *Journal of Research & Development* 56, 3-4: 1-15.

Gannes, L. (2014) 'Google to Buy Artificial Intelligence Startup DeepMind for $400M', *Re/code*, available at: http://recode.net/2014/01/26/exclusive-google-to-buy-artificial-intelligence-startup-deepmind-for-400m.

Garofalakis, M., J. Gehrke and R. Rastogi (2002) 'Querying and Mining Data Streams: You Only Get One Look', SIGMOD *Conference.*

Ghemawat, S., H. Hobioff and S. Leung (2003) 'The Google File System', ACM SIGOPS *Operating System Review*, ACM: October 19–22.

Gilbert, S. and N. Lynch (2002) 'Brewer's Conjecture and the Feasibility of Consistent', available at partition-tolerant web services, ACM SIGACT *News*: 51-59.

Goldsmith, P. (2014) 'Broad Institute and University of California Team Awarded NCI Cancer Genomics Cloud Pilot Contract', *Broad Institute*, available at: www.broadinstitute.org/news/6166.

Gray, J. and A. Reuter (1993) *Transaction Processing*, Burlington Massachusetts: Morgan Kaufmann.

Groves, P. et al. (2013) *The 'Big Data' Revolution in Healthcare*, McKinsey & Company.

Gurrin, C., A. Smeaton and A. Doherty (2014) 'Lifelogging: Personal Big Data', *Foundations and Trends in Information Retrieval* 8, 1: 1-125.

Haerder, T. and A. Reuter (1983) 'Principles of Transaction-Oriented Database Recovery', ACM *Computing Surveys* 15, 4: 287-317.

Hair, J. et al. (2006) *Multivariate Data Analysis*, Pearson Prentice Hall.

Halevy, A., P. Norvig and F. Pereira (2009) 'The Unreasonable Effectiveness of Data', IEEE *Intelligent Systems* 24, 2: 8-12.

Harte, M. (2014) 'How Predictive Analytics Improves Wind Turbine Maintenance', *Algoritmica*, available at: http://algoritmica.nl/how-predictive-analytics-improves-wind-turbine-maintenance.

Hennis-Plasschaert, J. (2011) 'Schriftelijke vragen over de verkoop van gegevens aan de politie door Vodafone en TomTom', *Nieuwsarchief*, available at: http://jeaninehennisplasschaert.vvd.nl/nieuwsarchief/38787.

Hildebrandt, M. (2014) 'Criminal Law and Technology in a Data-Driven Society', pp. 174-197 in *The Oxford Handbook of Criminal Law*, Oxford: Oxford University Press.

Hinton, G., S. Osindero and Y. Teh (2006) 'A Fast Learning Algorithm for Deep Belief Nets', *Neural Computation* 18: 1527-54.

Jue, N. (2014) 'ING en het gebruik van klantgegevens', *Nieuws- en persberichten*, available at: www.ing.nl/nieuws/nieuws_en_persberichten/2014/03/ing_en_het_gebruik_van_klant_brief.html.

Kaloxylos, A. et al. (2012) 'Farm Management Systems and the Future Internet Era', *Computers and Electronics in Agriculture* 89: 130-44.

Karaiskos, D. et al. (2015) 'Social Network Addiction: a New Clinical Disorder?', *European Psychiatry* 25, 1.

Klein, A. and W. Lehner (2009) 'Representing Data Quality in Sensor Data Streaming Environments', *Journal of Data and Information Quality* 1, 2.

Klous, S. (2015) 'A New Reality Requires New Ecosystems', *Proceedings of* HPCS 2.

Klous, S. and N. Wielaard (2014) *Wij zijn Big Data*, Amsterdam: Business Contact.

KRO/NCRV (2015) 'Dokters in de knel', *De Monitor*, available at: http://demonitor.ncrv.nl/dokters-in-de-knel.

Kurzweil, R. (2012) *How to Create a Mind: The Secret of Human Thought Revealed*, New York: Penguin.

Lakshmanan, V. et al. (2015) 'Machine Learning and Data Mining Approaches to Climate Science', *Proceedings of the 4th International Workshop on Climate Informatics*, Springer.

Layton, R. (2013) 'Net Neutrality in the Netherlands: Dutch Solution or Dutch Disease?', *24th European Regional Conference of the International Telecommunication Society*, Florence: Econstor.

Lessig, L. (1999) *Code and Other Laws of Cyberspace*, New York: Basic Books.

Libert, B., Y. Wind and M. Fenley (2014) 'What Airbnb, Uber, and Alibaba Have in Common', *Harvard Business Review*, November 20.

Lin, J. and M. Schatz (2010) 'Design Patterns for Efficient Graph Algorithms in MapReduce', *Proceedings of the Eight Workshop on Mining and Learning with Graphs*, ACM: 78-85.

Loshin, D. (2010) *Master Data Management*, Burlington: Morgan Kaufmann.

Mayer-Schönberger, V. and K. Cukier (2013) *Big Data: A Revolution that Will Transform How We Live, Work, and Think*, Boston: Houghton Mifflin Harcourt.

Moise, C., F. Antonelli and M. Vescovi (2012) 'How Do I Manage my Personal Data', *International Conference on Data Technologies and Applications (DATA 25-27 July)*: 123-8.

Moore, G. (1965) 'Cramming More Components onto Integrated Circuits', *IEEE Solid-State Circuits Newsletter*: 33-5.

Morozov, E. (2012) *The Net Delusion: The Dark Side of Internet Freedom*, New York: Public Affairs.

Nakamoto, S. (2008) 'Bitcoin: a Peer-to-Peer Electronic Cash System', *Consulted* 1: 2012.

O'Leary, D. (2014) 'Embedding AI and Crowdsourcing in the Big Data Lake', *Intelligent Systems* 29, 5: 70-73.

Olson, P. (2014) 'Facebook Closes $19 billion WhatsApp deal', *Forbes*, available at: www.forbes.com/sites/parmyolson/2014/10/06/facebook-closes-19-billion-whatsapp-deal.

Olston, C. et al. (2008) 'Pig Latin: a Not-So-Foreign Language for Data Processing', *Proceedings of the ACM SIGMOD International Conference*: 1099-110.

Porter, M. and M. Kramer (2011) 'Creating Shared Value', *Harvard Business Review*: 62-77.

Russel, S. et al. (2015) 'Research Priorities for Robust and Beneficial Artificial Intelligence', *Futureoflife.org*, available at: http://futureoflife.org/static/data/documents/research_priorities.pdf.

Schellevis, J. (2014) 'Winkels volgen je voetsporen – De opkomst van tracking via wifi-signalen', *Tweakers*, available at: http://tweakers.net/reviews/3385/1/wifi-tracking-winkels-volgen-je-voetsporen-inleiding.html.

Schumpeter, J. (1934) *The Theory of Economic Development: An Inquiry into Profits, Capital, Credit, Interest, and the Business Cycle*, New Brunswick: Transaction.

Shvachko, K., K. Kuang, S. Radia and R. Chansler (2010) 'The Hadoop Distributed File System', *Mass Storage Systems and Technologies*: 1-10.

Silberg, G. (2012) 'Self-Driving Cars: The Next Revolution', *KPMG LLP and Center of Automotive Research*, available at: www.kpmg.com/US/en/IssuesAndInsights/ArticlesPublications/Documents/self-driving-cars-next-revolution.pdf.

Snijders, T. (2011) *Multilevel Analysis*, Springer.

Thusoo, A. et al. (2009) 'Hive: a Warehousing Solution over a Map-Reduce Framework', *Proceedings of the VLDB Endowment*: 1626-9, available at: www.vldb.org/pvldb/2/vldb09-938.pdf.

Toshniwal, A. et al. (2014) 'Storm@Twitter', *Proceedings of the SIGMOD International Conference on Management of Data*, ACM: 147-156.

Ventor, J. (2001) 'The Sequence of the Human Genome', *Science* 291, 5507: 1304-1351.

Vinge, V. (1993) 'The Coming Technological Singularity: How to Survive in the Post-Human Era', *Vision-21: Interdisciplinary Science and Engineering in the Era of Cyberspace*: 11-22.

Weij, M. (2013) 'Equens' Big-Dataproject te vroeg afgeschoten', *AutomatiseringGids* June 19: 15

Wolf, G. (2010) 'The Data-Driven Life', *New York Times* April 28.

Wu, T. and M. Vietor (2011) *The Master Switch: The Rise and Fall of Information Empires*, New York: Vintage.

Xu, Z. and K. Hwang (1996) 'Modelling Communication Overhead: MPI and MPL Performance on the IBM SP2', *Parallel and Distributed Technology: Systems and Applications* 4, 1: 9-24.

Yi, X., G. Wei and F. Dong (2010) 'A survey on NoSql Databases', *Communications of Modern Technology*: 46-50.

Zaharia, M. et al. (2010) 'Spark: Cluster Computing with Working Sets', *Proceedings of the 2nd Conference on Hot Topics in Cloud Computing*, Berkeley, CA: USENIX.

Zaharia, M. et al. (2012) 'Discretized Streams: an Efficient and Fault-Tolerant Model for Stream Processing on Large Clusters', *Proceedings of the 4th USENIX Conference on Hot Topics in Cloud Computing*, Berkeley, CA: USENIX.

Zikopoulos, P. and C. Eaton (2011) *Understanding Big Data: Analytics for Enterprise Class Hadoop and Streaming Data*, New York: McGraw-Hill Osborne Media.

Zimmerman, M. (2008) 'The Singularity: a Crucial Phase in Divine Self-Actualization' *Journal of Natural and Social Philosophy* 4, 1-2: 347-370.

NOTE

1   McKinsey claims that health care benefits from Big Data could be as high as 300 billion dollars per year and European Government administration could save more than 100 billion euros in operational efficiency improvements alone. This excludes the reduction of fraud, errors and tax gaps.

3 CRYPTOLOGY AND PRIVACY IN THE CONTEXT OF BIG DATA

Seda Gürses & Bart Preneel

Executive Summary

'Big Data' has become the term of art to refer to a number of distinct socio-technical phenomena in present-day infrastructures. The objective of this paper is to discuss the potentials and limitations of using technical means to address privacy challenges associated with the technologies lumped together under the umbrella term Big Data. In order to do so, we will first unpack the technical elements implicit in the term Big Data and provide a short summary of privacy and fairness challenges associated with them. Next, we will provide an overview of the state of the art in cryptology and privacy technologies as it relates to Big Data. We conclude with a short analysis of whether and how some of the privacy challenges of Big Data can be addressed using technical means.

3.1 INTRODUCTION

'Big Data' is a popular term that is used to refer to the increased use of data-driven socio-technical infrastructures in everyday life. From an interdisciplinary perspective it has been defined as the combination of three elements:

technology: maximizing computation power and algorithmic accuracy to gather, analyse, link and compare large data sets.

analysis: drawing on large data sets to identify patterns in order to make economic, social, technical and legal claims.

mythology: the widespread belief that large data sets offer a higher form of intelligence and knowledge that can generate insights that were previously impossible, with the aura of truth, objectivity and accuracy (Boyd and Crawford 2012).

This popularly cited account shows that Big Data, as a term, unifies discussions that are related to separate technical phenomena. When applied in concert, proponents and opponents speculate that these phenomena may bring great societal benefits and costs. When we break this cloudy term down into its technical counterparts, we find that it consists of two parts: Big Data(bases), on the one hand, and the family of techniques called data science, data mining and machine learning, on the other. Stitching these two parts together is the concept of 'Software as a Service' (SaaS) as reflected in the 'cloud', the 'Internet of Things', and social and mobile networks.

In order to be more precise, we will refer to Big Data infrastructures, data analytics and SaaS architectures instead of Big Data (section 3.2) in the remainder of this text. By focusing on concrete technologies, we move away from the depiction of Big Data as large data sets that are like 'natural resources' waiting to be exploited (McClure 2015) and as a technological paradigm shift that invalidates all prior innovation in privacy and security technologies. Rather, we show the technological decisions made in developing hardware, software architectures and analytics that are pertinent to the feasibility of deploying techniques that intend to address privacy and security concerns around Big Data technologies. Section 3.3 introduces the state of the art of cryptology, followed by an evaluation of the feasibility of successfully deploying these technologies to protect digital information in section 3.4. We then introduce privacy technologies that are relevant in the context of Big Data. The application of data analytics on such a large scale also raises novel privacy and fairness challenges that call for new techniques. In particular, researchers have shown that how and what data is collected and collated, and what algorithms are applied, may amplify discrimination, unfair treatment and privacy violations. After briefly discussing the potential challenges to privacy and security by design in section 3.5, we conclude with some recent proposals to address these issues as well as innovative methods for ensuring accountability in algorithmic decision-making. We also map out gaps in research and practice.

3.2   UNPACKING BIG DATA: THE TECHNOLOGY BEHIND THE HYPE

In the context of this paper, we discuss the application of cryptology and privacy technologies to Big Data infrastructures and data analytics in the context of SaaS. By these we mean the following:

Big Data infrastructures
The term Big Data infrastructures refers to processes and technologies for managing large amounts of data. The associated challenges have been summed up in the Four Vs: Volume (size), Velocity (speed), Variety (formats) and Veracity (accuracy). In essence, these challenges have remained the same over recent decades; however, they now are comparatively 'bigger' (Jacobs 2009). Big Data engineers need to "scale out to thousands of commodity servers, replicate data across geographically remote data centers, and ensure high availability of user data in the presence of failures" (Agrawal et al. 2015). Given these capabilities, what distinguishes Big Data is the ability to accumulate observations over time and space (Jacobs 2009). These capabilities open the path to analysing how things have changed over time, providing real-time services using analytics or evaluating predictions based on past occurrences.

Implementing data analytics on such a large scale requires rethinking the way we organize data acquisition, storage and transfer. For example, databases have traditionally been designed to privilege fast input over output of data. This asymmetry inherent in traditional databases, together with the desire to do more complex analyses, has led to the redesign of databases, that is, moving away from rows and tables in a relational database to more flexible formats. The expansion in volume has also demanded the rapid development of applications for distributing large datasets across databases and data centres, progress in parallel computing capabilities and improvements in data transfer capabilities. Responding to all of these challenges has led to enormous breakthroughs in hardware and software design: Google, for example, boasts that its networking technology can read all of the scanned data in the Library of Congress in less than a tenth of a second (Lardinois 2015).

Data analytics

A number of terms are used to refer to different families of analytical techniques for discovering and predicting patterns in data. Data science, for example, is becoming the popular term of art in the industry. It refers to the "set of methods used to capture patterns in complex and large datasets for the sake of business applications, online services and data products" (Loukides 2010). Computer scientists have proposed 'data analytics' and more recently 'data science' to "support and guide the principled extraction of information and knowledge from data" (Provost and Fawcett 2013). The ongoing terminological quagmire suggests that we are witnessing a nascent field of study propelled by business interests rather than a mature science. For simplicity's sake, if we want to point to advances in research, we refer to machine learning. By this we mean techniques, methods and processes for analysing datasets in order to provide useful summaries or using models developed on sample data to make predictions. We use data analytics to talk about the application of machine learning in practice to everyday situations.

Software as a service

SaaS and underlying centralized architectures bootstrap most user-facing Big Data infrastructures and data analytics (Kaldrack and Leeker 2015). The SaaS model replaces the 'shrink-wrap' software model, where purchased software and data generated using that software reside on a personal device. In the SaaS model, all applications are hosted by the service provider, meaning that data collection and processing happens on the provider's servers. The consumers either 'rent' the services or use them for free over a network. SaaS helps reduce end-user hardware costs and allows organizations to reduce technology integration costs. It also allows customers to try software before purchasing and to scale their technology on demand.

The SaaS model builds upon two underlying layers: Infrastructure as a Service, which provides computing and storage resources, and Platform as a Service, such as the Google App engine. In the vernacular, the many ways in which these services can be mixed and matched on demand is shorthanded as 'the cloud'. Service architectures imply that computation is done mainly on the server side, which also means that all data users generate while interacting with the services flows to the service providers. With services provided by companies like Facebook, Google or Amazon, data generated by millions of users can be analysed (in real time) to improve efficiency and serve other organizational interests. These companies can use this data to do rapid development, determine new features and reshape services. A service can integrate multiple services on demand. This increases the number of entities that have access to user data, while decreasing the transparency of their transactions. As a consequence of these practices, there is little transparency, legibility or constraint regarding the activities that data collection and processing services engage in on the cloud or on user devices.

The challenges that Big Data infrastructures, data analytics and SaaS present to cryptology and privacy can be summarized as follows:

1. *Erosion of data confidentiality*: Services are organized to do computation on the server side, meaning that all data generated in using the services flows to the service providers to be stored in Big Data infrastructures.
2. *Intensification of identity management and tracking*: SaaS providers require user authentication as a prerequisite to service use and user tracking as central to their business models and licensing schemes. This has culminated in what we might call 'tracking and data analytics as a service'.
3. *Reconfiguration of service provision*: User-facing services are typically made up of multiple services, implying that the number of entities with access to user data increases while transparency decreases.
4. *Integrity of user devices, servers and algorithms*: Increasingly, service providers limit the ability of users to view or control what services are doing on their devices or their servers. This issue is intensified with accelerated feature updates.
5. *Ethics of experimenting with (user) populations for service optimization*: Machine learning is applied to the user data troves to scale and shape services and profile users. The application of this nascent technology to populations and their environments in order to optimize organizational interests amplifies concerns about discrimination, unfair treatment, and human experimentation.

3.3   STATE OF THE ART OF CRYPTOLOGY

3.3.1   WHAT IS CRYPTOLOGY?

Cryptology is the science that deals with the protection of information and computation using mathematical techniques. Historically, the primary goal of cryptology was confidentiality, that is, hiding the content of information to outsiders (Kahn 1996; Singh 2011). The advent of electronic communications brought to the fore the challenge of authenticating information, that is, establishing the source of information and making sure that information has not been tampered with. Cryptographic techniques can also be used to identify entities such as users or devices. Recently, there has been a growing interest in protecting metadata: this includes hiding the identities, locations or devices of communicating parties. Cryptography is also used increasingly to protect computations. We distinguish between symmetric cryptography and public-key cryptography.

Symmetric cryptography

Senders and recipients use a publicly known algorithm to transform the *plaintext* into *ciphertext* and vice versa. The operation of the algorithm is controlled by a secret key. The protection of information is thus shifted to protecting secret keys. Since the late 1990s, efficient solutions have been available for *authenticated encryption*: this operation hides the content of the plaintext (confidentiality) and allows recipients to detect modifications (authenticity). Secret keys can be agreed by physical means (e.g., the SIM card in a mobile phone). For large-scale systems, a Trusted Third Party (TTP) may act as intermediary. An example of a system with a TTP is Kerberos (Steiner et al. 1988), which is used in Windows Active Directory.

Public key cryptography

In the mid-1970s, Diffie and Hellman proposed a more elegant solution to the key distribution problem (Diffie and Hellman 1976). They invented *public-key cryptography*, in which the key used to encrypt information is different from the key to decrypt information. Senders encrypt the plaintext with the public encryption key of the recipient, and recipients decrypt the information with their private decryption key. As a consequence, the key for encryption can be made public, and there is no need for the parties to agree on a common secret in advance. Nevertheless, it is still important that senders know the correct public key of recipients: public-key encryption shifts the confidentiality of messages to the authenticity of public keys.

As a public encryption key is public, anyone can encrypt a message for the owner of the public key: hence public-key encryption provides confidentiality protection but does not authenticate the sender. Diffie and Hellman also proposed a second concept that solves the authentication problem, which they called *digital signatures*: senders transform a message with their private signing key; anyone can verify that it was created by this person by verifying this message with the sender's public verification key. This verification key can be widely distributed. Digital signatures are, to some extent, the electronic equivalent of manual signatures on a paper document. In order to verify that a digital signature on a message was generated by a specific person, one needs an authenticated copy of this person's public key.

Certification authorities and certificates

With public-key cryptography, the confidentiality and authentication of data can be shifted to the authenticity of public keys. Worldwide there a billions of users and devices with public keys, so keeping track of all these keys is very hard.
In order to make public-key cryptography scalable, a Trusted Third Party is introduced that is called a Certification Authority (CA). The CA digitally signs a statement that contains someone's name and public key. Other pieces are added to this statement, such as the validity period and the cryptographic algorithms that have been used. Such a statement is called a *certificate*. Certificates can be compared to paper passports or identity cards, which link a person's name to an attribute (e.g., a photo); such documents are typically signed by a civil servant. How do you verify a certificate? This requires the public verification key of the CA. In some contexts (such as e-government), there is only one CA, and it is not too difficult to widely distribute this one public key in many locations. On the web, there are more than 600 CAs.

Key generation

Cryptology shifts problems of securing data to securing keys. An important problem is how to generate those keys. For this purpose, you need random inputs. These inputs can be generated by electronic or optical circuits or by measuring the behaviour of systems and users. This random data is collected and combined; a cryptographic Pseudo-Random Number Generator (PRNG) (Barker and Kelsey 2012) is then used to process this data and stretch it into random and secret key bits.

3.3.2   ROLE OF CRYPTOLOGY IN PROTECTING DIGITAL INFORMATION

Communication security and secure storage are very important for military and government systems. Cryptography has been deployed in the banking sector since the 1970s and in the telecommunications industry since the late 1980s. The explosion of the Internet and the expansion of content protection mechanisms have resulted in large-scale deployments during the 1990s. For the future, there is a strong need for integrating cryptographic protection in e-health, critical infrastructures (e.g., smart grid, industrial control systems) and the Internet of Things (IOT).

Communications

Cryptography is essential to protect communications from passive and active adversaries: it allows you to establish a secure channel between senders and recipients over an insecure network such as the Internet and to control access to communication systems. Properly deployed cryptography allows end-to-end encryption between senders and recipients: this implies that no intermediate party is able to decrypt.

Network layer. IPsec (Kent and Sero 2005) is the standard for secure channel establishment and key management on the Internet. IPsec can be configured to work between any two individual nodes, but organizations tend to dislike encrypted tunnels through the gateways that guard the entry and exit points of their networks; their concern is that such tunnels could be used by attackers to inject malware or to steal information. A solution to this problem is to start or end the encrypted tunnel at the gateway. The IPsec standard is very complex and has many options, which makes it difficult to implement and configure IPsec securely. The Snowden documents show that intelligence agencies can intercept and decrypt tens of thousands of secure IPsec connections per hour. IPsec is supported by the major operating systems, but its deployment is limited by its complexity.

Transport layer. For web applications, the TLS standard (Dierks and Rescorla 2008) was established more than 20 years ago. More than 10 million servers and several billion devices (smart phones, tablets, laptops) communicate securely over SSL/TLS; it is used for secure e-commerce, e-banking, access to webmail and health applications, but also for protecting the network infrastructure such as routers, cameras and industrial control systems. SSL/TLS is much easier to deploy than IPsec. The protocol is more complex than it should be and the development and deployment of solutions for security flaws is often very slow. OpenSSL is a widely used open source library; a number of serious flaws (e.g. Heartbleed (Carvalho et al. 2014)) has resulted in increased security awareness and improvement of its governance. The Achilles heel of SSL/TLS is the more than 600 certification authorities (cf. Eckersley and Burns 2010); by default, browser users trust all of them. If a single one of them is subverted, this can lead to fraudulent certificates that allow to intercept or spoof communications. Several cases have shown that this is a realistic threat (e.g., Diginotar[1], Turktrust, CCNIC). Some products even add an additional CA to browsers that issue fake certificates to widely used domains in order to allow companies to intercept the web traffic of their employees.

Data link layer. Even if communications over wires and optical fiber can be intercepted on a large scale, it is clear that wireless communications are more vulnerable as radio waves spread over a very large area, typically much larger than what is required for the application. For this reason, separate standards have been developed to protect communication between mobile phones and base stations or base stations controllers (2G/3G/4G standards), between laptops, smart phones and tablets (WLAN standards) and for Personal Area Networks (Bluetooth and Bluetooth Low Energy or BLE). The first generations of wireless security standards had many flaws, but the recent versions have been improved substantially. The main limitation is that these standards do not offer end-to-end security: intermediate parties that control the end point of the wireless communication can see all the information. This is a concern for the GSM system and for WLANs, which have no proper method for authenticating the wireless access point. Medical devices (such as defibrillators and insulin pumps) are increasingly controlled over wireless channels but without proper protection.

Email. Emails are postcards and not letters. There are several solutions for securing email. The standardized solutions are S/MIME (Ramsdell and Turner 2010) and OpenPGP (Callas et al. 2007); the latter is supported by the open source library GPG.[2] Setting up secure email is still a challenge; it can work among groups of experts or can be configured in a corporation's email clients for internal email. Even then, most programs are very hard to configure and use securely. Global secure email is an even bigger problem: the most important challenges are key management and interoperability.

Voice calls and chat. Voice calls over the internet (VOIP) and chat sessions can also be protected using cryptographic methods. There are secure and open solutions such as OTR (Off The Record communications) (Goldberg et al. 2009), but most widely deployed systems do not have open specifications and have design flaws. The EFF has recently published a study[3] identifying shortcomings in many apps for secure communications. Skype has about half a billion users; the documents leaked by Snowden indicate that it can be intercepted by intelligence agencies.

Meta data. Network encryption hides the content of data but does not hide the amount of plaintext or the identities of the communicating parties. For high latency applications such as email, cryptographic remailers can be used (e.g. Mixminion by Danezis et al. (2003)). For low latency applications, a secure IPsec connection can be established to a proxy server. In both cases, compromise of the remailer or server (or a warrant) would undermine the security. Tor, designed by Dingledine et al. (2004), is a more robust and distributed scheme for low latency traffic. It encrypts traffic in three layers (called onions), and each of the three servers peels off one layer. The Tor network has more than 6,000 nodes, and there are about half a million users at any time.

Storage

Data on user devices. A second application of cryptography is the protection of data at rest. Each year, a huge number of USB drives, laptops and smart phones are lost, stolen or sold. If someone has access to the device, they can read all the private information stored on there: this may be financial information, commercially sensitive information or health-related information.

Data stored on a device should be protected with authenticated encryption, and the key (of at least 128 bits) should be stored in a secure place. A common solution is to store the decryption key on the device; this is clearly not an effective solution against a motivated opponent. A better option is to store the key in an external secure device (e.g., a smart card) or to use biometrics to authenticate the user and to derive a key that can be used to access the decryption key. Key management for the encryption of stored data is tricky as it requires a backup solution for most applications, in case something happens to the user or the user leaves the organization that owns the data.

There are several software tools that allow users to protect the data on their hard disk (e.g., Truecrypt, Veracrypt, Bitlocker). While Truecrypt was recently abandoned by its designer, it has recently undergone a serious security audit, and one can expect that the minor issues identified have been fixed in the fork Veracrypt. Today, many hard drives have built-in hardware encryption, but most drives come without key management software: if the drive is unplugged from one computer and plugged into a second computer, you can read all the data.

Data in the 'cloud'. Today, we store massive amounts of data in the cloud: this includes data at email providers (Gmail), social networks (Facebook), storage services (e.g., Dropbox, iCloud) or service providers such as Amazon EC2, the Google Cloud Platform and Microsoft Azure. The PRISM program, revealed by Snowden, gives the NSA access to the content stored in the clouds run by US companies. A related application requiring protection is databases: you want to protect the information in the database even if an attacker gets physical access to the server.

Authenticated encryption can offer effective protection, on the condition that the decryption key is stored locally under control of the data owner rather than in the cloud. However, the business model behind many cloud applications is that service providers can profile users based on the data and sell this profiling information to advertisers. If data (and metadata) were encrypted, this business model would no longer work. A surprising solution to this problem is to search in encrypted data: if the search terms are known in advance, you can encrypt data in such a way that the encryption is secure but you can still search the ciphertext for the search terms.

A second disadvantage of encryption of data in the cloud is that it seems to be impossible to perform operations on the data. However, this is not correct: there are many homomorphic cryptosystems that allow to add or multiply plain-texts by manipulating the ciphertexts. Gentry (2009) showed that Fully Homo-morphic Encryption (FHE) is possible in principle: in his solution, you can per-form both additions and multiplications on the plaintext, allowing you to com-pute any function in principle. Unfortunately, FHE is highly inefficient and, hence, very far from practical. For simple functions that only require a few multiplica-tions, however, this solution is becoming realistic. An important property of FHE is that the result is encrypted: the cloud provider can compute the result, but only the user can decrypt it. This implies that this solution brings benefits to users rather than cloud providers.

Media and software. Cryptography is widely used to protect media and software. The main goal of this technology is to enforce Digital Rights Management (DRM), that is, to ensure that only authorized users can access the content or use the soft-ware and that they cannot copy the bits or pass on the license to others (a limited number of copies or transfers is allowed in some cases). This is a very challenging problem, as the user of the device is the enemy in this setting. If you want to pro-tect content, the first step is to encrypt the information. This will preclude users from accessing the bits on their device and freely copying them. Access to the con-tent can then be controlled by controlling access to the decryption keys. Content protection is used in about 1.5 billion DVD and Blu-ray players. The pay TV market has just under 1 billion customers. There are about 250 million game consoles that protect the game software using cryptography.

Identification and access control

A cryptographic device can be authenticated by sending a challenge to the device and by asking it to encrypt this challenge with a symmetric algorithm; the result is sent as the response. If the verifier also possess the same key, he or she can verify the answer. In One Time Password devices, the challenge value is the time with a resolution of 30 seconds or 1 minute; this is more efficient as it is not necessary to transmit the challenge. If the cryptographic device is capable of computing digital signatures, it can sign the challenge. The advantage is that the answer can now be verified using the public key of the cryptographic device and that the verifier does not need to store sensitive secret keys.

Challenge response protocols are much more secure than passwords, but they require cryptographic computations. Moreover, they require an additional step in which users authenticate to the cryptographic device with a PIN code, a password or a biometric feature. The access control industry has deployed about 6 billion cards and 200 million readers; the main applications are access to buildings and public transport. The use of electronic fobs to open and start cars is also increasing rapidly. Both applications use symmetric cryptography.

The banking industry has deployed about 3.5 billion bank cards with symmetric cryptography and 2.7 billion EMV cards with public-key capabilities. These cards securely identify the account and the account holder and also authenticate and possibly encrypt the payment transaction. In many countries, governments are issuing Electronic Identity Cards (eID), e-passports and e-driving licenses with public-key capabilities; the total deployment is several 100 millions. eID cards can be used to access e-government services and some commercial services and to create digital signatures that are legally compliant. The usage of e-passports is restricted to local authentication such as border controls.

Update and boot

The software on many devices and apps is updated on a regular basis. Modern processors can even be updated remotely. The role of these updates is to fix security flaws but also to continuously enhance functionality. In order to prevent attackers from injecting malicious updates, all updates are digitally signed with the private key of the software vendor or app developer. This requires that the user device has an authenticated copy of the corresponding public key. This public key is typically inserted at installation and protected by several integrity mechanisms. The software update mechanism is available on billions of devices and is one of the largest applications of public-key cryptography.

Every time a computer starts up, a large number of programs are loaded and executed. It is important for users to know that the correct programs have been loaded and executed correctly. This can be guaranteed by cryptographically protecting the software and verifying the status of the computer. For many vendors and content owners, secure boot is also important to prevent illegal software or software that allows to circumvent DRM restrictions to be installed on a device. For this purpose, remote attestation protocols have been invented that allow someone to remotely verify the status of a machine after start-up. While secure boot is an important component of secure computation, this technology also brings up issues of control and autonomy: users have paid for hardware and software but may be prevented from freely using them. It also brings up competition issues, as these mechanisms can be used to exclude competing software from a given hardware platform.

Computation

The problem of secure execution goes beyond the boot phase: how can users (or a third party) verify that application software is executing correctly and that no information on the computation inputs or outputs is leaking to outsiders? This problem is relevant for DRM but also for the gaming industry, which wants to address cheating in multi-player online games. Secure execution can be supported by cryptographic techniques but also requires many other modifications to our current computer and software architectures.

Multi-Party Computation (MPC) is a cryptographic technique that allows for secure computation without having to trust a centralized entity (Yao 1982). Consider an application in which multiple data owners have sensitive data sets, such as a country's tax, social security and health databases, the buying patterns of users on multiple e-commerce sites or the bidding strategies in an auction. If you want to mine or analyse these Big Data sets, the easiest solution is to share the data and run the mining algorithms on the complete set. However, the parties may not trust each other with their valuable data. A simple solution is to send all the data to a TTP and ask this TTP to perform the mining. This assumes that there exists such a party that is trusted by all; this may not be realistic. Moreover, legal barriers may forbid sharing this data with a TTP. MPC can solve this problem if a large enough fraction of the parties is honest and if the parties are online: any problem that can be solved with a TTP can be solved without such a TTP; the parties can be sure that nothing leaks beyond the outcome (which is public) and that the results are correct. In the last decade, the efficiency of these protocols have been improved substantially, to the point that they can be applied to large databases and complex auctions in a realistic time frame. The difference between MPC and FHE is that, in FHE, the parties do not need to be available online and the result is always encrypted.

3.3.3   REGULATION OF CRYPTOLOGY

Cryptography is a dual-use good, and countries have tried to control its import, export and use to avoid hindering the operations of their intelligence and law enforcement services. In 1977, the US government published an open cryptographic standard for the protection of sensitive but unclassified data: the Data Encryption Standard. The key length of the DES was restricted to 56 bits, which meant that the NSA could decode any ciphertext in a reasonable amount of time, while it offered a reasonable protection against more modest adversaries.

Until the late 1980s, cryptography could only be implemented in expensive hardware; this meant that it was sufficient to control these hardware devices. Telecommunications was in the hands of state-controlled monopolies, which made things easier. There have been attempts in several countries to discourage research in and teaching of cryptology, e.g., by threatening with secrecy orders. Perhaps a more effective approach (still used in some countries) is to channel research funding through national cryptographic agencies, which would then require security clearances and/or impose publication restrictions. The EU did not fund any open cryptographic research between 1992 and 1999, but open research in cryptology was funded by several organizations in many European countries.

In the mid to late 1980s, the telecommunications monopolies were broken up, cryptography started migrating to software and, in the early 1990s, the quick growth of the Internet allowed low-cost global data communications. This made it much more difficult to control cryptographic software. A famous example is the source code of the email encryption tool PGPi 5.0, which was printed as a book in 1997 and legally exported from the US under the First Amendment. In response to the broad availability of cryptographic software, the US government proposed in 1993 that secure communications should use the Clipper chip; this chip had a secret algorithm and gave US government agencies access to the keys using a key escrow method. The US government tried to muddle the key-escrow debate by pointing out the importance of backup keys for stored data, while the Clipper chip would escrow keys for communications, for which a backup is not needed. Both the industry and academia protested vehemently and pointed out serious flaws in the key-escrow approach and in the specific details of the Clipper chip. The Clipper chip was abandoned by 1996. The wider belief was that the crypto wars had been won.

The export of cryptography from the Western world was controlled by COCOM (Coordinating Committee for Multilateral Export Controls), which was replaced by the Wassenaar arrangement on Export Controls for Conventional Arms and Dual-Use Goods and Technologies in 1995. Most countries (excepting a few, including the US) made exemptions for mass-market and public-domain crypto software. In 1998, these exemptions for mass-market software were limited to symmetric encryption algorithms with keys up to 64 bits and for encryption for DRM; at the same time, export controls were strongly reduced for cryptosystems with short keys[4] – which could easily be broken by intelligence agencies. In 2000, the export controls on mass-market crypto software and hardware were lifted completely. Worldwide, there are still many regulations on importing and export-ing crypto and for offering certain cryptographic services. China, for example, has a law that requires that every cryptographic algorithm used in China has to be designed in China. Russia also has its own cryptographic standards. Moreover, a recent attack on TLS/SSL enabled parties to fall back on the key lengths specified in the 1998 Wassenaar arrangement; while those keys were easy to break by an intel-ligence agency at that time, they can be broken by a team with a budget of a few thousand euros 17 years later (for more details, see the Crypto Law Survey of Koops[5] and Diffie and Landau 1998).

3.4   STRENGTH AND WEAKNESSES OF CRYPTOLOGY

Today we have a broad availability of strong cryptographic algorithms and proto-cols that can be implemented at very low cost to secure our communications and stored information. If you properly use well-configured open source crypto, you are protected against any opponent, with the exception perhaps of a few intelligence agencies. The main challenge is to make cryptography easy to config-ure and as transparent as possible for the end user. There are still challenges in developing robust and secure cryptographic code and in securely deploying and upgrading cryptography. In spite of this, only a small fraction of all Internet traffic is properly protected; even if there is a push of security by default for many appli-cations and devices, one should be concerned about the slow adoption of the exist-ing solutions and backdoors for intelligence agencies.

3.4.1   CRYPTANALYSIS

This section discusses several attacks on cryptosystems: mathematical attacks, attacks using quantum computers and side-channel and fault attacks.

Mathematical cryptanalysis

Exhaustive key search. The easiest way to break a cryptosystem is to try all possible keys. There are extensive reports that make recommendations for key lengths as a function of the length of the protection required and the budget of the opponent (e.g., ENISA 2014). In 2015, key lengths of 80 bits were the bare minimum. There is no reason why one would not use a 128-bit or even 256-bit key: the extra cost to distribute, store or use such a key is very small compared to an 80-bit or 100-bit key. If a cryptosystem is used by billions of users to encrypt large data volumes, 128-bit keys may be too short to secure protection for 20 years or more; a mini-mum length of 160 bits or 192 bits would be more appropriate in this case.

Shortcut attacks. For a well-designed symmetric cryptographic algorithm, no shortcut attack exists that has a cost that is substantially less than exhaustive key search. It is recommended to stick to widely used and thoroughly evaluated standards such as the AES. It is also recommended to carefully plan the replace-ment or upgrade of cryptographic algorithms.

For public-key cryptography, there are always algorithms that can exploit the mathematical structure and that are, therefore, more efficient than exhaustive key search. For the RSA algorithm, the public key consists of the modulus that is the product of two large primes, and the public exponent. The most straightforward method to break RSA is to compute the private key from the public key by factor-ing the modulus. In 2015, a 512-bit RSA modulus could be factored in 1 core-year (or in 1 hour on a network with 1000 8-core processors) (Adrian et al. 2015). The 512-bit discrete logarithm problem can be solved in 90 seconds on 2500 cores. If RSA is properly implemented, factoring the modulus is the best possible attack. However, there are some deployments of public-key cryptography using outdated standards for message formatting, specific optimizations and implementation weaknesses that allow for more efficient attacks.

Quantum computers

In a classical computer, information is represented in the form of bits; a bit can take the value 0 or 1. In a quantum computer, information is represented as qubits; a qubit can be in a superposition of states, that is, it can be 0 and 1 at the same time. Quantum computers can be realized by exploiting quantum-mechanical phenomena, that is, certain physical objects can be used to realize qubits and perform operations on them. Quantum computers can give an enormous speed-up to computations. If you have 30 calculation units on a classic computer, you can compute 30 times faster. In a quantum computer, 30 qubits can represent $2^{30} \approx 1$ billion values at the same time, and hence a speedup with a factor of 1 billion can be achieved in principle.

Operations on a quantum computer are more restricted than on a classical computer; hence, to fully exploit quantum computers, you have to invent new algorithms. The most important useful computations that could be performed on a quantum computer are the simulation of quantum many-body systems but also many cryptanalytic algorithms. Grover showed in 1996 (Grover 1996) that the time of a search operation (e.g., exhaustive key search) can be reduced on a quantum computer to a square root compared to a classical computer. This means that an exhaustive key search for a 128-bit key on a quantum computer takes the time of a 64-bit key on a classical computer (as $\sqrt{2^{128}} = 2^{64}$). For symmetric cryptography, the key lengths need to be doubled to resist attacks by quantum computers. In practice, you would need key lengths of 256 bits. For public-key cryptography, the impact of quantum computers would be much more dramatic. The security of the widely used public-key algorithms is based on two problems from algebraic number theory: factorization and discrete logarithm. Shor (1994) pointed out that quantum computers are extremely well suited to solving these problems. If a large quantum computer can be built, these systems would be completely insecure.

Many approaches are being tried to create quantum computers such as superconductors, trapped ions, optical lattices, quantum dots and nuclear magnetic resonance. The biggest challenge is controlling or removing quantum decoherence: interference with the outside world will disturb the quantum computations and render the result useless. Decoherence can be addressed by combining physical isolation techniques with quantum error correction. It is very hard to predict when the first large quantum computer will be available. There has been steady progress over the last two decades, and there are very large investments, by intelligence agencies, for instance, which would be interested in the cryptanalytic capabilities. Some experts believe that there is a 10-15 percent chance that a large quantum computer can be built by 2025 and that this probability will increase to about 1 in 2035. You may anticipate that the first quantum computers will be owned by intelligence agencies and that, hence, we may not be aware of their existence.

For the past two decades, researchers have been working on novel cryptographic algorithms that would resist quantum computers. Their focus has been on public-key algorithms, but it cannot be excluded that novel quantum algorithms will be discovered that reduce the strength of symmetric cryptographic algorithms beyond the quantum square root attacks known today. For public-key cryptography (both encryption and digital signatures), approaches are being studied based on lattices, codes and multivariate equations; for digital signature schemes, constructions based on hash functions can also be used. These schemes are typically faster than the current schemes, but most of them have much larger keys. For some of them, evaluating the concrete security level is challenging, and it cannot be excluded that novel quantum algorithms will be discovered that may weaken their security. It is expected to take 3-5 years before these schemes will start appearing in cryptographic standards, and it will take another 2-4 years before efficient implementations are widely available. This is a concern for encryption schemes because even in 2015 there is information we would like to protect for 10 years; this would mean that we should start using those schemes today. For digital signatures, this is less of an issue, and all documents could be re-signed every 3-5 years with improved algorithms with larger keys.

Side-channel and fault attacks

Cryptographic systems are mathematical algorithms. However, if we use them in practice, they are running on real devices. Attackers can take advantage of the physical properties of these devices.

Cryptographic implementations do not get a result instantaneously: there is always some delay. These implementations also consume power, emit electromagnetic radiations and emit photons. If these signals depend on the data and the key and if they can somehow be obtained by attackers, they may be able to deduce part of the secret key; this is known as a side-channel attack. If you want to protect implementations against these attacks, you should prevent the opponent from accessing these physical quantities, e.g., by shielding the implementation and providing an internal power source. However, perfect shielding is not possible, and timing information can be obtained remotely. A second approach is to add countermeasures to the implementation, e.g., by ensuring that the implementation is constant time, by making the power consumption independent of the key and by adding noise.

An even more powerful attack model consists of injecting faults in an implementation, e.g., by clock or power glitches or by shining with a laser on the chip surface. If a cryptographic device outputs incorrect results as a consequence of such a fault, the implications are typically devastating: you can easily recover the key. Protection against fault attacks typically includes verification of the intermediate or final results and error-detection codes.

Many implementations of cryptography are still vulnerable to these attacks, either because they have no protection against them or because the protection is insufficient. In many cases, the countermeasures are confidential, which makes it difficult to evaluate their strength.

3.4.2   **BYPASSING OR UNDERMINING CRYPTO**

Cryptography is a very powerful mathematical tool that can offer strong security, but it can be bypassed in many cases. Sometimes crypto can be switched off, for example, without the user noticing anything.

Cryptography moves the protection of information to the protection of keys, and attackers, therefore, try to get the keys. There are several approaches: I) you may ask for the key based on a key disclosure law, a court order or a security letter; II) you may use techniques to extract the secret keys from software or hardware; III) several attempts have been made to impose key escrow solutions, in which law enforcement agencies can get access to the key through a government-controlled backup option.

Crypto implementations may contain accidental errors or deliberate backdoors. A common problem is that implementations do not generate keys properly. A typical mistake is that not enough randomness is used in the key generation process; this makes the keys easy to predict to an attacker. A backdoor could consist of a key generation algorithm that only generates a small subset of the keys. The most extreme example known is the DUAL EC random bit generator, designed by the NSA and standardized by ANSI, ISO and NIST. This generator has two parameters; there are very strong suspicions that the NSA has generated these parameters in a special way such that they (and no one else) can predict future outputs from seeing a single output string. The risk of a backdoor was pointed out in a presentation at a conference in 2007, but the standard was only withdrawn after Snowden documents leaked in September 2013 referred to NSA's Bullrun program, which includes the undermining of crypto standards. Another type of backdoor is the deliberate insertion of a side channel. For example, an encryption device could deliberately leak information about the secret key through a timing channel.

Users and systems act upon information presented to them in clear. This implies that the unprotected information is processed by a computer, which is very often a complex device with several large integrated circuits and millions of lines of code. It is beyond the state of the art to make a computer 100 percent secure. There are many ways to get malware on a computer: through email attachments, malicious websites, worms, Trojans, thumb drives or even through official updates of the vendor. Sophisticated malware can then steal data and exfiltrate it through hidden channels. Examples of such malware are the German Bundestrojaner and the FBI's Magic Lantern software. Over the last five years, highly sophisticated malware such as Stuxnet and Regin have been exposed; there are serious concerns that many nations and organized crime will build on this leaked code and spread advanced malware on a much larger scale.

Yet another way to get access to information on a computer is to add hardware devices that extract information. The Snowden documents have revealed a trove of data on NSA's Tailored Access Operations (TAO)[6] and have given us a glimpse of some of the devices developed for this purpose. One such device intercepts the connection between the motherboard and the screen of a PC. A second type is modified USB and Ethernet connectors that can be used to insert malware and that work as wireless bridges, providing covert remote access. Some of these devices are inserted by intercepting devices in transit from suppliers to customers, raising the issue of supply chain security.

3.4.3   BARRIERS TO DEPLOYMENT OF CRYPTO

Cryptographic operations have the reputation of being very cost-intensive. However, computing power has progressed tremendously over the last decades, while cryptographic algorithms have not become much more complex. Today, the overhead in terms of computation of cryptography is low for most applications, perhaps with the exception of cryptography for tiny energy-constrained devices such as implanted medical devices. A cost barrier for cryptographic deployment is the cost of key management; this includes not only key establishment but the full life cycle management, which includes generation, revocation, archival and destruction. Moreover, if you want implementations that offer a high security level against physical attacks, the cost and complexity of the devices is rather high.

A second barrier to widespread use of cryptography is government-imposed limitations; the most frequently used argument for this purpose is lawful access to communicated or stored data. For cloud applications, it has been argued in section 3.2 that cryptographic protection of user data is considered to be incompatible with revenue models based on personalization and targeted advertising. The current alternatives such as searchable encryption are computationally more expensive and are more complex to deploy. Sophisticated cryptographic techniques for computing on encrypted data and secure computation are substantially more expensive at this stage than regular cryptography, and in some cases even completely impractical. It is expected that they will be restricted to niche applications, such as medical data and selected government databases.

3.5   PRIVACY ENGINEERING AND BIG DATA

Privacy research as a field of study originated primarily as a subtopic in security engineering. Its maturation over the years has led to a whole palette of 'privacy solutions' that originate from diverse subfields of computer science, such as security engineering, databases, software engineering, HCI and artificial intelligence. From a bird's eye view, all of these solutions address privacy using technical means. However, a closer look reveals that communities of researchers and practitioners rely on different definitions of privacy and on a variety of social and technical assumptions. As a result, they address different privacy and related concerns in the context of Big Data. We will identify three predominant approaches and give examples of how they apply to Big Data.

3.5.1   PRIVACY AS CONFIDENTIALITY (PETS)

The most popular conception of privacy relies on the binary that exposure of information leads to loss of privacy, while guaranteeing the confidentiality of information is a way to 'preserve' or 'enhance' privacy. Privacy solutions based on this approach rely on this binary understanding of unwanted disclosures to unauthorized parties as privacy violations. Hence, the capabilities of unauthorized parties (also called adversaries) are an important driver in the design of privacy solutions. These solutions intend to protect confidentiality of communications as well as traffic data (also called metadata) from unintended parties. Precautions are also taken to avoid inadvertent inferences from any data disclosed that could lead to privacy violations. Solutions in this approach foresee the protection of the disclosure of such data to all third parties, including the service provider itself. Many of the techniques make use of the cryptographic mechanisms discussed above but with the objective of protecting individual privacy rather than organizational assets. This means that, at times, securing privacy may be at odds with the security goals of the organization that is serving the user.

The emphasis on privacy leads to three important principles that are central to solutions in the privacy-as-confidentiality paradigm:

Data minimization: Designing systems and mechanisms that limit disclosure of information to that which is absolutely necessary for a given functionality.

Avoidance of a single point of failure: Abstaining from designing architectures for information collection and processing with a 'single point of failure', that is, data remains on users' devices or is distributed across multiple entities that have to collaborate to solve a computational problem.

Openness to scrutiny: Keeping the protocols, codes and processes of development that underlie the privacy tools open to public scrutiny in order to increase trust in the privacy solution itself.

Privacy-enhancing technologies (PETs) are those technologies that leverage all three principles above. These principles are fundamental to developing technologies for anonymous use of Big Data services like Tor (cf. section 3.1), and for providing users with the option of using services without disclosing sensitive data. PETs are aligned with the objectives of constitutional protections of the right to privacy more so than with the assumptions, principles and goals of data protection frameworks. Data protection frameworks put information stewardship ('accountability') obligations on data controllers, who act as custodians of personal data. The notion of the data controller as a trusted party is ill at ease with the anti-surveillance gist of constitutional privacy and privacy-as-confidentiality solutions (Diaz et al. 2013). In fact, most PETs function on the diametrically opposed perception of the data controller as an adversary. Frequent security breaches, lack of assurances of computations on the cloud as well as reports of data abuse by companies have served to confirm the importance of solutions in this approach.

Typical examples of this approach include encryption tools to protect digital communications discussed in section 3.2 as well as mechanisms to obfuscate user entries so that the service provider cannot infer with certainty a user's location, actual search engine queries (Balsa et al. 2012) or writing style (McDonald et al. 2012). While many PETs require service providers to take positive action, others are collaborative applications: users collectively act as the service providers, without the involvement of an actual data controller in the provision of the service. For example, the Tor network relies on a decentralized architecture run by volunteers to enable users to communicate anonymously. Multi-party computation (MPC) techniques are another example of collaborative solutions that allow parties to do data analytics without revealing their datasets to each other.

In addition to their role in upholding fundamental rights to privacy in the technical domain, PETs can be essential to establishing trust in Big Data infrastructures. Interesting examples are e-petition systems, which allow for anonymous participation but protect against fraud (Diaz et al. 2009), and privacy-preserving smart meters, which allow users to benefit from smart meters while avoiding disclosure of fine-grained meter measures to the service provider (Rial and Danezis 2010). These solutions are key to citizens' participation, when people regard anonymity as a precondition to signing e-petitions or to responding to situations in which people protest the intrusiveness of Big Data infrastructures, as in the case of smart meters in the Netherlands.

Relatedly, privacy-as-confidentiality techniques are used to ensure accountability in information systems (cf. section 3.2). Technically, accountability is often equated with integrity of systems, for example, improving the accountability of services by securing the integrity of (privacy-enhanced) system logs (Peeters et al. 2013). If transparency of service provisioning becomes an important mode of protecting privacy, such integrity measures will be key to auditing its infrastructures. Recently, accountability of algorithms has also attracted attention (Felten 2012).

Such mechanisms can be used, for example, to guarantee that users' newsfeeds on online social networks are not manipulated without the users' awareness (Feldman et al. 2012), as was the case in the Facebook emotion contagion study that led to an uproar from users and experts alike (Grimmelmann 2014; Kramer et al. 2014).

3.5.2 PRIVACY AS CONTROL (COMPLIANCE)

In the privacy-as-control paradigm, researchers and practitioners focus on developing mechanisms to provide individuals with greater control over their data flows and with technical means to enhance the ability of organizations using personal information to achieve data protection compliance. In this paradigm, it is assumed that, in an increasingly networked world, personal information will have to be disclosed. Hence, individuals must be empowered to make informed decisions about using services. This can partly be achieved through greater transparency as well as increased control over personal information flows. In this approach, organizations are expected to combine technical, legal and organizational means to protect users' data. In some cases, data subjects may not be users of the system (e.g., patients in a hospital). Nevertheless, privacy-as-control solutions may be instrumental in protecting subjects' data in such systems.

In data protection legislation, data controllers and processors are expected to provide some transparency to data subjects about the collection and processing of personal information, typically communicated through 'privacy policies'. Experience has shown that the language of privacy policies is difficult for users to comprehend. Privacy researchers have studied ways to ease the burden of reading privacy policies and improve their effectiveness through, for example, labelling mechanisms comparable to those in the food industry (Kelley et al. 2009), as well as designing machine-readable privacy policies that can be matched to user preferences (Cranor and Wenning 2007). Where interacting with a service implies sharing information with multiple service providers, user agents have been proposed that make (semi-)automated decisions regarding the acceptability of the associated privacy policies (Langheinrich et al. 2002).

The enforcement of promises made in privacy policies can be formalized using machine-readable privacy policy languages and applied using policy enforcement mechanisms (Petkovic et al. 2011) that provide organizations with technical controls over appropriate use of data. Recent work has addressed the use of policy languages to ensure that all providers involved in provisioning a cloud service comply with the user-facing legal privacy policy (Breaux et al. 2014; Sen et al. 2014).

Privacy policy languages can also be used to express user privacy preferences in context. Mechanisms for this purpose, often called 'privacy settings' (Johnson et al. 2012), are proposed that are closer to the users' mental models of services. Studies have shown that users are better served if privacy controls are set to privacy-friendly defaults (Angulo and Wästlund 2013), but that these defaults may vary across users and contexts. Given the mental load of managing multiple services, researchers propose using machine learning to assist users in keeping their privacy settings up to date and fit to their needs (Sayaf and Clarke 2012). Data analytics have also been proposed to semi-automatically extract the main tenets of privacy policies in order to assist users in making privacy decisions (Sadeh et al. 2014; Schaub et al. 2014).

Data subject access rights – i.e., the ability of data subjects to access, rectify or delete the data collected by a service provider – is another challenging requirement in Big Data infrastructures. Some service companies have proposed privacy dashboards (Google 2015) and identity management schemes (Chadwick 2009; Bhargav-Spantzel et al. 2007). These solutions aim to make the personal information held by (multiple) service providers transparent to data subjects. They also integrate reasonable controls over the collection and future use of this information. These mechanisms are increasingly important in SaaS, where users have to manage dozens of identities. However, the protections that identity management schemes provide are limited: many service providers will only make transparent information that has been volitionally disclosed by the user, not disclosing all the data captured through service use. Furthermore, 'anonymous' or aggregated use of data for analytics (e.g., profiling) is typically not made transparent since such data is no longer considered 'personal information'.

The claim that anonymizing data provides sufficient protection to individuals is misleading, however. Database anonymization consists of mechanisms to manipulate datasets so that a privacy requirement is fulfilled – e.g., individual users cannot be re-identified – while retaining maximum utility of the dataset. Research on databases has shown that even the most elaborate anonymization techniques do not provide sufficiently robust guarantees. Analysts may (inadvertently) recover the supposedly unlinked identities or find additional information about these data subjects by using auxiliary information (Sweeney 2002; Kifer and Gehrke 2006; Domingo-Ferrer and Torra 2008; Narayanan and Shmatikov 2010).

Differential privacy, an increasingly popular technique, avoids some of the known formal weaknesses of database anonymization by redefining the protection afforded using the technique. It ensures that only a limited amount of additional risk is incurred by participating in databases. In other words, the information that can be inferred from the dataset can be inferred regardless of whether a specific person's data is in the database. Differential privacy can be guaranteed independent of the computational power and auxiliary information available to an adversary (Dwork and Smith 2009). As a result of the way differential privacy lends itself to automation and quantification of privacy protection (Erlingsson et al. 2014), it is likely to gain in popularity in the context of Big Data services.

3.5.3   PRIVACY AS PRACTICE (TRANSPARENCY AND FEEDBACK)

In privacy as practice, engineers and designers focus on socio-technical designs to improve users' agency with respect to privacy in social settings. This approach captures privacy matters that arise from the mediation of communications, for example, between peers or in a workplace. These concerns are related to but often distinct from concerns about organizations collecting and processing data (privacy as control) or unintended observations that can be made by unauthorized parties (privacy as confidentiality). The social computing perspective, in which information systems are seen as facilitating social interactions, informs the methods and techniques used in this approach. The idea is to design systems that respect social norms with regard to information flows (Nissenbaum 2009) and that address privacy in the context of collective information practices (Palen and Dourish 2003). Techniques include providing users with feedback about system functionality as well as making transparent the potential impact of complex information systems on individual and social privacy, for example, addressing matters of discrimination.

Design researchers focus on supporting users in developing good privacy practices with others over time. If the consequences of users' actions can be made transparent to them, they may be able to make better decisions about their future interactions. Similarly, users may learn from their (mediated) social surroundings: information about how other people manage their privacy settings may provide guidance to the users. 'Socially translucent systems' using visibility, awareness and accountability of users' actions among peers can make it easier for users to create, notice and conform to social conventions (Erickson and Kellogg 2000).

Behavioural economists study how collective privacy practices can be improved at the level of individual decision-making. A number of studies point to failures in individual decision-making as the source of many social privacy problems that arise when using applications. These show that users systematically fail to correctly estimate privacy risks (Acquisti and Grossklags 2005) and to match their privacy preferences to their actual behaviours (Berendt et al. 2005). These failures motivate the exploration of design mechanisms that aid users in making better privacy decisions, especially when they lack complete information, are subject to cognitive and behavioural biases and are uncertain about the outcomes of their decisions. All in all, given the multitude of decisions using dozens of services, users may simply experience cognitive overload. In order to address these problems, interface improvements and corrective feedback mechanisms that aspire to make the potential effects of an action more visible have been explored. In one solution, users are able to view their effective permissions as they change their privacy settings (Lipford et al. 2010); in another, they are aided by recommender algorithms that predict the privacy setting preferences of users in their context (Xie et al. 2014); and in yet another, crowdsourcing is used to improve the performance of recommendations for default privacy-friendly settings (Lin et al. 2014).

From these examples, it seems evident that the increased use of data analytics to aid users with the immense cognitive overload of data flows in the cloud is inevitable. Ironically, this means that data analytics can also be seen as a tool to address potential privacy violations due to automation, and, in some cases, due to data analytics itself. However, even when serving users, these algorithms need to be made transparent and accountable. Furthermore, in addition to methods to ensure algorithmic accountability discussed earlier, in the privacy-by-practice approach, we find techniques that focus on making data-mining algorithms more transparent (Pedreshi et al. 2008) and fair (Dwork et al. 2012). The objective, therefore, is not only to make sure that the algorithms function as expected, but also to address societal harms resulting from the discriminatory impact of automated profiling and decision-making (Barocas and Selbst 2014).

3.6   CHALLENGES TO REGULATION BY DESIGN IN ASSURING PRIVACY AND SECURITY IN BIG DATA

Privacy by design, a concept that has risen to prominence over the last twenty years, is an instantiation of regulation by design: the act of embedding certain standards into design in order to foster social outcomes. Regulation by design has been gaining traction in policy circles (Yeung 2014). This is particularly true in addressing privacy and security in information and communication systems. The ambitions of regulation by design are in line with the aspirations of information system engineers to specify and implement systems that will reach a desired outcome in a specific environment (Zave and Jackson 1997), promising a natural match between policymakers, computer scientists and practitioners. Next, we will address some of the challenges associated with these nascent fields of regulation-by-design.

Providing normative guidance in substantive protection of privacy
In the context of privacy by design, the plurality of privacy concepts in law and technology has had positive and negative consequences. Privacy is a 'contested concept': it involves endless disputes about its 'essence or central meaning' that are both paramount and central to the term itself (Mulligan and Koopman 2015).

In fact, the vagueness of the term 'privacy' functions as part of its strength and allows the concept to be leveraged for the protection of individual and social privacy in very different contexts. Technically speaking, this has led to the impressive palette of privacy solutions sketched in the previous sections. Ideally, the solutions from the various approaches can together help address privacy and data protection compliance through technical means in Big Data settings. However, the lack of normative guidance has meant that organizations collecting and processing data often deploy privacy solutions selectively. Experience suggests that the preferred solutions can lean towards cosmetic changes in public-facing interfaces rather than fundamental changes to system architectures (Bonneau and Preibusch 2010). Reasons for favouring cosmetic changes vary. First, interfaces are where the rubber meets the road: 'creeping out' users with intrusive systems can easily jeopardize the systems' future success. This incentivizes organizations to manage privacy expectations and perceptions at the interface level. Second, there is path dependency: if the underlying infrastructure is built upon personal data markets and surveillance as its driving (economic) forces, those building services above the infrastructure will be hard pressed not to replicate and reinforce these aspects.

It is possible to address these challenges by providing normative guidance and incentivizing the implementation of privacy technologies. Such guidance can stipulate that organizations go beyond cosmetic and procedural measures in order to achieve effective protections and could require the deployment of technical measures across the layers of Big Data infrastructures. The path dependency and centralization of services in the hands of a few players can be turned to an advantage by promoting the integration of privacy technologies and cryptological advances in the underlying cloud infrastructure, and by requiring similar steps to be taken in service agreements.

Supporting privacy and security by design in infrastructure

At least since the Snowden revelations, it has become clear that privacy and security on the Internet must be addressed at the infrastructure level, a matter that has so far been neglected. Technology standards are a prime example of technological infrastructure of grave importance for privacy and security. In 1990, for example, the IETF decided that all standards documents (known as RFCs) should include security considerations. This led to increased attention to matters of security in RFCs. Initiatives are currently being launched to address privacy considerations in internet standards (Doty 2015), but this work is led by a few volunteers and needs to be supported more generously. Similar initiatives should be considered for other infrastructures such as browsers, cell phones, telecommunication networks, and wireless standards.

In the current regulatory and market landscape, organizations often get away with deploying intrusive systems. Because of how service provisioning in Big Data infrastructures has been reconfigured, it is difficult for policymakers and the general public to experience, recognize, understand and reasonably react to intrusive practices. Privacy violations may also emerge from the interaction of different services. Privacy and security researchers can play an important role here in identifying potential privacy problems due to the way information systems are implemented in practice. Examples of such research include studies of intrusive web and phone tracking (Acar et al. 2013), showing risks of re-identification in anonymized datasets (Sweeney 2002; Narayanan and Shmatikov 2008), and exposing discrimination in data analytics (Hardt 2014). This work is invaluable for generating public discussions and developing appropriate regulation mechanisms. In this context, it is also likely that organizations running intrusive systems will resort to countering such studies. This makes it necessary to protect independent studies of currently deployed systems.

Reconciling conflicting regulation-by-design projects

Cyber security is another growing regulation-by-design project. A closer look at the current proposals in legal and technical projects to improve the cyber security of critical infrastructures suggests that these policies actively contest some of the assumptions that undergird traditional security and privacy engineering practice. Most significantly, the current cyber security strategy sees resilience rather than classic security as its main objective. It is argued that "it is very difficult to retrofit trust mechanisms into the Internet" and, hence, impossible to achieve dependable security using preventive mechanisms (Executive Office of the President National Science Technology Council 2011). Instead, a unified approach in partnership with private and public organizations is called for that rests on the application of 'game changing' pre-emptive security techniques for guaranteeing resilience (Executive Office of the President National Science Technology Council 2011).

According to the US Strategic Plan for a 'Trustworthy Cyberspace', resilient services are those that can 'fight through, survive and recover' from attacks. For this purpose, the development of capabilities to learn from past attacks using data analytics in order to mitigate future ones is seen as necessary (NITR 2014). These techniques are designed to enhance the availability of systems, often at the cost of confidentiality and integrity guarantees, if necessary. Most importantly, protection of confidentiality of information is seen as secondary to methods that provide 'system agility, diversity and adaptability'. For example, it is argued that adaptability can be achieved through intensive surveillance and pre-emptive filtering of undesirable activities on networks and the dynamic redistribution of data across cloud computing networks. Integrity guarantees can also be sacrificed in order to increase the cost and effectiveness of attacks; for example, cyber-deception and obfuscation techniques are proposed to decrease the replicability of attacks across systems. However, sacrificing integrity may come at the cost of the mechanisms proposed for achieving accountability in Big Data infrastructures.

In addition to the implementation of the proposed technical plans, legislation such as the recent Cyber Intelligence Sharing and Protection Act (CISPA) bill in the United States (114th Congress 2015) foresees a unified action plan for sharing information between service providers and federal agencies about system vulnerabilities, cyber threats and attacks. Companies that participate in CISPA will be granted immunity even if they violate privacy and data protection laws. The European Network and Information Security (NIS) Directive is advancing along the same lines. These legal proposals demonstrate that cyber security agendas on both sides of the Atlantic are moving policies toward a resilience model that prioritizes surveillance and deception as methods of protection at the cost of privacy and civil liberties.

If these proposals materialize, we will very likely experience a sea change in security practice and research. This change is likely to affect the feasibility of successfully developing technical approaches to privacy: currently these contradictory regulation-by-design projects implicitly encourage computer scientists to make an either-or choice between privacy and surveillance. The conflicts between privacy and cyber security regulation should be attended to at the policy level. The impressive efforts to train cyber security professionals should be equally reflected in capacity-building for privacy professionals.

In summary, privacy and security by design can play an important and positive role in Big Data. The success of regulation by design in this context depends on a comprehensive understanding of the information systems that we want to build; public and expert understanding of associated privacy problems in Big Data infrastructures; and the evaluation of appropriate technical, legal and organizational measures to address these. In ensuring the success of privacy and security by design, various parties have argued for the importance of using market incentives.

Governments can also play an active role by participating in a market for such technologies. In this context, innovation procurement can be explored as a way to increase the prominence of such technologies (Edquist and Zabala-Iturriagagoitia 2012). At the end of the day, the success of privacy by design will hinge upon consistently upholding it alongside potentially competing projects like cybersecurity.

3.7   BIG DATA'S UNIQUE CHALLENGES TO PRIVACY AND SECURITY BY DESIGN

We will finally discuss ways to address the challenges specific to Big Data infrastructures, data analytics and cloud services that we identified in the introduction. Most recommendations are about encouraging or regulating the use of existing privacy and encryption technologies, while others point to the need for further research on articulating and addressing the problems associated with Big Data technologies:

1. Data confidentiality:
   – Privacy-as-confidentiality solutions can help ensure that services can be offered without collecting unnecessary data on the server side. Cryptographic techniques can be useful in making sure that unintended and unauthorized parties cannot easily access this data and that parties can perform collaborative computations without centralizing or disclosing sensitive information to each other, while benefiting from Big Data infrastructures.

2. Intensification of identity management and tracking:
   – Privacy-as-confidentiality solutions can help enable anonymous use of services despite intrusive tracking practices. The use of PETs as personal protection should be promoted but is not sufficient to address the negative consequences of the current tracking infrastructure. Privacy preserving mechanisms can also be developed for license tracking without user tracking.
   – Many trackers claim that their practices are not intrusive because they do not collect personal information or because they use data anonymization techniques. Applying data anonymization may not be sufficient to address all the problems associated with the increased application of tracking and data analytics. Even after data anonymization, given the powerful advances in machine learning today, a company may infer sensitive information about a person from commonly observable attributes, such as shopping patterns associated with early pregnancy (Wagstaff 2012). Organizations are increasingly acting on such uncertain inferences, raising questions about responsible use of data analytics (Ellenberg 2014). Even the mathematical guarantees afforded by differential privacy fail to address the wide variety of problems associated with the quality of the information used for profiling, the resulting future opportunities users are offered or the way people are treated (Barocas and Nissenbaum 2014) as a result of automated decision-making. Policymakers can leverage existing research and commission empirical studies to inform the development of constructive rules limiting or regulating the use of ubiquitous tracking.

3. Reconfiguration of service provision:
   – Cryptographic methods can be applied to increase the accountability of cloud services and data analytics algorithms, allowing individuals and organizations to share data with others more confidently.
   – If data must flow to multiple service providers, privacy-as-control solutions can be used to make transparent where information is flowing and for what purposes. Policy languages and enforcement schemes can be applied within and across services.

- Case studies of service provisioning are needed to identify practices that negatively impact users and define best practices, e.g., limitations on rapid feature release in services.

4. Integrity of user devices, servers and algorithms:
   - Secure logging and mechanisms for algorithmic accountability can provide ways to make Big Data and SaaS practices more transparent to oversight boards, civil society and regulatory bodies as well as end users.
   - Privacy-as-practice solutions can be used to support users in managing services in their social settings and to provide the public with greater knowledge of the societal impact of services and Big Data infrastructures.
   - With the integration of services and the Internet of Things, and the increased influence of data analytics in everyday life, data-centric definitions of privacy violations may prove insufficient. We are beginning to see privacy violations that result from having access to persons and actively influencing their behaviour (Singer 2015) through control over their 'things'. Internet-of-Things applications can be used to manipulate users' behaviours (e.g., Pavlok), manage health and fitness (e.g., Fitbit) and organize learning (e.g., Muse). These systems 'access' individuals through data, but the resulting manipulation of behaviour may give rise to ethical concerns as well as violations of privacy and autonomy. Finally, user devices are increasingly controlled by companies for security and 'convenience' reasons, limiting users' ability to control, maintain, or fix their devices. The lack of autonomy over your own 'things' is likely to raise questions about fundamental freedoms. These issues require urgent attention in research and policymaking.

5. Ethics of experimenting with user populations for service optimization:
   - Some experts argue that data analytics must be explored further as, with the volume of current datasets, classic tests for significance of results are likely to be misleading, resulting in false correlations. Hence, experts recommend experimenting and exploring the patterns found in such datasets, in the wild if possible (George et al. 2014). The increased use of these methods means that, in many instances, populations, cities and regions are simply seen as 'fields' or laboratories for experimentation (CUSP 2015). The uproar against the recent 'emotion contagion study' on Facebook suggests that measures will need to be taken to avoid using data analytics for population experiments. Ideally, only methods that have achieved a certain level of maturity should be released to affect large populations. Measures should be taken to allow for informed participation in such studies, and for providing due process in case of undesirable consequences and harms.

– We generally lack professional and ethical guidelines for data analytics. Collaboration with computer scientists and professional associations can be leveraged to develop technical best practices and regulatory mechanisms. Some of these practices can be standardized. Regulatory frameworks that build on the precautionary approach may also be leveraged to deploy machine learning on populations in a responsible, transparent and accountable manner (Narayanan et al. 2015). Scholars working on this topic have invited us to ask at least some of the following questions (Hildebrandt and Vries 2013): Whom do we collect data from? Under what conditions? How is this data organized and cleaned up? By whom? How is the appropriateness of this data evaluated? How are vulnerable communities and minorities treated throughout the process? What algorithms are selected? Why? If different algorithms return different results, who decides which one is to be selected? For every benefit analysis, is there also an analysis of the costs to the communities affected by the data analytics? In current practice, many of these questions are answered by using 'common sense', if at all. Addressing these questions requires privacy technologies, but also good engineering practice, ethical reflection, public discussion and robust policies that integrate these questions into the data analytics process.

In conclusion, privacy technologies are fundamental to enabling good Big Data infrastructures. None of the five challenges listed above are new, but they appear in new configurations and at a different scale in the context of Big Data. The centralization inherent to Big Data infrastructures, however, means that there is a potential for making more effective changes at these central nodes and at the level of infrastructure. Normative guidance on privacy by design in Big Data settings should stipulate going beyond cosmetic and bureaucratic measures and should include the deployment of technical measures across the layers of Big Data and cloud infrastructures. The deployment of privacy technologies should be coupled with evaluation mechanisms that will help feed the development of best practice and regulatory mechanisms. The conflicts between privacy and cybersecurity regulation should be attended to at the level of policy, and training efforts for cybersecurity professionals should be equally reflected in capacity-building in privacy professionals. Finally, attending to the ethical challenges raised by experiments with user populations requires focused and interdisciplinary attention, as well as greater participation of civil society. While technical means will continue to be developed to address them, these issues require greater expertise and public opinion than is currently available.

REFERENCES

114th Congress (2015) *H.R.234 – Cyber Intelligence Sharing and Protection Act*, Library of Congress, January 2015.

Acar, G. et al. (2013) 'Fpdetective: Dusting the Web for Fingerprinters', pp. 1129-1140 in *Proceedings of the 2013 ACM SIGSAC Conference on Computer and Communications Security*, New York: ACM.

Acquisti, A. and J. Grossklags (2005) 'Privacy and Rationality in Individual Decision Making', *IEEE Security and Privacy* 3, 1: 26-33, January/February.

Adrian, D. et al. (2015) 'Imperfect forward Secrecy: How Diffie-Hellman Fails in Practice', *Pre-Print*, available at: https://weakdh.org/imperfect-forward-secrecy.pdf.

Agrawal, D. et al. (2015) 'Mind Your PS and VS: A Perspective on the Challenges of Big Data Management and Privacy Concerns', pp. 1-6 in *Big Data and Smart Computing (BigComp)* International Conference on, IEEE.

Angulo, J. and E. Wästlund (2013) 'Identity Management through 'Profiles': Prototyping an Online Information Segregation Service', pp. 10-19 in *Human-Computer Interaction. Users and Contexts of Use*, Springer.

Balsa, E., C. Troncoso and C. Diaz (2012) 'Ob-pws: Obfuscation-Based Private Web Search', pp. 491-505 in *Security and Privacy (SP)*, IEEE Symposium, May 2012, Doi: 10.1109/SP. 2012.36.

Barker, E. and J. Kelsey (2012) 'Recommendation for Random Number Generation Using Deterministic Ran-Dom Bit Generators', *Nist Special Publication* 800-90a, available at: http://csrc.nist.gov/publications/nistpubs/800- 90A/sp800-90A.pdf.

Barocas, S. and H. Nissenbaum (2014) 'Big Data's End Run around Procedural Privacy Protections', *Commun. ACM* 57, 11:31–33, ISSN 0001-0782, available at: http://doi.acm.org/10.1145/2668897 [October 2014].

Barocas, S. and A. Selbst (2014) *Big Data's Disparate Impact*, available at SSRN 2477899: http://papers.ssrn.com/sol3/papers.cfm?abstract_id=2477899.

Berendt, B., O. Günther and S. Spiekermann (2005) 'Privacy in E-Commerce: Stated Preferences vs. Actual Behavior', *Communications of the ACM* 48, 4: 101–106.

Bhargav-Spantzel, A., A. Squicciarini and E. Bertino (2007) 'Trust Negotiation in Identity Management', *Security Privacy, IEEE* 5, 2:55–63, ISSN 1540-7993, Doi: 10.1109/MSP. 2007.46 [March 2007].

Bonneau, J. and S. Preibusch (2010) 'The Privacy Jungle: On the Market for Data Protection in Social Networks', pp. 121-167 in *Economics of Information Security and Privacy*, Springer.

Boyd, D. and K. Crawford (2012) 'Critical Questions for Big Data', *Information, Communication and Society* 15, 5: 662–667.

Breaux, T., H. Hibshi and A. Rao (2014) 'Eddy, a Formal Language for Specifying and Analyzing Data Flow Specifications for Conflicting Privacy Requirements', *Requirements Engineering* 19, 3: 281–307.

Callas, J., L. Donnerhacke, H. Finney, D. Shaw and R. Thayer (2007) 'Open PGP Message Format, RFC 5581', *Internet Engineering Task Force (IETF)*, available at: https://tools.ietf.org/html/rfc5581.

Carvalho, M., J. DeMott, R. Ford and D. Wheeler (2014) *Heartbleed 101. IEEE Security and Privacy* 12, 4: 63–67, Doi: 10.1109/MSP.2014.66, URL http://dx.doi.org/10.1109/MSP.2014. 66.

Chadwick, D. (2009) 'Federated Identity Management', pp. 96-120 in A. Aldini, G. Barthe and R. Gorrieri (eds.) *Foundations of Security Analysis and Design* V 5705 of Lecture Notes in Computer Science, Berlin Heidelberg: Springer, ISBN 978-3-642-03828-0. Available at: http://dx.doi.org/10.1007/978-3-642-03829-7_3.

Cranor, L. and R. Wenning (2007) 'Platform for Privacy Preferences (p3p) Project: Enabling Smarter Privacy Tools for the Web', *Technical report, World Wide Web Consortium*, available at: www.w3.org/P3P.

CUSP, Center for Urban Science and Progress: NYC as a Laboratory (2015), available at: http://cusp.nyu.edu/about.

Danezis, G., R. Dingledine and N. Mathewson (2003) 'Mixminion: Design of a Type III Anonymous Remailer Protocol', pp. 11-14 in *IEEE Symposium on Security and Privacy* (S&P 2003) 11-14 May 2003; Berkeley, CA, USA, pp. 2-15, IEEE Computer Society 2003, ISBN 0-7695-1940-7, available at: http://dx.doi.org/10.1109/SECPRI. 2003.1199323.

Diaz, C., E. Kosta, H. Dekeyser, M. Kohlweiss and G. Nigusse (2009) 'Privacy Preserving Electronic Petitions', *Identity in the Information Society* 1, 1: 203–209.

Diaz, C., O. Tene and S. Gürses (2013) 'Hero or Villain: The Data Controller in Privacy Law and Technologies', *Ohio State Law Journal* 74: 923-964.

Dierks, T. and E. Rescorla (2008) 'The Transport Layer Security (TLS) Protocol version 1.2, RFC 5246', *Internet Engineering Task Force* (IETF), available at: https://tools.ietf.org/html/rfc5246.

Diffie, W. and M.E. Hellman (1976) 'New Directions in Cryptography, Information Theory', *IEEE Transactions on* 22, 6: 644-654.

Diffie W. and S.E. Landau (1998) *Privacy on the Line: The Politics of Wiretapping and Encryption*, Cambridge, MA: MIT Press.

Dingledine, R., N. Mathewson and P. Syverson (2004) 'Tor: The Second-Generation Onion Router', pp. 303-320 in M. Blaze (ed.) *Proceedings of the 13th USENIX Security Symposium*, August 9-13, 2004, San Diego, CA, USA, USENIX 2004, available at: www.usenix.org/publications/ library/proceedings/sec04/tech/dingledine.html.

Domingo-Ferrer, J. and V. Torra (2008) 'A Critique of K-Anonymity and Some of Its Enhancements', in *Third International Conference on Availability, Reliability and Security* 2008, ARES, August.

Doty, N. (2015) 'Reviewing for Privacy in Internet and Web Standard-Setting' in *First International Workshop on Privacy Engineering at the IEEE Security and Privacy Symposium*.

Dwork, C., M. Hardt, T. Pitassi, O. Reingold and R. Zemel (2012) 'Fairness Through Awareness', pp. 214-226 in *Proceedings of the 3rd Innovations in Theoretical, Computer Science Conference, ACM*.

Dwork, C. and A. Smith (2009) 'Differential Privacy for Statistics: What We Know and What We Want to Learn', *Journal of Privacy and Confidentialit* 1, 2, available at: http://repository.cmu.edu/jpc/vol1/iss2/2 [2009].

Eckersley, P. and J. Burns (2010) 'An Observatory for the SSLiverse', Presented at DefCon 18, Las Vegas (NV), USA July; Electronic Frontier Foundation (EFF) 2010, available at: http://www.eff.org/files/DefconSSLiverse.pdf.

Edquist, C. and J. Mikel Zabala-Iturriagagoitia (2012) 'Public Procurement for Innovation as Mission-Oriented Innovation Policy', *Research Policy* 41, 10: 1757–1769.

Ellenberg, J. (2014) 'What's Even Creepier than Target Guessing that You're Pregnant?' *Slate* 9, June, available at: www.slate.com/blogs/how_not_to_be_wrong/ 2014/06/09/big_data_what_s_even_creepier_than_target_guessing_that_ you_re_pregnant.html.

ENISA (2014) 'Algorithms, Key Size and Parameters Report', *Technical report, ENISA*, available at: www.enisa.europa.eu/activities/identity-and-trust/library/ deliverables/algorithms-key-size-and-parameters-report-2014.

Erickson, T. and W. Kellogg (2000) 'Social Translucence: An Approach to Designing Systems that Support Social Processes', *ACM Transactions on Human Computer Interaction* 7, 1: 59-83.

Erlingsson, U., V. Pihur and A. Korolova (2014) 'Rapport: Randomized Aggregatable Privacy-Preserving Ordinal Response', pp. 1054-1067 in *Proceedings of the 2014 ACM SIGSAC Conference on Computer and Communications Security*, ACM.

Executive Office of the President National Science Technology Council (2011) 'Trustworthy Cyberspace: Strategic Plan for the Federal Cybersecurity Research and Development Program', *National Coordination Office*.

Feldman, A., A. Blankstein, M. Freedman and E. Felten (2012) 'Social Networking with Frientegrity: Privacy and Integrity with an Untrusted Provider', pp. 647-662 in *USENIX Security Symposium*.

Felten, E. (2012) *Accountable algorithms*, available at: https://freedom-to-tinker.com/ blog/felten/accountable-algorithms.

Gage Kelley, P., J. Bresee and L. Faith Cranor (2009) 'A 'Nutrition Label' for Privacy, pp. 4:1-4:12 in *Proceedings of the 5th Symposium on Usable Privacy and Security, SOUPS '09*, New York, NY, USA 2009, ACM, ISBN 978-1-60558-736-3, available at: http://doi.acm.org/10.1145/1572532.1572538.

Gentry, C. (2009) 'Fully Homomorphic Encryption Using Ideal Lattices', pp. 169-178 in *Proceedings of the Forty-first Annual ACM Symposium on Theory of Computing, STOC '09*, New York, NY, USA: ACM, ISBN 978-1-60558-506-2, available at: http://doi.acm.org/10.1145/ 1536414.1536440.

George, G., M. Haas and A. Pentland (2014) 'Big Data and Management', *Academy of Management Journal* 57, 2: 321-326.

Goldberg, I., B. Ustaoglu, M. van Gundy and H. Chen (2009) 'Multi-Party off-the-Record Messaging', pp. 358-368 in E. Al-Shaer, S. Jha, and A.D. Keromytis (eds.) *Proceedings of the 2009 ACM Conference on Computer and Communications Security, CCS 2009*, Chicago, Illinois, USA, November 9-13, ACM 2009, ISBN 978-1-60558-894-0, available at: http://doi.acm.org/10.1145/1653662.1653705.

Google (2015) *Google Dashboard 2015*, available at: www.google.com/dashboard.

Grimmelmann, J. (2014) *The Facebook Emotional Manipulation Study: Sources 2014*, available at: http://laboratorium.net/archive/2014/06/30/the_facebook_emotional_manipulation_study_source.

Grover, L. (1996) 'A Fast Quantum Mechanical Algorithm for Database Search', pp. 212-219 in *Proceedings of the Twenty-Eighth Annual ACM Symposium on the Theory of Computing*, Philadelphia, Pennsylvania, USA May 22-24, available at: http://doi.acm.org/10.1145/237814.237866.

Hardt, M. (2014) 'How Big Data is Unfair: Understanding Sources of Unfairness in Data Driven Decision Making', *Medium*, available at: https://medium.com/@mrtz/how-big-data-is-unfair-9aa544d739de [26 September 2014].

Hildebrandt, M. and K. de Vries (2013) *Privacy, Due Process and the Computational Turn: The Philosophy of Law Meets the Philosophy of Technology*, New York, NY: Routledge.

Jacobs, A. (2009) *The Pathologies of Big Data*, ACM Queue 7, 6.

Johnson, M., S. Egelman and S. Bellovin (2012) 'Facebook and Privacy: It's Complicated', pp. 9:1-9.15 in *Proceedings of the Eighth Symposium on Usable Privacy and Security, SOUPS '12*, New York, NY, ACM, ISBN 978-1-4503-1532-6, available at: http://doi.acm.org/10.1145/2335356.2335369.

Kahn, D. (1996) *The Codebreakers: The Story of Secret Writing*, New York: Scribner.

Kaldrack, I. and M. Leeker (2015) 'There Is No Software, there Are Just Services: Introduction' in I. Kaldrack and M. Leeker (eds.) *No Software, Just Services*, Lüneburg: Meson Press.

Kent, S. and K. Sero (2005) 'Security Architecture for the Internet Protocol, RFC 2401'. *Internet Engineering Task Force (IETF)*, available at: https://tools.ietf.org/html/rfc4301.

Kifer, D. and J. Gehrke (2006) 'L-Diversity: Privacy beyond K-Anonymity' in *IEEE 22nd International Conference on Data Engineering (ICDE)*, July.

Kramer, A., J. Guillory and J. Hancock (2014) 'Experimental Evidence of Massive-Scale Emotional Contagion through Social Networks', *Proceedings of the National Academy of Sciences* 111, 24: 8788–8790, available at: www.pnas.org/content/111/24/8788.abstract.

Langheinrich, M., L. Cranor and M. Marchiori (2002) 'Appel: A p3p Preference Exchange Language, *W3C Working Draft*.

Lardinois, F. (2015) *How Google's Networking Infrastructure Has Evolved over the Last 10 Years*, available at: http://techcrunch.com/2015/08/18/how-googles-networking-infrastructure-has-evolved-over-the-last-10-years/#.k68low:LG00.

Lin, J., B. Liu, N. Sadeh and J. Hong (2014) 'Modelling Users' Mobile App Privacy Preferences: Restoring Usability in a Sea of Permission Settings' in *Symposium on Usable Privacy and Security* (SOUPS).

Loukides, M. (2010) 'What is Data Science?', *Technical Report, O'Reilly Radar Report.*

McClure, S. (2015) *Data Science and Big Data Two Very Different Beasts*, available at: http://kdnuggets. com/2015/07/data-science-big-data-different-beasts.html.

McDonald, A., S. Afroz, A. Caliskan, A. Stolerman and R. Greenstadt (2012) 'Use Fewer Instances of the Letter 'I': Toward Writing Style Anonymization', pp. 299-318 in S. Fischer-Hübner and M. Wright (eds.) *Privacy Enhancing Technologies* 7384 of *Lecture Notes in Computer Science*, Berlin Heidelberg: Springer, ISBN 978-3-642-31679-1, available at: http://dx.doi.org/10.1007/978-3-642-31680-7_16.

Mulligan, D. and C. Koopman (2015) *Theorizing Privacy's Contestability: A Multi-Dimensional Analytic of Privacy*, available at: http://cra.org/ccc/files/docs/meetings/Privacy/Koopman%20and%20Mulligan.pdf.

Narayanan, A., J. Huey and E. Felten (2015) 'A Precautionary Approach to Big Data Privacy', *Technical Report, CITP*, Princeton University.

Narayanan, A. and V. Shmatikov (2008) 'Robust De-Anonymization of Large Sparse Datasets', pp. 111-125 in *SP '08 Proceedings of the 2008 IEEE Symposium on Security and Privacy*, Washington: IEEE Computer Society.

Narayanan, A. and V. Shmatikov (2010) 'Myths and Fallacies of Personally Identifiable Information, *Communications of the ACM* 53, 6: 24-26.

Nissenbaum, H. (2009) *Privacy in Context: Technology, Policy and the Integrity of Social Life*, Stanford University Press.

NITR (2014) *Report on Implementing the Federal Cybersecurity Research and Development Strategy*, National Coordination Office.

Palen, L. and P. Dourish (2003) 'Unpacking Privacy for a Networked World', pp. 129-136 in *Proceedings of the SIGCHI Conference on Human Factors in Computing Systems*, ACM.

Pedreshi, D., S. Ruggieri and F. Turini (2008) 'Discrimination-Aware Data Mining', pp. 560-568 in *Proceedings of the 14th ACM SIGKDD International Conference on Knowledge Discovery and Data Mining*, ACM.

Peeters, R., T. Pulls and K. Wouters (2013) 'Enhancing Transparency with Distributed Privacy-Preserving Logging, pp. 61-71 in *ISSE 2013 Securing Electronic Business Processes*, Springer.

Petkovic, M., D. Prandi and N. Zannone (2011) 'Purpose Control: Did You Process the Data for the Intended Purpose?', pp. 145-168 in *Proc. of Secure Data Management*, LNCS 6933, Springer.

Provost, F. and T. Fawcett (2013) 'Data Science and Its Relationship to Big Data and Data-Driven Decision Making', *Big Data* 1, 1: 51-59.

Ramsdell, B. and S. Turner (2010) 'Secure/Multipurpose Internet Mail Extensions (S/MIME) version 3.2 Message Specification, RFC 5751', *Internet Engineering Task Force (IETF)*, available at: https://tools.ietf.org/html/rfc5751.

Rial, A. and G. Danezis (2010) 'Privacy-Preserving Smart Metering', *Microsoft Technical Report MSR-TR-2010-150*, Microsoft Research, November.

Richter Lipford, H., J. Watson, M. Whitney, K. Froiland and R. Reeder (2010) 'Visual vs. Compact: A Comparison of Privacy Policy Interfaces, pp. 1111-1114 in *Proceedings of the 28th International Conference on Human Factors in Computing Systems*, CHI '10, New York, NY, USA, ACM, ISBN 978-1-60558-929-9, available at: http://doi.acm.org/10.1145/1753326.1753492.

Sadeh, N. et al. (2014) 'Towards Usable Privacy Policies: Semi-Automatically Extracting Data Practices from Websites' Privacy Policies' in *SOUPS*.

Sayaf, R. and D. Clarke (2012) 'Access Control Models for Online Social Networks' in *Social Network Engineering for Secure Web Data and Services*, IGI – Global (in print).

Schaub, F., T. Breaux and N. Sadeh (2014) 'Crowdsourcing The Extraction of Data Practices from Privacy Policies' in Second AAAI Conference On Human Computation and Crowdsourcing.

Sen, S., S. Guha, A. Datta, S. Rajamani, J. Che Tsai and J. Wing (2014) 'Bootstrapping Privacy Compliance in Big Data Systems', pp. 327-342 in *Security and Privacy (SP), IEEE Symposium on*, IEEE.

Shor, P. (1994) 'Algorithms for Quantum Computation: Discrete Logarithms and Factoring', pp. 124-134 in *35th Annual Symposium On Foundations Of Computer Science*, Santa Fe, New Mexico, USA, 20-22 November, available at: http://Dx.Doi.Org/10.1109/SFCS.1994.365700.

Singer, N. (2015) *Technology that Prods You to Take Action, Not Just Collect Data*, New York Times, 18 April, available at: www.nytimes.com/2015/04/19/technology/technology-that-prods-you-to-take-action-not-just-collect-data.html?_r=0.

Singh, S. (2011) *The Code Book: The Science of Secrecy from Ancient Egypt to Quantum Cryptography*, Anchor 2011.

Steiner, J., B. Clifford Neuman and J. Schiller (1988) 'Kerberos: An Authentication Service for Open Network Systems, pp. 191-202 in *Proceedings of the USENIX Winter Conference*, Dallas, Texas, USA, January, USENIX Association.

Sweeney, L. (2002) 'K-Anonymity: a Model for Protecting Privacy', *International Journal on Uncertainty, Fuzziness and Knowledge-Based Systems*, 10, 5: 557–570.

Wagstaff, K. (2012) 'How Target Knew a High School Girl was Pregnant before Her Parents Did', *Time* 12, February.

Xie, J., B. Knijnenburg and Hongxia Jin (2014) 'Location Sharing Privacy Preference: Analysis and Personalized Recommendation', pp. 189-198 in *Proceedings of the 19th International Conference on Intelligent User Interfaces*, IUI , New York, USA, ACM, ISBN 978-1-4503-2184-6, available at: http://doi.acm.org/10.1145/2557500.2557504.

Yao, A. (1982) 'Protocols for Secure Computations (Extended Abstract), pp. 160-164 in *23rd Annual Symposium on Foundations of Computer Science*, Chicago, Illinois, USA, 3-5 November , IEEE Computer Society, available at: http://dx.doi.org/10.1109/SFCS.1982.38.

Yeung, K. (2014) *Design for Regulation*, Legal Studies Research Paper Series 2014-2, London: King's College London Law School.

Zave, P. and M. Jackson (1997) 'Four Dark Corners of Requirements Engineering', *ACM Transactions on Software Engineering and Methodology* (TOSEM) 6, 1: 1–30.

NOTES

1   Diginotar was compromised in 2010: a hacker managed to subvert its system and issue false certificates. Diginotar went out of business shortly after the breach was made public.

2   See www.gnupg.org.

3   See www.eff.org/secure-messaging-scorecard.

4   DES with a 56-bit key, RSA with a 512-bit key, and ECC with a 112-bit key.

5   See www.cryptolaw.org.

6   See http://leaksource.info/2013/12/30/nsas-ant-division-catalog-of-exploits-for-nearly-every-major-software-hardware-firmware.

PART II

EMPIRICAL PERSPECTIVES ON BIG DATA

4 POLICING, BIG DATA AND THE COMMODIFICATION OF SECURITY

Gemma Galdon Clavell[1]

Security (social, legal and otherwise) has been one of the great achievements of the modern era. However, the challenges of providing security services and of making people feel safe change across times and cultures. Recently, the proliferation of technological solutions and devices is not only modifying the face of policing but is also bringing about broader social changes that influence our society's understanding of what constitutes security. The next few pages are an attempt to link the recent evolution of policing and security provision with the possibilities and risks of new technologies and Big Data solutions.

4.1 POLICING AND SECURITY IN THE LATE 20TH CENTURY

After the fall of the Berlin Wall in 1989, the new global scenario brought a novel geostrategic balance and an innovative public management agenda. This was known as 'new public management' (NPM), and was based on public choice theory and managerialism. Since then, market principles have permeated the public agenda in its entirety (O'Malley 1997; O'Malley and Palmer 1996), first in the United Kingdom and the United States and later in most OECD countries (Gruening 2001). Many public bodies have chosen to separate the provision of public services from the production by contracting out, either by privatizing services or by creating public-private partnerships (PPPs). The logic of these shifts was, and still remains, economically and operationally driven: it is a way to reduce costs, promote decentralization and gain a greater role for citizens in certain services. In this context, as the symbolic importance of the public realm diminishes, responsibility is shifted away from the government and onto the people, thus encouraging citizens to play a larger role in taking care of themselves and their property. This has had a tangible impact on policing and security.

In the 70s and 80s, increasing crime rates and an overall erosion of the traditional social control mechanisms that are characteristic of individualized societies (Jones and Newburn 2002) put an immense pressure on budgets. This subsequently led to an increasing demand for efficient policing. This shift was coupled with growing appeals for community involvement, participation and police collaboration to achieve the goal of maintaining safety, especially at the local scale. This was also the period in which criminologists began to identify a new problem: the feeling of insecurity as a phenomenon independent of objective insecurity stats. Although many violence-related risks disappeared in this period, people still expressed grave fear of crime which exists externally to the possibility of being a victim of a criminal act. The general climate of insecurity, the media and the 'signal crimes' (crimes of great media impact) emerged as decisive factors in the demand for citizen security in much of the Western world, especially in large cities.

Understanding the highly subjective experience of insecurity has allowed for the development of more comprehensive, community-based policies which are structured around the central ideas of improving community components, solidarity and collective efficacy over police intervention. It was within this context that Wilson and Kelling published a theory in 1982, known as 'Broken Window theory', which would prove to have a profound impact on the security policies of the next 20 years and also inspire contradictory developments in the field. According to these authors, urban disorder in the form of neglect and abandonment of public spaces, attracts antisocial and criminal behaviour. It suggests that in order to reduce violence, law enforcement should identify triggers that often escalate to large problems, and intervene with force before a harmful event occurs. In this sense, the tenants of the theory are 'repressive interventions' and 'preventative action', and both should be undertaken in order to reduce urban disorder and crime rates.

Over time, it has become apparent that these developments are especially felt at the local level and in local policy, more so than in the national, regional or federal sphere, where this relaxation of the public 'monopolistic' role concerning the use of force is taking more time to permeate the public agenda. In the 1990s, cities increasingly ceased to be recipients or 'enablers' of national, regional or federal policies, and instead sought to become major actors and agents in international politics and global change (Gilling 1999; Cochrane 2007). The victory of Rudolph Giuliani in the NYC elections in 1993 was the first example of the way in which cities and security forces directly relate to urban insecurities. With the help of leading transnational security consulting firms, the NYC security agenda – based on both the Broken Windows theory (Wilson and Kelling 1982) and a 'zero tolerance' approach to urban disorder – made its way to the global security agenda (Dixon and Maher 2005; Mitchell and Beckett 2008). This happened at a time when most Western cities were beginning to claim a newly-found leading role in the regulation of social conflict and disorderly behaviour (Cochrane 2007).

This process of decentralization, however, coexists with the emergence of 'global policing'. Through ICTs, shared databases and personnel exchange, global surveillance and policing networks are deployed to enhance prosecution of transnational crime. In this context, Europol and Interpol agencies are key examples of security organizations aiming to overcome the problems that arise when the police is confined to national borders. Despite this global reach, police forces in Europe continue to be fragmented due to geographical, functional, historical, cultural or administrative factors. In many countries, several police forces with overlapping functions coexist (Mossos d'Esquadra, Ertzaintza, Guardia Civil and local forces in Spain; Carabinieri and Polizia di Stato in Italy; Bundespolizei, Landespolizei, etc. in Germany; or Police Nationale and Gendarmerie Nationale in France). EU police forces, therefore, are experimenting contradictory changes and pressures, with the local and the global taking prominence over the national, which had traditionally been the space for the monopoly of the use of force.

Besides the potential interconnection of functions and competences, an important question emerges around the issue of information exchange. Security is a significant area of sovereignty which member states are hesitant to delegate to the EU. This means that the information gathered by certain security forces is often inaccessible to other agencies, thus increasing required effort and decreasing efficiency. Data sharing among EU countries may bring valuable insight to nations. However, there are issues of national sovereignty, the protection of one's own citizens under the precepts of national legal frameworks and matters related to ethics and privacy that emerge as extremely complex and controversial. There is a complex balance which each country must grapple with, and so far, in practice, data sharing among EU law-enforcement agencies continues to be more of an aim than a reality.

In this context of data splintering, privatization processes may introduce additional forms of fragmentation. As private companies grow and the number of security businesses increase, there is an expanding amount of security-related information spread across a broadening number of organizations. This distribution of resources across a large range of actors can provide access to new sources of data, but it also leaves organizations without a centrally accessible system. Without clear legal frameworks, sharing protocols and data-sharing technologies, the complexity of the new public-private data sharing systems could worsen access to useful information, and not the other way around.

Overall, the combination of budget constraints, city-led decentralization, demand for greater citizen involvement in policing activities, commodification and the need to a landscape of deep decentralization (at both the global and data level) has fundamentally transformed the nature of policing and security in most Western societies. The main trends that can be observed in policing and security provision since the late 90s are explored in the following sections and can be summarized as follows: an increased blurring of the lines between defence, policing and intelligence; an increased emphasis on data and prediction (as opposed to prevention); and an increasing reliance on technological solutions to increase efficiency. These developments intensified after two notable events: the 9/11 attacks on the Twin Towers in the US and the increasing commodification of security. The latter is a novel phenomenon in which security is heightened in order to face a global threat which manifests itself locally, irrespective of geopolitical boarders and divisions.

4.1.1   HYBRIDIZATION: THE BLURRING LINES BETWEEN DEFENCE, POLICING AND INTELLIGENCE

Traditionally, States and the military dealt with defence policy, while local authorities acted as enablers of centrally-decided police and crime prevention lines of action (Gilling 1999). However, interrelated phenomena such as the increased powers at the local level, Zero Tolerance practices, the global War on Terror and the drive to fortify cities and borders against powerful, unpredictable, global enemies of the Western 'way of life' (Graham 2010) have been increasingly blurring the lines between defence policy, crime prevention and intelligence, especially in urban environments. Trapped between global threats and growing local fears, cities are increasingly the spaces where the boundaries between homeland security and community safety collapse, where the elimination of risk and the *other* become an omnipresent electoral promise and social expectation, and where public space is securitized and re-moralized (Cochrane 2007) in the name of law and order.

In many cases, the rhetoric around security shifts between terrorism, crime and incivility with an incredible ease. Devices once only used against foreign military threats, such as legal tools, control mechanisms and rationales of action, are now deployed within cities to give people a sense of security in their everyday use of public space. In the same way, the outcry for security at the community level reinforces a tougher approach to issues related to defence and international security. CCTV cameras and biometric identification are tools being used to fight terrorism, but also to prevent theft and anti-social behaviour. Although this is an example of *function creep*, and the legal, ethical and policy implications are seldom acknowledged, society's use of these technologies is growing rapidly, blurring the lines between previously-separated phenomena through the deployment of similar technologies.

In this new reality, rationales and powers usually deployed beyond national borders and against global threats find their way to the management of urban scenarios, and roles traditionally responsible for dealing with law-breaking are increasingly asked to address complex social matters. As social problems increasingly fall within the purview of local authorities, the police are now asked to monitor and fine deviant or 'annoying' behaviour and to intervene as social-penal agents (Wacquant 2000). At the same time, city dwellers witness an enormous increase of (armed) private security to control access to shops, public transport and special events.

This blurring of lines also happens between police forces and intelligence agencies. Law-enforcement agencies used to rely on information that was passed on to them from the intelligence services, but with growing fears and technological possibilities at the local level, this top-down approach no longer holds. Today, police forces collect and analyse information just like intelligence agencies would, looking for patterns and trying to predict future events. Intelligence-led policing has made it to most Western police policies, imposing an 'analysis-driven approach to decision-making' (Ratcliffe 1998: 4) that demands a command of sources much greater than that necessary to fulfil a traditional, reactive police role.

This means, on the one hand, that data has become essential in police work, both in terms of investigation, intervention and evaluation (the quality of all police work is measured from an intelligence perspective, and intelligence-led policing has become the template for police work in many countries and cities). It also means that police officers are being converted to intelligence actors and intelligence material 'users', as policing becomes an 'informationalized' activity (Loader 2002: 142). The police have been resorting to ever more sophisticated surveillance technologies in recent years and have been granted much more intrusive investigative powers in order to use them. In doing so, the Police have brought their modus operandi closer to that of intelligence agencies. This process has not only brought intelligence into policing but has also shifted the intelligence focus towards matters of internal security, calling into question the need for such traditional divisions to continue to exist (Završnik 2013).

4.1.2   PRE-EMPTION AND PREDICTION

This new paradigm, in which the definition of security is enlarged to find risks and threats in a myriad of scenarios, local and foreign, finds its logic in the politics of pre-emption. While outlined as doctrine in the 2002 US National Security Strategy, the idea of anticipatory action in cases of urban disorder had been guiding domestic policing for several years before the 9/11 attacks. The 'preventionist consensus' finds its recent origins in the Broken Windows theory put forward by Wilson and Kelling in 1982. What is interesting here is that, whereas focusing on maintaining order, looking after the physical environment and caring about some people's 'quality of life' spells care and proximity and can be seen as an attempt to build more democratic and representative police forces (O'Shea 2000), this same rhetoric is underpinning harsh 'zero-tolerance' and 'three strikes' sentencing approaches.

Going beyond the original analysis laid out in the Broken Windows theory, the policy adaptation of the general principles laid out by Wilson and Kelling has stressed pre-emption and proximity, but reducing them to the role of the police forces has tended to privilege harsher sentencing and increased disciplinary powers over welfarist measures. Therefore, the Broken Windows theory seems to have informed a rhetoric of prevention, community, partnership and empowerment, while at the same time providing the logic for an increase in the repressive and pre-emptive tools of the police.

In the field of public policy, the idea of network management, participation and multi-level governance assumes that, in the transition between the traditional local government model and the urban governance paradigm, public roles go from imposing and regulating to leading and enabling, and government instruments move from regulation and sanctioning to participation and co-management (Blanco 2004). If we pay close attention to the reality of policing and tackling crime and disorder, however, what we find is a new-found emphasis on the tradi-tional roles and tools together with a rhetoric of governance. In the post-9/11 world, community police seems to be less about policing for the community and more about policing the *community –just in case.*

This focus on pre-emption and prediction has heightened after 9/11. A lower toler-ance for risk and uncertainty at a societal level has meant that the current demand to stop harmful events before they happen is widespread and popular. This search for certainty often relies on an overtly optimistic belief in the possibilities of tech-nological solutions when it comes to drawing patterns and predicting events before they happen. Equipped with a myriad of gadgets, the security forces of the 21st century seem convinced that Big Data can – and will – predict the future.

4.1.3   THE IMPACT OF TECHNOLOGY

Technology has been at the centre of many of the police-related developments of recent years. However, budget cuts and growing security concerns in a globalized society have increased this trend, pushing towards an increased 'informationaliza-tion' of the police and security forces (Završnik 2013). Technology has always been present in policing: pictures of suspects were used by the police quickly after the invention of photography, and the first CCTV cameras for security purposes were introduced in the 1950s, for instance. Databases have also been used for a long time in police departments, initially in the form of physical files and more recently in digital form. Back in the 80s, and through crossing different sources of data using computers, using statistics and figures to produce crime maps, and geolocating different categories of events on these maps, police officers began to realize that patterns could emerge, intelligence could be derived and more efficient security services could be provided. In the 21st century, however, the possibilities of new technologies seem endless.

The current economic crisis has turned towards a path of political discourse based mainly on the reduction of public budgets. To maintain the current level of serv-ices, there is a need to increase the efficiency and efficacy of public administration, avoiding unnecessary expense and maximising the impact of the services provided. In this context, the introduction and use of IT applications is one of the solutions of choice to help to cut costs and administrative procedures. All in all, the combination of increasing pressure on budgets; more availability of new technologies and data; the need for immediate, 'tangible' solutions to growing insecurities; a general belief in the 'neutrality' of technology solutions; and the optimism surrounding technology's ability to solve social challenges found in public discourse, is likely to drive and intensify this process of informationalization of the police and security forces.

This is both an opportunity and a challenge. New technologies are an opportunity because they can improve procedures and outcomes. However, introducing technological processes in public administration is no easy task. Technologies can produce significant changes in police agencies, but these changes may have unanticipated and collateral consequences for organizational structures, functions, goals and mandates (Manning, 1992). Therefore, special attention should be paid to matters of information sharing, training and coordination of operators, communication, clear management structures and roles, leadership and intelligence.

There are several ways in which security companies and organizations may use information and ICTs to be more competitive. The list of information sources may include:
- statistics (e.g., predictive policing systems, criminal records);
- sensors (CCTV, smart cameras, unusual activity detection, smart city devices, etc.);
- biometric records (fingerprints, DNA, etc.);
- mapping: Geolocalization of minors and elderly people, pedestrians flow, traffic heatmaps, etc.;
- license plates records;
- mobile devices: Automotive Navigation Systems, mobile phones;
- private and public e-services: e-shopping, social media activity, e-mail, IM, e-government;
- 'Internet of Things': wearables, smart devices and home automation, etc.;
- citizen and customer records: financial records, passenger name records, criminal records, vehicle records, tax information, paying information.

The use of ICT in policing is aimed at fighting major security threats such as terrorism and organized crime, but also petty crime. Regular crime (Pleasance 2014) or online offensive comments (Sawers 2015) might also be addressed with the support of digital resources. Online and offline resources can be combined to enhance investigation results: for instance, fingerprints obtained at a crime scene may lead to an official name and date of birth; this name can be linked to numerous additional records like credit card utilization, telecommunications, travelling routines or online social network activities. As all these pieces of information are owned by

different public or private organizations, it is of the utmost importance that cooperation through data and metadata transfers is adequately regulated through sound
protocols and policies which guarantee the accomplishment of individual rights
and ethical standards. Security organizations must deal with a wide range of
threats and risks (from Advanced Persistent Threats to regular crime), which
require different intervention levels (international, domestic, local…) as well as
varying degrees of resource allocation.

While all these technologies carry the promise of more efficient policing and predictive analytics, over-reliance on technology in the field of policing is problematic. Issues related to the legality, ethics and social acceptability of the technological processes developed, as well as training and understanding of technological
biases are still open to discussion.

This is especially the case when technologies are used to promote citizen collaboration with the police, as 'outsourcing' investigative capabilities can lead to the
erosion of the presumption of innocence (citizens sharing with the police images
or information related to objectively non-suspicious people), profiling (when citizens' prejudices are translated into how they perceive specific minorities and how
likely they perceive them to commit crimes) and a general loss of social cohesion
and trust as vigilantism proliferates. This has proven to be an issue before, in the
context of high-profile crimes where the police have asked for citizen involvement
and collaboration (Galdon Clavell and Zavala 2014). This will be explored further
throughout the chapter.

4.1.4   A GROWING GLOBAL PRIVATE SECURITY BUSINESS

The processes laid out above have coincided with a massive expansion of the private security industry. While trading in security services is not new to policing
nor to the protection of national security, the number of private security firms
engaged in these areas and the scope of their business activities have increased
exponentially since the mid-20th century, especially after 9/11. At the same time,
police have increasingly engaged in the commercial security marketplace through
outsourcing and user-pays services. According to some authors, public policing
has in many ways become a business run by business men and women (Ayling,
2014: 16).

The largest of these private security firms are based in Europe. The world's biggest
private security company, Group4Securicor (G4S), is one of the UK's 100 largest
corporations by capitalization, and the largest employer listed on the London
Stock Exchange. With operations in 115 countries, it employs over half a million
people. Following a similar pattern of expansion, the Swedish-based Securitas has
also become a significant provider of security services across Europe and beyond.
As the world's second-largest private security company, Securitas has

implemented more than 60 acquisitions over the past two decades, employs more than 240,000 people in thirty-seven countries, and now has 12 percent of the global outsourced security market. The company's total sales in 2007 amounted to approximately $6.9 billion, with an organic sales growth of 5 percent. The third largest security-related firm in the world, the Spanish Prosegur, also mirrors this trend. Founded in 1976, the firm employed more than 75,000 people in 2009 and has extensive operations in Europe and Central and South America (PRIO 2009: 4).

Overall, the private security industry is estimated to have a world-wide market value of over $165 billion, and growth rates of over 8 percent. In many countries, private security employees now outnumber their public counterparts, often considerably. This growth has been accompanied by the evolution of commercial security companies with extensive resources and geographic reach. As some authors highlight, it is difficult to precisely estimate the amount of private security in the total range of security services. However, the available figures all point in the same direction. Private security nowadays covers a multitude of industries, large and small, all related to the provision of security services, investigations, crime prevention, order maintenance, intelligence collection and military services (Van Steden and Sarre 2007: 226; Van Buuren 2010: 1). The main subareas in the security field to be provided by private actors are those destined to the protection of private spaces and individuals: home security systems, anti-theft devices for stores, personal safety (self-defence, bodyguards, etc.), among other things. The protection of the public space itself is still largely reserved to public-managed organizations, even though this may change in the near future. Nevertheless, a wide range of outsourced services are provided by the free market: fine management systems, LEAs training academies, LEAs equipment, etc.

Figure 4.1   British Security Industry Turnover

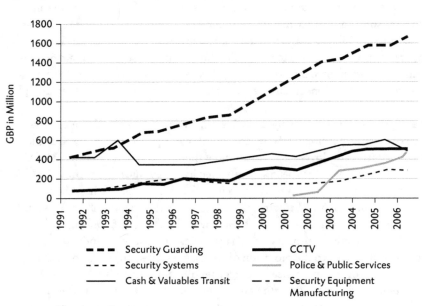

Source: Krahman 2008b

In much of Europe and North America, private protection has become the norm in areas that were previously publicly protected, such as shopping malls, housing estates and parks, as well as private property. In 1999, US spending on private security was 73 percent higher than for public law enforcement, and private security officers outnumbered public police in the region of three to one (Altheide and Michalowski 1999: 481; Krahman 2008: 140-41). In the UK alone, between 1991 and 2005, the turnover of private security companies rose by no less than 330 percent (an average of 23 percent annually). In the US, the average growth of the private security sector is around 8-10 percent per year. By comparison, the UK manufacturing sector only expanded on average by 0.5 percent in the same period, and even the IT sector grew only by 6-8 percent annually (Krahman 2008b: 16). Private security companies with publicly traded stocks grew at twice the rate of the Dow Jones Industrial Average in the 1990s. Some 2,003 estimates suggested that the revenues had already reached $100 billion by then. Others claim that the US military market alone (excluding combat services) was already $100 billion strong in 2003 (Avant 2006: 509).

In the UK, investment in private security is four times as high as it was in 1990. Moreover, the cost of national security products and services has typically increased on average by 10 percent per year in real terms (Hartley undated). In 1945, the UK government spent £1 million on each Lancaster bomber airplane, whereas the government had to pay £20 million per aircraft for its successor, the

Tornado, in 1980 (Alexander and Garden 2001: 516; Krahman 2008a: 138-39). As a result, private citizens and businesses currently make up between 70 and 90 percent of the contracts of internationally operating private military and security companies. While citizens in Europe and North America have supported cuts in their security and defence budgets, the turnover of these companies has quadrupled since 1990 (Krahman 2008: 141).

Over the course of the last fifteen years, the use of markets to organize for security has also grown rapidly. Consider the recent experience in Iraq. When the US defeated the Iraqi Army in 2003, at least one out of every ten people deployed in the conflict were hired by private security companies (PSCs) to perform work that was previously performed by soldiers. In May 2004, it was estimated that in excess of 20,000 private security personnel from countries as varied as Fiji, Israel, Nepal, South Africa, Chile, El Salvador, the United Kingdom, the United States and many more employed by some 25 different PSCs worked for the US government, the British government, the Coalition Provisional Authority (CPA), private firms and international non-governmental organizations (INGOs) in that country (Avant 2006: 507-8).

As mentioned above, the global recession, which started in 2007, intensified the pressure to leverage the impact of public services into the budgets, increasing the need for security agencies to 'do more with less' (Ayling et al. 2009). The subtle, strategic and gradual nature of the privatization process implemented to this key area allows for the avoidance of major criticism. Furthermore, the shift to a private-supported security is often accompanied by the broadening and development of new consumption trends and social phenomena: new residential and shopping areas, or entertainment complexes, for example, which provide the illusion of being public spaces while being only subject to private regulations and private security. The growth of such so-called 'mass private property' (public venues that are privately owned) (Shearing and Stenning 1983) has driven the privatization of security in developing economies (Kempa et al. 2004). Accompanying this trend, the expansion of intangible private property and the growing demand for covering security needs related to the informational economy (e.g., cybersecurity, intellectual property rights, etc.) generates policing expectations that can only be adequately covered through the private sector (Tusikov 2012).

Private security and the Information Economy
The rise in importance and numbers of private actors who conduct policing has been defined as nothing less than a "profound development in the securing of society" (Spearin 2004: 1), with vast implications for how security is provided at the local and global levels, but also for the data-sharing landscape that characterizes the Big Data society. The process of commodification of policing and security has taken place in the context of the Information Economy (Castells 2010), in

which information, processed through a global network of interconnected ICTs, is the key resource for organizations to increase added value in their operations. In his context, resources are optimized not so much through better deployment strategies or organizational decisions, but instead by identifying and processing a broad range of information inputs, thus improving the quality of the decisions made on the basis of this for each given situation.

Companies working in the field of security are also adapting their strategies; rather than only providing mass-consumption commodities (e.g., security guards, alarm systems, etc.), they now supply customized services that are personalized for each client. 'One-size-fits-all' strategies are perceived as ineffective at mitigating risks, whereas tailored solutions based on the growing availability of information sources allows providers to adapt security approaches and save efforts. The use of ICTs allows for the adaptation and optimization of resources required in each situation through the collection, processing and analysis of available data.

Because risk detection must be based on quality information, the adequate combination of multiple sources through Big Data technologies can meaningfully enhance the actual performance of security systems and strategies. In this context, the commodification of security is linked to the commodification of digital identities and personal data. According to J. van Dijck, "metadata appear to have become a regular currency for citizens to pay for their communication services and security." Moreover, people's digital profiles (also known as 'digital shadows' or 'data doubles') hold the promise of immense profits in the foreseen digital identity market. The commodification of identities and personal data has led to the appearance of a new category of actors, the 'data brokers';

> "companies whose primary business is collecting personal information about consumers from a variety of sources and aggregating, analyzing, and sharing that information, or information derived from it, for purposes such as marketing products, verifying an individual's identity, or detecting fraud. Significantly, data brokers typically collect, maintain, manipulate, and share a wide variety of information about consumers without interacting directly with them."

In a world in which the boundaries between publicly and privately owned data are increasingly difficult to establish, the possibilities of this new data landscape appear to be endless. So are the risks.

4.2   PRIVATIZATION, COMMODIFICATION AND PUBLIC-PRIVATE PARTNERSHIPS

This process of outsourcing security services from the public to the private sphere is based on the assumption that it is a cost-effective activity, although there is no evidence which comes to this conclusion. As some authors have noted, circumventing public expenses through privatization and civilianization has not been costless, as state and local government spending on private services escalated from $27 billion in 1975 to some $100 billion in 1987, with the federal sector contributing another $197 billion of public expenditures to private security services in 1987 (Lo Turco 2009). Citing the observation that the number of public police officers have also risen alongside private sector growth, and that the economic and political capital associated with public policing has also increased (Zedner 2006: 269), some authors suggest that private and public security sectors are expanding, and that an appropriate term to describe this process, therefore, would be the 'commodification of security' (Van Buuren 2010: 2).

This idea is somewhat contested because in certain cases the expansion of the private sector has coincided with lower public protection. In Canada, for instance, conservative estimates place the ratio of those employed in private security to those employed in public security – meaning public police officers – at 2: 1. More generous estimations place the figure at 4: 1. It is estimated that the private security industry grew ten times in size between 1988 and 1995. In contrast, Statistics Canada reported in 1998 that the ratio of police officers to population stood at its lowest level since 1970 (Spearin 2004: 1). In the US, the number of sworn officers exceeded the number of people employed in the private security field in the 1960s, but the numbers had shifted to the point where an estimated three people were employed in private security for every sworn officer in the United States by 1990 (Forst and Manning 1999; Lo Turco 2009). This would point to a process of both commodification and privatization, with an increasing role for public-private partnerships (PPPs).

There are additional trends that have reinforced this move away from a public monopoly of the provision of security. The growing role of local and regional authorities, described above, which has imposed an agenda centred around decentralization, means that local police forces and regional security provision departments have proliferated in search of better collaboration between the police and society. Additionally, calls to people's participation in policing, through neighbourhood watch schemes[2] or technologically-aided new communication means (applications, instant messaging, etc.) have led to the dissolution of a public monopoly on security provision. It is apparent that security is no longer dominated by the State and is instead a continuum of collaboration between public actors, private actors and citizens. These partnerships establish complex webs of data flows and dependencies that, at the same time, shape the possibilities and limits of these new arrangements.

PPPs are "forms of cooperation between actors from the public and the private sector that are set-up with the intention to continuously exist over a long period of time and that are organized according to different characteristics" (Paun 2013: 31). Examples of PPPs operating today are InfraGard and the FBI/Department of

Defense and the Defense Industrial Base (DIB)/Cyber Security/Information
Assurance Program (CS/IA) IDB and Saab in the US (McNally 2012). They proliferate in the fields of Airport Security Management or in Major Events and Sport
Infrastructures Security Management such as the Olympic Games and Stewarding
System at Stadiums (Lo Turco 2009: 63-64). In early July 2012, for instance, just a
few weeks before the opening of the London Olympics on 27 July, the multina-
tional security company G4S defaulted on its £284m contract to provide 10,400
security personnel for the event, citing recruitment and scheduling difficulties.
Around 4,700 members of the armed forces had to be drafted in to cover the short-
fall in security employees (Aljazeera 2012; Ayling 2014: 2). Many countries, such as
much of Great Britain and Australia, have developed PPPs in policing. This
includes both the police department's contracting out of policing functions to private agents, and the development of collaborations between sworn police and private security agents operating independently in a particular jurisdiction (Sturgess
2002). The Vera Institute has reported a similar array of public-private policing
partnerships in Brazil, India, Indonesia, Kenya, Nigeria and South Africa (Bhanu
and Stone 2004; Lo Turco 2009).

PPPs proliferate because they often allow for a minimal financial commitment from
the government at the outset and share the risks between public and private actors
(thus not falling entirely into the hands of the public bodies). It is also believed that
the private sector is more efficient and less bureaucratic, which could facilitate the
completion of new projects on time and in an effective manner. As for the private
partners, they acquire substantial long-term contracts, visibility, image and access
to political figures that can be useful in furthering their market scope. PPPs, however, can also have long tendering periods and high transaction costs, and run the
risk of sacrificing quality for cost. Absence of an effective pre-coded channel of
communication between public and private sectors, both on the local and the
national level, can lead to lack of information, coordination, trust and reciprocity
in the relationships among constituents.

Regardless of the pros and cons, today's security landscape is increasingly characterized by plural policing partnerships and other contractual arrangements
between public and private providers. While there is a need for more concrete
empirical research in hybrid security practices at different levels (Van Buuren
2010: 4), all evidence and observation suggests that such practices are here to stay.

The proliferation of policing technologies increases this trend, as Big Data technologies and infrastructures (sensors and devices, telecommunication networks and
servers, databases, specialized analysis software and hardware, etc.) are often
owned by private actors, even when developed for or used by public police forces.
Public organizations often do not own, develop or acquire resources such as collected information, technologies or expertise. They also need the ability to extract

useful and understandable information: complete, comprehensive, truthful, reliable, timely and regularly updated. Often it does not make strategic sense for public bodies to develop their own data processing technologies, and so the best option is to make use of existing resources available on the market. Big Data technologies that are already developed are offered globally, and a vast amount of useful personal data is currently being collected by private actors (Internet Service Providers, online services, etc.). For certain tasks, outsourcing is the most sensible option as private companies already own a large amount of digitalized and shared information as well as cloud systems with a competitive storage capacity, bandwidth and performance.

In this data context, PPPs allow for existing infrastructure to be taken advantage of, while simultaneously exerting public control and accountability mechanisms that minimize the severity of collateral damages. In the European case, the joint research frameworks FP7 or Horizon 2020 organize public-private partnerships to foster research and development initiatives. An important role of these initiatives is to develop security research projects. In 2012 it was possible to list up to 268 projects in this area, and the budget invested by the EU for the 2007-2013 period amounted to €1.4 billion (European Union 2014).

In the context of PPPs for security purposes based on ICTs, there is a remarkable shift of power relations. On the one hand, corporations may acquire questionable quotes of power and controlling capabilities. Because private corporations are not subject to the same accountability measures as public bodies, and are instead held to other market principles, their bad practices may only be unveiled once the harm is irreversible. On the other, the interests and negotiating capacities of ISPs and e-services (e.g., to develop PETs, to avoid backdoors and reject data access requests etc.) may change following regulation variations, governmental discourse and societal attitudes, in a moving landscape that is often difficult to grasp. At the same time, security actors and decision-makers (LEAs, Intelligence agencies, governments, and security companies) may acquire increasing access to personal data that citizens may want to keep private or away from the authorities but still share with friends or acquaintances. Once the information is collected, however, it is very difficult to control whether it ends up in the hands of public bodies. In non-democratic contexts, this can be highly harmful to fundamental rights and freedoms and make protest and dissent more difficult if not impossible. Finally, as Big Data is currently a developing field, regulation is still being established, and the process is complex. Communication networks are global, and standardized control mechanisms are not easy to deploy throughout all the affected geographical areas and sectors, as evidenced by the cases of the secret mass surveillance programmes recently exposed by the ex-CIA consultant and whistleblower Edward Snowden.

4.3   BIG DATA IN A FRAGMENTED SECURITY CONTEXT

While most data used in an investigation is still police data (accessed through legal warrants and within the framework of an investigation), police forces find themselves increasingly relying on privately gathered data, both in the context of open investigations and when gathering information or carrying out regular prevention activities. Private CCTV cameras or privately owned social media are regularly accessed and used by the police, and in most countries the legal framework establishes this need to share data between private and public actors.

Large internet and social media companies are a case in point here. Of the worldwide requests received by Google from law enforcement authorities from July to December 2012, for instance, 32 percent where made from the EU. In 40 percent of the cases, Google complied and provided the requested information. Concerning Microsoft, up to 47 percent of the worldwide requests received from law enforcement authorities in 2012 came from the EU, and 79 percent of them where complied with. In the case of Twitter, only 10 percent of the requests received came from the EU, and 2 percent were serviced (Boulet and Hernanz 2013).

In the UK, communications data were intercepted on 514,608 occasions in 2013. Of these requests, 76.9 percent were made to 'prevent crime or disorder'; 11.4 percent were made for National security reasons; 11.3 percent were justified by 'emergency' situations (preventing death or injury); and the final 0.4 percent fall into the category of 'other' causes, such as tax purposes. During these requests, 970 errors occurred, leading to the arrest of two innocent people (Worth 2014).

The exploitation of ICTs for security purposes is no longer just a matter of LEAs wiretapping phone lines and intervening communications. It embraces a remarkable phenomenon that consists of people actively keeping track of their own lives through a wide variety of formats: detailed social network profiles, blog and microblogging posts, personal pictures and videos shared through public or semi-public social networks, IM and VoIP conversations, geolocalization social sharing, etc. All these informational inputs are being used by the authorities as evidence to motivate investigations and to support accusations in trials (as well as by private actors to conduct market research and segmentation).

However, the relationships and dependencies established between public and private actors through data is much more complex than the 'I can access your data' message seemingly spread by the stakeholders involved. Often, accessing the data is not easy, especially if the company holding the data is outside the jurisdiction of the police filing the request. Moreover, data is not just a resource but a game changer. Boulet and Hernanz (2013) present four possible scenarios for law enforcement agencies in the EU when requesting access to private data from companies that host or process the desired information:

- Voluntary cooperation: Law enforcement authorities get access to their desired data by bilaterally contacting a private party who hosts the data of interest. This approach requires the private company to cooperate voluntarily with the law enforcement authority requesting the data. As recent examples have shown, this voluntary cooperation cannot be taken for granted as it creates a burden for private companies. If the requested data is stored on a server located in another country, most law enforcement authorities (depending on national law) will need to notify the country concerned, in a process that can take a long time.
- Direct access: Law enforcement authorities get access to private databases without the knowledge or the consent of the private company. Some law enforcement agencies can also obtain remote access to data through special software or by technical means ('key loggers', 'sniffers') in very exceptional circumstances. A related scenario in this category would be the observation by police authorities of social network activity (Facebook, Twitter, Instagram, etc.).
- Mutual legal cooperation: Law enforcement authorities use mutual legal cooperation as the old-fashioned way of obtaining requested data when the private party is located outside their territory. Police often complain about the technical difficulties and length of this procedure.
- Europol: A fourth possible scenario in the future could be for police agencies to turn to a centralized EU law enforcement authority (for instance, Europol) which could adopt a standardized and streamlined approach. This process would allow for a direct request for private data from Internet companies in the EU, who would then share the data with the requesting national police authority. This scenario would require upgrading the mandate of EU agencies to include such responsibility.

A fifth, important scenario is crowdsourcing. There is a growing trend among police forces to request the collaboration from citizens using social media channels (Trottier 2014). In this case, the gathered data is obtained lawfully by the police as it is made available to them purposefully by citizens who are willing to cooperate and help the security forces. However, this scenario raises important ethical concerns, as, to a certain extent, it effectively turns citizens into police agents.

While this debate is only incipient, it should be tackled before such crowdsourcing schemes proliferate, to make sure that their legal, social and ethical implications can be fully grasped. Crowdsourcing in the field of policing could be also seen as a form of 'hyperfragmentation', where each person acts as an information source.

Private surveillance cameras installed in places like stores or private spaces are a form of security outsourcing and fragmentation as public agencies are not required to oversee their management, but LEAs can take advantage of the existence of a private decentralized surveillance network. However, this also implies risks, as private surveillance operators are not subject to the same regulations as public officials, and cases like the live streaming of the images captured by over 73,000 cameras whose owners had not changed their default passwords (Jawad 2014) can proliferate.

In this data-dominated context, it is worth noting that data in itself is not automatically 'Big Data'. Security-related organizations have always used information as a key resource for operations. The difference in the present day is that Big Data is not about data being inputted into a database, but it implies the processing of large quantities of complex information in a short period of time. Laney (2001) listed three key tendencies that make up Big Data: volume, velocity and variety:

1. Data volume: e-commerce enables the collection of up to 10x the amount allowed by conventional transaction channels; this information serves as a key additional value input for companies.
2. Data velocity: not only in terms of physical bandwidth and protocol issue, but also considering the capacity to access and analyze the information in near real time.
3. Data variety: the integration of wide and diverse sources of data with different formats and structures.

The combination of Big Data and quantum computing improves the chances of solving more complex problems at a faster speed than is possible with classic computing, as processing more information can lead to identifying previously neglected or overlooked patterns and connections. Additional information about an individual can be derived, moreover, by using segmentation and building profiles on the basis of individual data.

The current 'datafication' of daily routines feeds into this process, as individuals leave a vast registry of their actions that constitute their 'data doubles' or 'quantified selves', a data shadow they cannot control nor shape or delete. Mayer-Schoenberger and Cukier (2013) understand 'datafication' as the transformation of social actions into online quantified data, enhancing real-time tracking and predictive analysis. This situation enables what R. Clarke in 1988 called 'dataveillance': the "systematic use of personal data systems in the investigation or monitoring of the actions or communications of one or more persons." In this context, it is possible to find out and visualize simple behavioural patterns from online traces left by digital platform users. For instance, applications like *Twaps* or *Tinfoleak* enable the tracking of Twitter users who post geo-tagged content or allow for the extraction of related statistics and data about their activity on the website. This information can be used by any public or private actor with no need to inform the user nor gather their consent.

Nonetheless, it is important to highlight that Big Data does not necessarily include the utilization of personal data, nor does it need to generate detailed personal records; in many cases, it is used in the context of climate statistics or other non-human related purposes. However, when original databases include personally identifiable data, simple anonymization techniques currently fail to ensure that re-identification cannot happen, and that identities cannot be inferred from the combination of multiple sources of information, especially when geolocation is part of the mix. This difficulty is one of the main reasons behind one of the most important principles of data protection: data minimization. In a context in which digitalized information cannot be properly secured against any threats not permanently deleted, the best way to protect people's privacy is by making sure that only the data that is immediately relevant and useful to a given process or service is collected.

A parallel challenge concerns the quality and usefulness of decisions made on the basis of Big Data. If data collection is undertaken by a single organization intending to enhance their predictive or investigative strategies, it is possible that shallow or narrow data collection strategies could generate a poor data sample, thus contributing to potentially misleading results. Here, the idea that more information always leads to better decision-making should be challenged, as it remains to be proven that the main obstacle towards evidence-based policy is lack of information (and not, for instance, lack of resources or political pressure). The best diagnosis can also perish when facing the challenges of implementation: lack of financial planning, training, information and communication channels can turn good ideas into failures (Pressman and Wildavsky 1984), particularly in the context of fragmented information sources that require very effective communication, coordination and leadership.

For instance, a control room with dozens of CCTV monitors does not automatically result in enhanced security simply through the wide-scale collection of information (Barret, 2013). This technique is deemed to be effective because it serves as a tool that takes advantage of the ability of ICTs to save human resources; it functions as just one technique in a broader strategy implemented by society to achieve the goal of enhanced security. For example, the detection of unusual events may also be carried out by computerized systems (smart cameras, noise thresholds, etc.), but, to be effective, the location and position of CCTV cameras must work in collaboration with existing informational inputs (mappings and crime stats, among many others). Efficiency is increased by knitting a network of informational sources that, when strategically implemented and critically evaluated, provide a valuable collection of information from which to make important decisions.

It is worth noting however, that Big Data can both contribute to increased fragmentation and lead to its overcoming, as security agencies can shorten distances by using data and new technologies. Investigating procedures can be made easier through the processing of vast volumes of digitalized data, and Big Data analytics can allow for the 'de-fragmentation' of this information, knitting together different sources. Data brokers compile multiple information sources, software programs help to analyze and process them and data scientists are prepared to make useful interpretations. Seamless, rights-based interaction and collaboration between these actors can yield productive results from the interaction between policing and Big Data.

Moreover, the relationship between security and privacy is bound to evolve in the near future. As new data crimes proliferate (cybercrime, identity theft, etc.), people will most likely grow concerned about what use is made of their personal data, and privacy may emerge as a new sphere of protection –just like property. LEAs and corporations may increasingly find that the sources they used to rely on are either better protected by privacy-enhancing and encrypting solutions or that new regulations limit the use that third parties can make of user-generated content and data. The current social climate surrounding Big Data poses a significant challenge for private and public organizations that are interested in collecting personal and non-personal data for their own use, as society becomes increasingly aware and vocal about their privacy concerns surrounding the deployment of omniscient 'Orwellian' systems, based on black-box systems and ubiquitous surveillance practices.

4.4   CONCLUSION: ADVANTAGES, RISKS AND RECOMMENDATIONS

The rise of security technologies and the remarkable growth of the security business are clear evidence of the transformation of public policing. What once was an endeavour that was exclusively under the purview of the State and public bodies is now a marketable service. Security-related routines have also experienced a transformation, as seen in the shift from human-driven tasks to computer-driven tasks fuelled by informational inputs. Moreover, this intensive technification of security systems and strategies has provoked a shift from mitigation of risks by prosecution and enforcement, to minimization of risks through prevention and prediction.

But while Big Data has accompanied these processes and often increased the efficiency and innovation opportunities of security organizations, it is necessary to balance out both the advantages and risks of this data-intensive context. It is also important to establish recommendations and best practices in order to improve processes and outcomes, but also to monitor how the interaction between security and fundamental rights and values evolves, with a view to creating innovative processes and technologies that leave behind the trade-off of rights (where one wins, one loses) to encourage the joint promotion of both security and privacy.

A good starting-point would be to train public servants to identify the difference between personal data (information linked to an identified person) and datasets that do not reveal personal details. The use of predictive policing tools such as pseudonymized maps and calendars that give information on how statistically likely a crime is to occur in a certain area or at a specific time is very different from the use of lists of identifiable names ('heat lists') with the intention of determining if these specific people are actively committing crimes (Strawd 2014; Upturn 2014). Moreover, the management of personal data requires specific measures to avoid risk practices, starting from data minimization and avoiding the routine mass collection of data which is not needed in first place. Even though potential access to data has to be guaranteed for law-enforcement purposes, strict protocols have to be observed throughout the data management cycle (collection, distribution, storage, access and deletion). Another distinction may be made in the case of telecommunications, as metadata can still reveal a great deal of personal information about a specific individual. Intercepting communications metadata, therefore, is not a minor infringement of a data subject's privacy (Farivar 2014; Opsahl 2013) and should be regulated, controlled and accountable.

It is difficult to deny that the use of ICT solutions and Big Data processes for security purposes can introduce unexpected informational factors that enhance the quality and efficiency of investigations, that transnational investigations can be enhanced with the use of data-sharing mechanisms, that the real-time analysis of risks can improve rescue missions and that data analysis can lead to better prevention strategies. However, it is also true that data is only as neutral as those designing the data collection mechanisms and algorithms. Therefore, data can also be used for unjustified or illegal profiling based on ethnic, religious or socio-economic characteristics. Increasing networking and interconnection of devices may weaken the control and security of information: cloud services, mobile devices and online sharing practices demand additional security measures and attitudes, which are still not fully developed. There is also the related risk of 'datacentrism', which may lead to a sort of data despotism or minimization of the digital divide, thus privileging those digitally included, or substituting actual citizens for their data doubles in policy-making. Delegating data processing to private actors may also lead to risk practices, as these may have perverse incentives and the regulation of private entities is still far away from that of the public sphere. The factual provenance of data is a related and often overlooked risk. Finally, privacy is a key right at stake in this new scenario, in which 'technological optimism' can lower controls and guarantees.

Bearing in mind this complex and dynamic combination of risk and potential, an initial toolset of recommendations for security organizations aiming to make use of Big Data could include the need to identify in advance information that is truly relevant and useful, and collect only that (data minimization), the creation of well-weighed indicators and profiles (variables) to guide data analysis, the requirement to seek informed consent for the use of personal data, avoid database re-utilization and establish accountability and transparency mechanisms. The development of privacy-enhancing technologies is also a crucial step, as is the need to develop protocols aimed at guaranteeing ethical standards and assessing the societal impact of new technological solutions and processes. In order to protect individual rights, data access logs need to be created; data interception and access warrants should be mandatory; and there should be oversight bodies to monitor and establish the limits of the collaboration between private companies, judicial bodies, police forces and intelligence agencies.

While blurring the lines between public and private bodies, and public and private data, is probably an irreversible trend, and one that can lead to improved policy-making and socially desirable outcomes, there is one line that should never be crossed in this new data scenario, as emphasized recently by both US[3] and UK[4] Courts: the line that distinguishes between the (data) rights of individuals subject to a legitimate police investigation, who may need to surrender personal information in a process with judicial oversight, and the rights of the men and women who, as citizens, should never have to fear that their communications, correspondence or daily routines are the subject of unwarranted mass surveillance.

REFERENCES

Al Jazeera (2012) *Will the London Olympics Be Safe?*, available at: www.aljazeera.com/ programmes/insidestory/2012/07/201271643930549890.html [16 July 2012].

Alexander, M. and T. Garden (2001) 'The Arithmetic of Defence Policy', *International Affairs* 77, 3: 509-29.

Avant, D. (2006) 'The Implications of Marketized Security for IR Theory: The Democratic Peace, Late State Building, and the Nature and Frequency of Conflict', *Perspectives on Politics* 4, 3: 507-528.

Ayling, J. (2014) 'Trading in Security: Issues in the Commodification of Public Security. *RegNet'*, *Working Paper* 38, Regulatory Institutions Network, available at: http://dx.doi.org/10.2139/ssrn.2463954.

Ayling, J.M., P. Grabosky and C. Shearing (2009) *Lengthening the Arm of the Law: Enhancing Police Resources in the 21st Century*, Cambridge: Cambridge University Press.

Barret, D. (2013) 'One Surveillance Camera for Every 11 People in Britain, Says CCTV Survey', *The Telegraph*, available at: www.telegraph.co.uk/technology/10172298/ One-surveillance-camera-for-every-11-people-in-Britain-says-CCTV-survey.html [8 June 2015].

Bhanu, C. and C. Stone (2004) *Public-Private Partnerships for Police Reform*, Vera Institute of Justice, available at: www.vera.org/publications.

Blanco, I. (2004) *Governance urbana i polítiques d'inclusió sòcio-espacial*, UAB: Doctoral Dissertation.

Boulet, G. and N. Hernanz (2013) 'Cross-Border Law Enforcement Access to Data on the Internet and Rule of Law Challenges in the EU', *SAPIENT Policy Brief D6.6*, available at: www.sapientproject.eu/docs/SAPIENT%20D66%20Policy%20Brief %20-%20final.pdf [July 2013].

Buuren, J. van (2010) 'Security as a Commodity: The Ethical Dilemmas of Private Security Services', *INEX Policy Brief* 6, March.

Castells, M. (2010) *The Information Age: Economy, Society and Culture Volume 1: The Rise of the Network Society*, 2nd ed., Oxford: Wiley Blackwell.

Clarke, R. (1988) 'Information Technology and Dataveillance', *Communications of the ACM* 31, 5: 498-512.

Cochrane, A. (2007) *Understanding Urban Policy*, Oxford: Blackwell Publishing.

Dixon, D. and L. Maher (2005) 'Policing, Crime and Public Health: Lessons for Australia from the 'New York miracle'', *Criminal Justice* 5, 2: 115-143.

Dijck, J. van (2014) 'Datafication, Dataism and Dataveillance: Big Data between Scientific Paradigm and Ideology', *Surveillance and Society* 12, 2: 197-208, available at: www.surveillance-and-society.org | ISSN: 1477-7487.

European Union (2014) *EU Research for a Secure Society*, available at: http://ec.europa. eu/dgs/home-affairs/financing/fundings/pdf/research-for-security/ security_research_catalogue_2014_en.pdf [May 2014].

Farivar, C. (2014) *Surprise, Surprise: My Online Metadata Actually Reveals Where I've Been*, [ArsTechnica blog], available at: http://arstechnica.com/security/2014/03/surprise-surprise-my-online-metadata-actually-reveals-where-ive-been/ [8 June 2015].

Forst, B. and P.K. Manning (1999) *Privatization of Policing: Two Views*, Washington, DC: Georgetown University Press.

Galdon-Clavell, G. and J.M. Zavala (2014) *Report on Societal Impact of Using Social Media in Security Context*, deliverable for SLANDAIL Project, European Commission.

Gilling, D. (1999) 'Community Safety: A Critique' in *The British Criminology Conferences: Selected Proceedings* 2.

Graham, S. (2010) *Cities Under Siege: The New Military Urbanism*, London: Verso.

Gruening, G. (2001) 'Origin and Theoretical Basis of New Public Management', *International Public Management Journal* 4: 1–25.

Hartley, K. (undated) 'The UK's Major Defence Projects: A Cause for Concern?' *Research Paper, Centre for Defence Economics*, available at: www.docstoc.com/docs/28359125/1-THE-UKS-MAJOR-DEFENCE-PROJECTS-A-CAUSE-FOR-CONCERN-Professor#.

Jawad, U. (2014) 'A Creepy Website Is Streaming from 73.000 Cameras; Some in the Bedroom', *NeoWin* [blog], available at: www.neowin.net/news/a-creepy-website-is-streaming-from-73000-cameras-some-in-the-bedroom, [8 June 2015].

Jones, T. and T. Newburn (2002) 'The Transformation of Policing? Understanding Current Trends in Policing Systems', *British Journal of Criminology* 42, 1: 129-146, doi: 10.1093/bjc/42.1.129.

Kempa, M., P. Stenning and J. Wood (2004) 'Policing Communal Spaces', *British Journal of Criminology* 44, 4: 562-81.

Krahman, E. (2008a) 'Security: Collective Good or Commodity?', *European Journal of International Relations* 14, 3: 379-404.

Krahmann, E. (2008b) 'The Commodification of Security in the Risk Society', *Working Paper 06-08*, University of Bristol, School of Sociology, Politics and International Studies, available at www.bristol.ac.uk/spais/research/workingpapers/wpspaisfiles/krahmann0608.pdf [8 June 2015].

Laney, D. (2001) *3D Data Management: Controlling Data Volume, Velocity and Variety Gartner*, available at: http://blogs.gartner.com/doug-laney/files/2012/01/ad949-3D-Data-Management-Controlling-Data-Volume-Velocity-and-Variety.pdf [8 June 2015].

Lo Turco C.C. (2009) 'The Field of Security. Public Private Partnerships', *SIAK-Journal – Zeitschrift für Polizeiwissenschaft und polizeiliche Praxis* 2: 62-67, available at: http://dx.doi.org/10.7396/2009_2_G [8 June 2015].

Loader, I. (2002) 'Policing, Securitization and Democratization in Europe', *Criminal Justice* 2, 2: 125-153.

Manning, P. K. (1992) *Organizational Communication*, Hawthorne, N.Y.: Aldine DeGruyter.

Mayer-Schoenberger, V. and K. Cukier (2013) *Big Data. A Revolution that Will Transform How We Live, Work, and Think*, London: John Murray Publishers.

Mcnally, S. (2012) 'The Evolution and Importance of the Private Security Sector', *AMUSecurityInfo* [blog], American Military University, available at: http://amusecurityinfo.com/the-evolution-and-importance-of-the-private-security-sector [8 June 2015].

Mitchell, K. and K. Beckett (2008) 'Securing the Global City: Crime, Consulting, Risk, and Ratings in the Production of Urban Space', *Indiana Journal of Global Legal Studies* 15, 1: 75-100.

O'Malley P. (1997) 'The Politics of Crime Prevention' in P. O'Malley and A. Sutton (eds.) *Crime Prevention in Australia*, Sydney: Federation Press.

O'Malley P. and D. Palmer (1996) 'Post Keynesian Policing', *Economy and Society* 25: 137-155.

O'Shea, T.C. (2000) 'The Political Dimension of Community Policing: Belief Congruence Between Police and Citizens', *Police Quarterly* 3, 4: 389-412.

Opsahl, K. (2013, June 7) 'Why Metadata Matters', *Electronic Frontier Foundation Blog* [Blog], available at: www.eff.org/es/deeplinks/2013/06/why-metadata-matters [8 June 2015].

Paun, C. (2013) 'Globalization of Law Enforcement. A Study of Transnational Public-Private Partnerships against Intellectual Property Crimes, Dissertation,' *Universität Bremen – BIGSSS*, available at: http://d-nb.info/1072047276/34.

Pleasance, C. (2014) 'Gang who 'Stole More than $ 1 million in Jewellery and Cash' Caught after Posting Pictures of Themselves Showing off Their Swag on Social Media', *Mail Online*, available at: www.dailymail.co.uk/news/article-2649491/Gang-stole-1million-jewelry-cash-caught-posting-pictures-showing-swag-social-media.html#ixzz3cTQyuBBX [8 June 2015].

Pressman, J. and A. Wildavsky (1984) *Implementation: How Great Expectations in Washington Are Dashed in Oakland; or, Why It's Amazing that Federal Programs Work at All, This Being a Saga of the Economic Development Administration as Told by Two Sympathetic Observers Who Seek to Build Morals on a Foundation of Ruined Hopes*, Berkeley: University of California Press.

Sawers, P. (2015) 'Facebook and Twitter Could Be Hate-Speech 'Accomplices' if New French Law Passes', *Venture Beat News*, available at: http://venturebeat.com/2015/01/27/facebook-and-twitter-could-be-hate-speech-accomplices-if-new-french-law-passes [8 June 2015].

Shearing C.D. and P.C. Stenning (1983) 'Private Security: Implications for Social Control', *Social Problems* 30, 5: 493-506.

Spearin, C. (2004) 'Mall Cops, Military Contractors, and Al-Qaeda: an Examination of the Commodification of Canadian Security and Contemporary Terrorism', *Journal of Conflict Studies* 24, 1, available at: http://journals.hil.unb.ca/index.php/JCS/article/view/291/463.

Steden, R. van and R. Sarre (2007) 'The Growth of Private Security: Trends in the European Union', *Security Journal* 20, 4: 222-235.

Strawd, M. (2014) 'The Minority Report: Chicago's New Police Computer Predicts Crimes, but Is It Racist?' *The Verge*, available at: www.theverge.com/2014/2/19/5419854/ the-minority-report-this-computer-predicts-crime-but-is-it-racist [8 June 2015].

Sturgess, G. L. (2002) 'Private Risk, Public Service', *Policy*, Autumn, available at: www.cis.org.au/images/stories/policy-magazine/2002-autumn/2002-18-1-gary- l-sturgess.pdf.

Trottier, D. (2014) 'An Overview of Police-Led and Crowdsourced Investigations on Social Media', *Journal of Law, Information and Science* 23, 1.

Tusikov, N. (2012) 'Measuring Organised Crime-Related Harms: Exploring Five Policing Methods', *Crime Law Social Change* 57, 1: 99–115.

Upturn (2014) 'Predictive Policing: From Neighborhoods to Individuals' in *Civil Rights, Big Data, and Our Algorithmic Future A September 2014 Report on Social Justice and Technology*, available at: https://bigdata.fairness.io/wp-content/uploads/ 2015/04/2015-04-20-Civil-Rights-Big-Data-and-Our-Algorithmic-Future- v1.2.pdf [8 June 2015].

Wacquant, L. (2000) *Las cárceles de la miseria*, Buenos Aires: Manantial.

Wilson, J.Q. and G.L. Kelling (1982) 'Broken Windows: The Police and Neighborhood Safety, *Atlantic Monthly* 249, 3: 29-38.

Worth, D. (2014) 'Police and Intelligence Agencies Overusing Data Request Powers', *V3.Co.Uk* [Blog], available at: www.v3.co.uk/v3-uk/news/2338780/police-and- intelligence-agencies-overusing-data-request-powers [8 June 2015].

Završnik, A. (2013) 'Blurring the Line between Law Enforcement and Intelligence: Sharpening the Gaze of Surveillance?', *Journal of Contemporary European Research*. 9, 1: 181-202.

Zedner, L. (2006) 'Liquid Security: Managing the Market for Crime Control', *Criminology and Criminal Justice* 6, 3: 267-288.

NOTES

1   The author would like to thank José Maria Zavala and Jennie Day for their inputs and contributions to this piece.

2   For more information on neighbourhood watch schemes in the EU, see the IRISS project: www.irissproject.eu.

3   'U.S. Court Rules NSA Mass Surveillance Illegal', see www.amnestyusa.org/news/press-releases/us-court-rules-nsa-mass-surveillance-illegal.

4   'GCHQ-NSA intelligence sharing unlawful, says surveillance tribunal', see www.privacyinternational.org/?q=node/482.

5 PRE-EMPTIVE BIG DATA SURVEILLANCE AND ITS (DIS)EMPOWERING CONSEQUENCES: THE CASE OF PREDICTIVE POLICING

Rosamunde van Brakel

5.1 INTRODUCTION

> "It's a poor sort of memory that only works backwards", the Queen remarked.
> "What sort of things do you remember best?" Alice ventured to ask.
> "Oh, things that happened the week after next", the Queen replied in a careless tone.
> "For instance, now" she went on, sticking a large piece of plaster on her finger as she spoke, "there's the King's messenger. He's in prison now, being punished, and the trial doesn't even begin till next Wednesday: and of course the crime comes last of all."
> "Suppose he never commits the crime?" said Alice.
> "That would be all the better, wouldn't it?" the Queen said, as she bound the plaster round her finger with a bit of ribbon. (Carroll 1896/1996: 181)

This quote from *Through the Looking Glass, and What Alice Found There* illustrates well the pre-crime of pre-emptive logic that hides behind several new surveillance technologies. Deploying new predictive technologies makes it possible to gather specific knowledge of the future. According to this logic, authorities can punish and intervene before a crime happens. The Queen "represents the contrary of a human knowledge conscious of its limits, its arbitrariness, its uncertainty, its ambiguity. She embodies the dream of an absolute power, presenting its decision as based on truth through a knowledge of the future" (Bigo 2010).

The pre-emptive society is not about taming uncertainty, which is characteristic of the risk society discourse (Rose 1998), but rather about imaginary surveillance control, which is:

> "a fantastic dream of seeing everything capable of being seen, recording every fact capable of being recorded, and accomplishing these things, whenever and wherever possible, prior to the event itself. (…) it circulates as an effective mechanism in the technical evolution of control in postindustrial societies" (Bogard 1996: 4-5).

The pre-emptive logic that is behind the trend in governments and corporations, who are increasingly turning to predictive analytics and data mining when examining behaviours[1], is characterized by a belief in (the objectivity of) statistics and technology as promoted by the private corporations that are developing the technology and that, in their enthusiasm, are often uncritical and fail to take into account their own limitations. A good illustration can be found, for instance, in what Tony Blair, former prime-minister of the United Kingdom, said in 2006:

"You can predict reasonably accurately the kids and the families who are going to be difficult. (...) If we are not prepared to predict and intervene far more early then there are children who are growing up, in families which we know are dysfunctional, then the kids a
few years down the line are going to be a menace to society."

Of course, the pre-emptive logic as described above is very generalizing, and not
all policymakers and law enforcement practitioners approach new technologies
uncritically.[2] It is undeniable, however, that this logic can be recognized in many
new surveillance practices, such as predictive policing, especially in the
United States. It is also evident, for instance, in technologies that try and predict
who is a terrorist, including risk profiling at airports and smart-CCTV with behavioural detection software, or in children's risk-profiling applications that try and
predict the risk of this child being more prone to committing a crime than that
child (Van Brakel, forthcoming).

These new types of surveillance technologies that employ such pre-emptive logic
are known as pre-emptive surveillance (Bogard 1996; Lyon 2007; Elmer and Opel
2008; Van Brakel, forthcoming); on the basis of Lyon's 2001 definition of surveillance, they can be defined as follows: 'the systematic or targeted collection and
processing of data of entities[3], which are used to make predictions about future
harm on the basis of profiles with the main goal of intervening before harm is
done' (Van Brakel, forthcoming). Just like other surveillance technologies,
pre-emptive surveillance may have both empowering and disempowering effects,
is neither good or bad in itself, and is not neutral: all that depends on the socio-
political historical context, on the reasons why a particular technology is being
implemented, and on the micro-practices that characterize the implementation of
the technology (Lyon 2001; Van Brakel 2013).

In the broader context of developments in pre-emptive surveillance, recent technological trends promise to change practices drastically. One of these trends is
known as 'Big Data' (Mayer-Schönberger and Cukier 2013). Many definitions of
Big Data can be found in the literature, and the '3V definition' is often brought forward as one that a significant number of people can agree on; in this definition, Big
Data is characterized by great data volume, data velocity, and data variety (Laney
2001). This definition focuses only on characteristics of the data. To be able to analyse the disempowering and empowering effects of Big Data, we need to use a
more encompassing definition of Big Data that also takes into account the socio-
historical context. Therefore, Big Data can be seen as a socio-technological phenomenon within the larger context of the emergence of pre-emptive surveillance,
offering the possibility of conducting predictive or real-time analyses of huge
amounts of data – structured or unstructured, in different formats, and taken from
different types of sources – which may lead to original new insights and knowledge and, as a result, change practices significantly.

An abundance of literature has been published on the empowering and disempowering effects of Big Data for advertising, medicine, climate change, social sciences, and many more social domains from a legal perspective, a business perspective, and a critical data/surveillance studies perspective (Manovich 2011; Boyd and Crawford 2012; Tene and Polonetsky 2012; Kitchin 2013; Mayer-Schönberger and Cukier 2013; Lyon 2014). However, not much attention has yet been paid to the effects of Big Data applications on citizens in the specific context of policing.[4] The main objective of this chapter, therefore, is to provide a better understanding of what predictive Big Data policing is and to discuss both the empowering and the disempowering effects of predictive Big Data policing as a form of pre-emptive surveillance.

The chapter is structured as follows: in the first part, the phenomenon of predictive policing will be explained, including examples of where Big Data is used and how effective it is. In the second part, we will explore the disempowering and empowering effects of predictive Big Data policing.

5.2   BIG DATA AND CRIME PREVENTION: THE CASE OF PREDICTIVE POLICING

Since the 1990s, developments in intelligence-led policing in Europe (see Maguire 2000; De Hert and Vis 2005) and increasingly popular theories of situational crime prevention (Benbouzid 2015) have led to the development of hotspot analysis and later to prospective hotspot analysis (Bowers et al. 2004). This then led to the development of one of the first 'predictive policing applications' in the United Kingdom, known as ProMap (Johnson et al. 2009). At roughly the same time as Promap was being developed in the UK at the end of the first decade of the 21st century, IBM was developing one the first predictive policing applications in the United States, using databases of past crimes and data such as typical times of the day and types of weather that correlated with crime to identify trends and map out prediction (Bachner 2013). Police officers were making the case that, as a result of budget cuts, predictive policing should be the future of policing (Beck and McCue 2009).

Predictive policing can be defined as: "any policing strategy or tactic that develops and uses information and advanced analysis to inform forward-thinking crime prevention" (Uchida 2009). The fundamental principle underlying the theory and practice of predictive policing is that it is possible to make probabilistic inferences about future criminal activity on the basis of existing data (Bachner 2013). Not all predictive policing applications are strictly Big Data, and many currently still work with 'small data', but what we can see is that they all have the potential to become Big Data as more and more data is becoming available and as the ICT infrastructure of law enforcement agencies is becoming more advanced.

As the result of the emergence of more accessible analytical methods and the development of more complex algorithms (Kitchin 2013; Rienks 2014) and efforts to make policing more cost-efficient and productive, crime analysts are now generating predictions about where crime is likely to occur and where suspects are likely to be located (Beck and McCue 2009; Rienks 2014; Van Brakel 2015). With software becoming smarter and more powerful and database storage capacity increasing, it is now also becoming possible to make predictions on the basis of enormous amounts of unstructured and structured Big Data from different sources and file types.

Types of predictive policing

A distinction can be made between two types of predictive policing: predictive mapping and predictive identification. The first type refers to the application of predictive analytics to predict when and where a crime may take place at an aggregate level of analysis. The second type is predictive identification, where the analysis is at the individual or group level; this can focus on predicting potential offenders, offenders' identities, criminal behaviour, and potential victims of crime. The most commonly used type is predictive mapping. Illustrations of this type of predictive policing software include, but are not limited to, PredPol in the US and UK (PredPol 2015; Kentonline 2013), Criminality Awareness System (CAS) in the Netherlands (Willems and Doeleman 2014) (see text box for more detailed discussion), Precobs in Germany and Switzerland (Simon 2014), and KEYCRIME in Milan, Italy (Mastrobuoni 2014).

New applications are experimenting with combinations of different data sources. Bogolomov et al. (2014), for instance, present a type of predictive policing in which they use data abstracted from mobile phones and demographic data. Another emerging trend that is the use of hotspot methods, which are linked to social media data from Twitter and Facebook, for instance, to make predictions. In this case, the algorithm searches for particular language use that indicates a bigger chance of crime in a certain area. For example, if people are talking about going out, going to pubs, and getting drunk, these are indicators that are identified by the data mining models. From the moment the data are collected, the GPS tags in the tweets make it possible to visualize the threats and hotspots for potential crimes (Gerber 2014).

Criminality Awareness System (CAS) Amsterdam[5]

The Criminality Awareness System (CAS) was mainly developed by the Regional Information Organization of the Amsterdam Police in response to the fact that traditional hotspot methodology was not reliable and that there was no standard methodology. The main goal of CAS is to make police work more efficient by optimizing where the police concentrate their efforts. In practice, CAS predicts in which areas specific high-impact crimes, such as burglary, will take place in a two-week period. The two-week period is necessary in the case of burglaries because displacement effects might happen as a result of increased surveillance in the area, and the situation might have changed after two weeks (in contrast to pick-pocketing, for example, which is pretty stable). The technology was piloted in Amsterdam and will be piloted in four other police units in the Netherlands (North-Netherlands, North-Holland, East-Netherlands and The Hague) from late 2015 on. CAS is currently only applied to high-impact crimes such as home burglaries, street robberies, and assaults, but there are plans to expand it to other crimes such as pickpocketing, business burglaries, and bicycle thefts. The pilot project in Amsterdam mainly focused on home burglaries.

CAS, which uses neural network techniques, divides Amsterdam into cells of 125 by 125m. Certain cells, such as water and fields, are not included in the analyses. A lot of data is gathered on these cells. The choice of data is based on previous criminological research and theories and includes general crime data, national statistics data, and geodata. The interesting cells light up in different colours: red, orange, and yellow. Red cells are hotspots: places where the probability of a home burglary taking place is the highest over the next two-week period. Orange and yellow squares have lower probabilities. As a result of this prediction, the police will increase their surveillance in the red areas to prevent burglaries from happening (Willems and Doeleman 2014).

An example of the second type of predictive policing, predictive identification using Big Data, is an application used in the US called Intrado Beware, which has been sold to police departments in the US since 2012. It is a mobile application, which works within Motorola Solutions new Intelligent Data Portal (IDP) platform, a mobile, cloud-based application that gathers contextual information from existing commercial and public databases (9-11.com Magazine 2014).

According to the company that makes the technology:

> "Accessed through any browser (fixed or mobile) on any Internet-enabled device including tablets, smartphones, laptop and desktop computers, Bewarefi from Intrado searches, sorts and scores billions of publically-available commercial records in a matter of seconds - alerting responders to potentially dangerous situations while en route to, or at the location of, a 9-1-1 request for assistance" (Intrado 2012).

After analysing commercial, criminal, and social media information, the Beware algorithm then assigns a score and a threat rating (green, yellow, or red) to a person, which is automatically sent to a requesting officer (Skorup 2014). The software was first piloted by the City of Thornton Police Department in Colorado and is currently piloted in Fresno (Intrado 2012; Hoggard 2015). However, there have also been police departments, such as Bellingham, that decided not to purchase the software after citizens raised concerns about cost and privacy implications, even though the police department had applied and received a federal grant to cover part of the $36,000 annual cost of Beware (Johnson 2014).

Effectiveness of predictive policing

In general, it is too early to draw any convincing conclusions about the effectiveness of the predictive policing applications discussed above. The new software has not been implemented long enough to get a clear picture, and only a few extensive independent evaluations have been performed (see, for example, Hunt, Saunders and Hollywood 2014). Studies conducted by the police themselves on PredPol pilot projects show that there is a significant effect for property crimes: burglars show territorial behaviour when they find an area where there is a lot to be stolen and keep returning to the same area (Berg 2014).[6] Other positive results were found by Mastrobuoni (2014), who conducted an evaluation of KEYCRIME. This author showed that KEYCRIME, which is being used by the police in Milan, can help reduce crime rates and can help the police cut costs. The positive results Mastrobuoni found were obtained in applying the software to burglaries of private companies.

Very little can be concluded from the results of a pilot project in Kent UK where PredPol has been implemented (Kent Police 2013). A more extensive evaluation of predictive policing software, which was used to predict property crime in the United States, was unable to find any statistically significant effects (Hunt, Saunders and Hollywood 2014). The main criterion that is used to measure effectiveness is change in crime statistics, but, as numerous criminological studies have shown, fluctuations in crime figures can be the result of a whole number of variables which cannot be kept under control in such a short pilot project only implemented in one city. The new CAS pilot in four cities in the Netherlands will provide a richer picture of the effectiveness of CAS for crime prevention when it will be evaluated.

Not only are the first evaluation results inconclusive, but they have often not been conducted properly either: they do not take into account other possible causal variables; they do not take into account broader crime trends; and they do not cover a broad enough time span to be able to draw conclusions about causal effects. It is very difficult, therefore, to conclude that there is a causal relation between a drop in crime and the implementation of the software (Van Brakel 2015). Moreover, a significant part also depends on what exactly is being measured. The technology is effective but effective in what? The implementation of some technologies might be effective in predicting but not in decreasing crime. Some might be very effective for police management but not for crime prevention. It should be made clear from the start of a pilot project what the main purpose of the technology is, and evaluations should focus on the effectiveness of the main goal for which the technology was implemented.

In conclusion, as these technologies are still very new, especially predictive identification technologies, future evaluations will have to shed more light on their effectiveness for crime prevention. Currently, no evaluations of predictive identification applications have been found. However, as long as the methodology behind these new technologies is not critically questioned, and as long as there are no mandatory quality standards of evaluation (see Farrington 2003) to make sure that evaluations are conducted properly, these types of evaluations need to be interpreted with due care (Van Brakel 2015).

5.3   (DIS)EMPOWERING EFFECTS OF PREDICTIVE BIG DATA POLICING ON CITIZENS

The previous section examined predictive policing and the effectiveness of the technology. In the following section, we will be exploring the disempowering and empowering effects of predictive Big Data policing on citizens.

5.3.1   DISEMPOWERING EFFECTS OF BIG DATA ON CITIZENS

The following section aims to show how predictive Big Data policing can contribute to disempowerment of individuals, groups, and society. The section is structured following the main disempowering effects that can be recognized; the survey does not pretend to be an exhaustive overview of all issues but rather an exploration of how certain characteristics of Big Data technology have an impact on individuals, groups, and societies.

Responsibilization of technology and transparency
Technology is becoming increasingly smarter and responsibilized. With a nod to Garland (2001), 'responsibilization' here refers to the fact that technology is increasingly made responsible for decision-making. Currently, this is only partially the case in law enforcement as the process has only been automated to a certain extent and the final decision to intervene is still mostly taken by a human being.

But it is not unlikely that future decision-making about interventions will increasingly be done by technology, especially in the context of smart video surveillance at mass transportation sites and mega-events, where the algorithm rather than the human being decides what is suspicious behaviour[7] (Heck 2014) or in the case of threat assessments as used by the Beware software, similar to current developments in credit scoring in the US (Zarsky 2016). There is still a lot of resistance to making technology autonomous, but recent developments relating to terrorist threats have clearly shown how easily laws can be changed in states of emergency. This will have potentially serious consequences for accountability if something goes wrong. It will be unclear who should be held accountable: the company developing the technology, the computer scientist who wrote the algorithm, or the policymaker who implemented the technology? It will be tempting to blame the technology, with the result that no one will be held responsible as long as no clear legal and policy safeguards are put in place (Van Brakel and De Hert 2011).

It is not only technology that is increasingly responsibilized in the Big Data era, but private companies are as well. Although the fragmentation and commodification of security and law enforcement is not a new phenomenon (Loader 1999; Garland 2001), Big Data will accelerate this process as more and more data is in hands of private companies and, faced with too little expertise and too few resources, police and other law enforcement agencies will turn to private companies to out-source work or to purchase software. In several European countries, the police are increasingly turning to public-private partnerships to outsource key service areas (White 2014; Ponsaers et al. 2015). This also implies that the private sector is becoming increasingly powerful. Software such as PredPol has a vendor lock-in, meaning that the police cannot tweak the software themselves and depend on the private company to adjust the software to fit their needs. One can also witness resistance against this kind of responsibilization of private companies; with CAS, for instance, the Amsterdam police have developed their own open-source soft-ware, which is transparent and provides much greater flexibility and control.

In addition to the increased responsibilization of technology and private compa-nies, another problem is the fact that technology is often not transparent and it is unclear who provided the information and who decided about the categories on the basis of which the algorithm was written. This is especially an issue with soft-ware that has a vendor lock-in such as PredPol, which is not transparent about what has been written into the algorithm (Pasquale 2015). This is also a serious problem with the Beware software, which is not transparent about what the 'sus-picious' profile is that leads to a red threat rating or how the algorithm is program-med. There are no clear safeguards or redress procedures in place for people to be able to see their 'threat ratings' or to find out what indicators gave them a high score.[8] A lot also depends here on who owns the algorithm and where the data has come from. There is no mechanism to correct errors, for instance, if someone has the same name as a convicted person. Secrecy is important for companies develop-ing such software, as being transparent about their algorithms will imply that other companies can steal their ideas.

Bias, algorithmic discrimination, and stigmatization
Rules or categories used in predictive policing software must be translated into computer code, and the translation itself may have several consequences (Kitchin 2014) as the original intentions may be lost in translation (Introna 2007) and the way examples in the data mining process[9] are labelled can lead to bias or error:

"The unavoidably subjective labeling of examples can skew the resulting findings in such a way that any decisions taken on the basis of those findings will characterize all future cases along the same lines, even if such characterizations would seem plainly erroneous to analysts who looked more closely at the individual cases" (Borocas and Selbst 2016:11).

Algorithmic discrimination may be a potential consequence (Van Brakel 2015), which can be the result of three types of bias creep. The first type is bias that unintentionally creeps into the labelling of examples or the rules that are coded into the algorithm.[10] The data the analysis is based on, secondly, may be biased as a result of biased assumptions that are baked into the data by the way it was collected (for instance, arrest rates; see below). And, thirdly, without this being explicitly written into the software, bias creep may occur due to technical defects, faults, and bugs in the system, which may lead to more false positives that meet certain criteria (Introna and Nissenbaum 2011) and false negatives.

Borocas and Selbst (2016) highlight the fact that, although data mining may inherit the prejudices of prior decision-makers or reflect the widespread biases that persist in society at large, the resulting discrimination is almost always an unintentional emergent property of the algorithm's use rather than a conscious choice by its programmers, with the result that it can be unusually hard to identify the source of the problem or to explain it in court. However, this observation is not underpinned by empirical evidence, and one can argue that, especially in the context of anti-terrorism and anti-radicalization policies, this observation does not ring true, and the discrimination is a conscious choice by the programmers as a form of ethnic profiling. This highlights the issue of the programmers' moral responsibility and accountability, which has received very little attention in the literature so far (see Rogaway 2015).

The risk of algorithmic discrimination is much higher with predictive identification systems such as BEWARE, and, as it concerns individuals, the consequences are also much more serious. As conclusions are drawn at aggregate level of analysis, one might easily conclude that bias is not an issue for predictive mapping applications such as CAS. However, this is not the case. Predictive mapping can potentially lead to ethnic profiling. If arrest rates are a measure for predicting in which areas most crime occurs, for instance, and if it is clear that arrest rates are disproportionately higher in particular population groups as a result of ethnic profiling (see Harcourt 2007; De Schutter and Ringelheim 2008; Open Society 2009; Weber and Bowling 2012), there is a clear bias in the prediction, and the mapping can lead to even more ethnic profiling. In the Netherlands, for instance, where the CAS system has been implemented, research has shown that ethnic profiling by the police is a significant problem (Van der Leun and Van der Woude 2011; Open Society Initiative 2013).

It should be underlined that this is not a problem that is inherent in Big Data, but rather a problem that is inherent in policing today and that may get integrated into Big Data analysis.[11] However, Big Data applications, such as pre-emptive surveillance technologies, will make it more difficult to scrutinize discriminatory effects as the technology and the aggregate level of analysis create an appearance of objectivity. What is specific for Big Data, however, is that the more different types of data are included in the analysis, the greater the likelihood of bias.

It is often claimed that Big Data is reliable and that causality seizes to matter because the sample size is so big (Mayer-Schönberger and Cukier 2013). However, error is a crucial problem with Big Data when it focuses on decision-making about individuals and groups, as with predictive identification. Reliability also depends on how the technology is implemented in an organization. Error is indeed less of an issue with predictive mapping such as CAS as the analysis is conducted at aggregate level, but, as we have seen above, Big Data is also being used for predictive identification. Threat assessment systems, such as Beware, employ algorithms that combine and analyse the incoming streams of data. The errors become even more frequent and unknown as a result of the above-mentioned types of bias creep. Therefore, these systems may cause certain people to be falsely identified (false positives) and 'real' criminals and terrorists to remain unidentified (false negatives).

A high rate of false positives increases the risk that certain individuals and groups are systematically and disproportionately targeted as potential criminals, a stigma that is almost impossible to shake off and may even lead to a self-fulfilling prophecy, with stigmatized individuals starting to show criminal behaviour (Jussim et al. 2003; Van Brakel 2016). Such stigmatization has very serious consequences for citizens' flourishing, well-being, and life chances as has been extensively shown in sociological and criminological research on stigmatization and labelling effects (Goffman 1963; Farrington et al. 1978). This is especially a concern with predictive identification applications, such as Beware.

Cumulative surveillance effect, cumulative disadvantage, and chilling effects
To be able to perform Big Data analyses, police and law enforcement agencies will require increasing amounts of data. Information has gone from scarce to superabundant, and everybody's data is collected everywhere, on social media, smartphones, loyalty cards, government databases, etc., and can be used to make analyses and predictions to improve all sectors of society (Lyon 2007; Mayer-Schönberger-Cukier 2013). This mass data collection will provide the police with the opportunity to apply Big Data analyses in several key services in the future. Rather than focusing only on the people who are 'suspected' of crime or *at risk* of crime, there is a shift to collecting everyone's data with pre-emptive surveillance technologies such as Big Data.

One result of this ubiquitous data collection and analysis is that, in combination with all other surveillance technologies that are around, there is a cumulative surveillance effect (Mitchener-Nissen 2014). Particularly with the Snowden revelations, this has led to 'chilling effects'. The unwillingness or inability of journalists and writers to write and publish solely on the basis of their professional judgement or whistle-blowers being afraid to speak out may cause increased distrust in police and authorities and can have an impact on social cohesion. These chilling effects are harmful to creativity and freedom of expression, breed conformity, and have an impact on people's ability to hold power to account through peaceful protest (PEN America 2013; Campbell and Van Brakel 2015).[12]

Furthermore, one can argue that, intertwined with this cumulative surveillance effect, a cumulative disadvantage effect is taking place. As law enforcement focuses on certain types of crime, such as the high-impact crimes that are more likely to be committed by the poor, and less on other types of crime, such as white collar crimes, which are more likely to be committed by the rich or by corporations, people who commit the first type of crime are more likely to have criminal records and be put under surveillance. The crime data that are available, therefore, will also tend to focus on these specific types of crime, with the result that predictive policing also focuses mainly on these high-impact crimes, causing the above-mentioned bias towards high-impact crimes to become even more entrenched. This data may not only be biased but may also be unreliable if it has been fiddled or inaccurately recorded, as has been shown in the UK, for instance, by UK Statistics Authority (2014) and evidence by Her Majesty's Chief Inspector of Constabulary (Winsor 2013).

These biased and unreliable statistics, generated as a result of targeted crime control efforts in an era of Big Data, moreover, can now potentially lead to even more intensive surveillance of these population groups (Gandy 2009). The presence of a significant group in law enforcement who have biased assumptions about crime and ethnicity is clearly demonstrated by the disproportionate number of deaths of people of colour by the police in the United States (The Guardian 2015)[13] and by the pervasive ethnic profiling by police forces in the EU (see above). People who fit into certain social or ethnic categories will potentially be disproportionately targeted by these systems, especially if their application will be used in the context of anti-terrorist or de-radicalization policies.

Impact on trust and democracy

As a result of the above-mentioned cumulative disadvantages, trust in police and government among certain groups in society may become so low that people who are in need of help will cease to turn to the government. A recent quantitative study by Brayne (2014), for instance, found that individuals who have been stopped by the police, arrested, convicted, or incarcerated are less likely to interact with surveilling institutions, including medical, financial, labour market, and educational institutions, than their counterparts who have not had contacts with criminal justice. As criminal justice contacts are disproportionately distributed, the study suggests that system avoidance is a potential mechanism by which the criminal justice system contributes to social sorting and increased marginalization. In a 'Big Data' society in which data collection is increasingly necessary to obtain rights, this will contribute to the social exclusion of already excluded social groups (Lerman 2013).

Apart from the above, there are a number of groups of people whose data is intentionally or unintentionally not included in databases such as the Amish people, Roma, travellers, but also Luddites and people who just do not like technology, are not on Facebook, avoid buying a smartphone, etcetera. This has consequences not only for those people themselves and how they obtain rights, but also for the effectiveness of the technologies, as someone who might have committed a crime may not have been included in all the databases. Not being included in government databases, finally, might become synonymous with being suspicious, with people who actively try and avoid being in the system automatically becoming more suspicious and considered riskier. They will be stigmatized as a result.

5.3.2   EMPOWERING EFFECTS OF BIG DATA ON CITIZENS

The potential disempowering effects of Big Data described above paint a bleak picture if policymakers and lawmakers do not take the datafication of society seriously and start devising policies and legal safeguards to protect citizens. However, discussing only the disempowering effects of these practices would run the danger of ignoring the agency and reflexivity of subjects of Big Data as well as the variable ways in which power and participation are constructed and enacted (Couldrey and Powell 2014). In addition, it would not leave any space for discussing the positive consequences or potentials of Big Data. Technology itself is neither good nor bad, nor is it neutral (Kranzberg 1986); it can be implemented for very different reasons, including control and care (Lyon 2001; Van Brakel 2013). Technology needs to be studied in its socio-political technical setting. Hence, thinking about the empowering effects of Big Data implies thinking about the broader socio-political context that should promote empowerment. In relation to crime prevention, this implies a shift in policymaking towards a more 'positive' criminology, that is, a different way of thinking about crime prevention.

Thinking about crime prevention both in policy and in certain academic criminological communities is often characterized by negative terms such as 'fighting', 'combating', 'tackling', 'controlling', 'punishing', and 'preventing' (Schuilenburg et al. 2014). More caring solutions are often portrayed as soft and ineffective or not a police task. With regard to predictive policing, very little is said about how this is going to improve trust in the police and empower communities; the emphasis

mainly lies on control, both internal control, that is, more effective police management, and external control, that is, controlling crime. The community policing
discourse has been pushed aside to make room for cost-efficient solutions and the
'technological fix', which will protect the future from danger and harm. By contrast, Schuilenburg, van Steden and Oude Breuil (2014) advocate a shift in thinking
towards a more 'positive' criminology, which is based on concepts such as care,
belonging, and trust and takes into account human connectedness and local
capacity building.

In this spirit, crime prevention policies should be shaped from the bottom up and
match community needs with law enforcement needs. Should law enforcement
not consider positive and caring alternatives that have as their goal to empower
communities and individuals and to remove conditions that tempt people into
crime? This implies a focus on long-term policies that will have a lasting effect,
instead of a focus on populist and immediately effective and visible repressive
measures by which certain policymakers, with their eye on upcoming elections,
are showing the public that they are doing something about it (Garland 2001).[14]
Part of this reaction can also be seen as a widespread disillusionment with the welfarist criminal justice policies of the previous decades, at least in the UK (Garland
2001). Now, however, we have got on the other end of the spectrum, where questions of care, human flourishing, and trust are not asked anymore.

Drawing attention to these issues, moreover, does not imply that law enforcement
should completely do away with control and repressive measures. The approach
advocated here, inspired by the idea of 'positive criminology', argues for an inclu-
sive and proportional policy that is characterized by control and care, protected by
checks and balances, and that takes pre-emptive surveillance technologies and
their empowering and disempowering effects seriously. This is not a new
approach. When you explore crime prevention literature and official UN crime
prevention guidelines, you find a similar approach which is evidence-based and
has provided many examples of best practices (Waller 2006; UNODC 2010).

How can Big Data contribute to positive criminology? How can Big Data applications empower people in the context of crime prevention? In the scarce literature
available about concrete ways in which Big Data can empower citizens, Big Data is
seen as a tool for fighting discrimination and empowering groups. Cedar Grove,
a non-profit initiative in the US, for instance, uses a combination of demographic
analysis, contextual investigation, housing and economic analysis, and geographic
information systems to explore potentially discriminatory implications of public
policy decisions (FPF 2015). In the context of policing and crime prevention, Big
Data can be used as a tool for predicting and visualizing what areas are unsafe for
people to walk home at night or applications that predict what communities
would benefit from extra community policing. Another example could be to use

Big Data applications to conduct more effective police work audits to increase effectiveness but also as an accountability and transparency tool to weed out bias and error from predictive policing applications.

To give a concrete illustration in the context of crime prevention, there are two ways in which you can think of using predictive Big Data policing for preventing people from committing crime in the future. The first response is the pre-emptive repressive response: to develop software that will analyse Big Data to predict what people are at risk of committing crime so the police can intervene before the crime is committed by them. An example here is the BEWARE software, which we discussed in section 5.2.

The second response is the positive criminology response: similar to the above-mentioned Cedar Grove initiative, a consortium of police, social workers, neighbourhood workers, schools, civil society organizations, and city planners could work together and use Big Data applications to identify what areas in a city need more attention (areas where, for example, an increasing number of young people are more at risk of radicalizing) and identify what specific problems in that area need to be addressed. Data could include school quality measures, percentage of neighbourhood green, crime rates, mean income, percentage of unemployment, etc. If you have areas that are run down, lacking green spaces, with a concentration of people who are disadvantaged or unemployed with no future prospects, crime figures will be higher than in other areas.

A caring intervention here might be to improve schooling and urban space, to invest in community policing, to invest in parenting and family support programmes, public health, building up trust with the community, empowering victims of crime, etcetera (for knowledge and evidence-based crime prevention policy, see Waller 2006; UNODC 2010). It is a more positive long-term strategy to change the conditions in society so as to prevent people from embarking on crime. A repressive intervention will only take place if it is really necessary, but budgets are divided equally over both controlling and caring measures.

These two responses are very different. The first type of response is known to have a lot of social and ethical consequences and may have a disempowering effect on citizens, particularly if it is implemented in a repressive way. Nor has it been demonstrated that it is effective. The second type of response, in contrast, can be underpinned with promising criminological empirical evidence and best practices, contributes to empowering citizens and society as a whole, and encompasses a long-term strategy, changing the structural sources in society that contribute to crime.

Finally, the question arises how can we make existing applications such as CAS and BEWARE more empowering for citizens and reduce the disempowering effects. One way forward would be for the police to have increased awareness of the potentially disempowering effects, as their only current concern is its compliance with data protection regulation. Secondly, policymakers could expect the police to comply with an independent evaluation with particular quality standards when they pilot a new technology, which includes a proportionality test. Furthermore, the police could provide clear redress procedures and compensation to citizens that have been negatively affected by a certain technology (who have been falsely accused, for instance). A final idea is for the police to consider the predictive mapping application as an opportunity not only to catch more criminals but also to provide citizens in burglary-prone areas with better information about securing their property and to increase trust between citizens and the police.

5.4   CONCLUDING REMARKS

A number of conclusions, points for discussion and pointers for future research can be identified in this chapter. A first conclusion is that Big Data is a new technological development that should be situated in its socio-historical context as part of a larger trend that can be described as pre-emptive surveillance. Just like other surveillance technologies, it can have good and bad effects, and it can empower and disempower individuals, groups, and society as a whole. Awareness is crucial. Time will tell if Big Data and predictive policing can indeed play a positive role for citizens in crime prevention. As we have shown, the effectiveness of these applications in cutting crime and improving security is still unclear, and several potential disempowering effects have been identified, particularly with regard to predictive identification.

Secondly, predictive Big Data policing should be seen as one of several tools to support existing practices. Many police officers using the technology might recognize this, though policymakers focusing on cutting costs or winning elections might invest all their money in the technology, with the result of minimizing investments in essential police work and effective crime prevention initiatives or best practices that are more caring and might not necessarily imply the use of technology. Police forces in many countries are investing in new ICT technologies and strategies (see Jackson et al. 2014; Nationale Politie 2015; College of Policing 2016). No reference is made to investing in existing best crime prevention practices or advancing knowledge of effective alternative (also non-technological) strategies. Welsh, Farrington and O'Dell (2010), for instance, showed how alternative public surveillance measures such as security guards, place managers, and defensible space, instead of CCTV, are encouraging approaches to reducing crime. This question, therefore, must be asked: why is little to no money being invested in exploring alternative strategies and measures or in rigorous evaluations of tried-out strategies? In relation to this, there appears to be a lack of knowledge-based and evidence-based crime prevention[15] policy (see also De Vroe and Ponsaers 2014), which will translate into what funds will be invested in what type of Big Data applications. Instead of investing in crime prevention strategies and best practices that have proven to work (Waller 2006; UNODC 2010), money is being invested in technologies that have not yet proven their effectiveness and that, predictive identification applications in particular, may have potentially disempowering effects on citizens and society.

Thirdly, what has become clear in this chapter is that predictive Big Data policing is a tool that can improve policy but that there is a serious potential for the disempowerment of individuals, groups, and society depending how it is implemented and with what intention. It is not just privacy and data protection that are an issue; there is a whole plethora of potential consequences that are often not taken into account when implementing such technologies.

Fourthly, more discussion and empirical research is needed to explore how Big Data can be implemented for crime prevention in a more positive, caring way that enhances social cohesion and empowers people and to explore how Big Data can contribute to the empowerment of citizens with the goal of preventing crime in sustainable ways. It should be noted, however, that the current neoliberal climate in many European countries, with its narrow focus on austerity measures, cost-effectiveness, and managerialism and its lack of knowledge-based and evidence-based policies, does not stimulate another way of thinking about crime or investments in evidence-based cost-effective policies.

Finally, a lot of critical academic literature on Big Data has tended to focus on the negative and disempowering effects of Big Data. Such a focus on the negative only, however, gives a distorted picture and bypasses the fact that the technology might have empowering effects on people and society if it is used in a different way with different motivations. As has been shown in the section on the empowering effects of Big Data, predictive Big Data policing can be used in different ways: it can be used in a repressive way, involving a lot of risk of disempowering citizens, and it can be used in a more positive way as advocated by positive criminology. By building trust in the community and exploring ways in which Big Data can play a bottom-up role, this may help to build community relations, and using predictive policing applications to prevent crime in this way can have empowering effects. Furthermore, first results show that Big Data applications might have an empowering effect on police officers and police work itself, although, to be effective, the police ICT systems need to be able to process the more powerful software, which is currently not the case in the Netherlands, Belgium, and the UK (De Ruyver 2010; Budget and Performance Committee Greater London Authority 2013; Jonker and Van Wely 2015). Further research is needed to explore what is possible. In addition, more attention needs to be paid to making the existing predictive policing practices more empowering for citizens by taking the risks into account and by making sure that efficient checks and balances are in place.

REFERENCES

9-11.com Magazine (2014) *'Intrado Beware' Integrates with Motorola Solutions' Intelligent Data Portal*, available at: www.9-1-1magazine.com/Corp-Intrado-Beware-Motorola-Solutions-Intell-Data-Portal.

Bachner, J. (2013) *Predictive Policing: Preventing Crime with Data and Analytics, IBM Centre for the Business of Government*, available at: www.businessofgovernment.org/report/predictive-policing-preventing-crime-data-and-analytics.

Beck, C. and C. McCue (2009) 'Predictive Policing: What Can We Learn from Wal-Mart and Amazon about Fighting Crime in a Recession?', *The Police Chief*, LXXVI, 11.

Beck, U. (1992) *Risk Society: Towards a New Modernity*, London: Sage.

Benbouzid, B. (2015) *From Situational Crime Prevention to Predictive Policing: Sociology of an Ignored Controversy, Champ Pénal/Penal Field* 7, Online Publication, available at: http://champpenal.revues.org/9066 [28 August 2015].

Berg, N. (2014) 'Predicting Crime, LAPD Style', *The Guardian* 25 June 2014, available at: www.theguardian.com/cities/2014/jun/25/predicting-crime-lapd-los-angeles-police-data-analysisalgorithm-minority-report [20 November 2015].

Bigo, D. (2010) 'The Future Perfect of (in)Security (P8): Pre-Crime Strategy, Proactivity, Pre-Emption, Prevention, Precaution, Profiling, Prediction and Privacy', *Interdisciplines*, available at: http://archive-org.com/page/3765529/2014-02-22 and www.interdisciplines.org/paper.php?paperID=342 [12 November 2014].

Blair, T. (2006) *Our Nation's Future – Social Exclusion*, Speech given in York, available at: www.britishpoliticalspeech.org/speech-archive.htm?speech=283 [3 June 2015].

Bogard, W. (1996) *The Simulation of Surveillance: Hypercontrol in Telematic Societies*, Cambridge: Cambridge University Press.

Bogolomov, A. et al. (2014) 'Once Upon a Crime: Towards Crime Prediction from Demographics and Mobile Data, *ICMI 14 Proceedings of the 16th International Conference on Multimodal Interaction*, New York: ACM, available at: http://dl.acm.org/citation.cfm?id=2663254.

Borocas, S. and A.D. Selbst (2016) 'Big Data's Disparate Impact, *California Law Review* 104, available at: http://papers.ssrn.com/sol3/papers.cfm?abstract_id=2477899 [2 May 2015].\

Bowers, K.J., S.D. Johnson and K. Pease (2004) 'Prospective Hot-Spotting; The Future of Crime-Mapping?', *British Journal of Criminology* 44, 5: 641-658.

Boyd, D. and K. Crawford (2012) 'Critical Questions for Big Data, Provocations for a Cultural, Technological and Scholarly Phenomenon', *Information, Communication and Society* 15, 5: 662-679.

Brakel, R. van (2013) 'Playing with Surveillance: Towards a More Generous Understanding', pp. 281-294 in W. Webster et al. (eds.) *Living in Surveillance Societies: The State of Surveillance*, CreateSpace Independent Publishing Platform.

Brakel, R. van (2015) 'Iedereen verdacht? De effectiviteit en impact van het gebruik van preëmptieve surveillance voor publieke veiligheid', *Orde van de Dag* 69: 35-42.

Brakel, R. van (2016) 'The Rise of Preemptive Surveillance of Children in England:
	Unintended Social and Ethical Consequences' in T. Rooney and E. Taylor
	Surveillance and Childhood, London: Ashgate.
Brakel, R. van and P. De Hert (2011) 'Policing, Surveillance and Law in a Pre-Crime Society:
	Understanding the Consequences of Technology Based Strategies', Journal of
	Police Studies 20, 3: 163-192.
Brayne, S. (2014) 'Surveillance and System Avoidance Criminal Justice Contact and
	Institutional Attachment', American Sociological Review 79, 3: 367-391.
Budget and Performance Committee Greater London Authority (2013) Smart Policing. How
	the Metropolitan Police Service Can Make Better Use of Technology, available at:
	www.london.gov.uk/sites/default/files/gla_migrate_files_destination/Police
	%20technology%20report%20-%20Final%20version.pdf.
Campbell, C. and R. van Brakel (2015) 'Privacy As a Line of Flight in Societies of Mass
	Surveillance', Ethical Space: International Journal of Communication Ethics:
	Special Double Issue the Press, Intelligence and the Ethics Debate 12, 3/4: 39-46.
Carroll, L. (1896) 'Through the Looking Glass, and What Alice Found there', pp. 121-250 in
	L. Carroll (1996) The Complete Illustrated Lewis Carroll, Ware: Wordsworth
	Editions Ltd.
College of Policing (2016) National Policing Vision, available at: www.college.police.uk/
	About/Pages/National-policing-vision-2016.aspx.
Couldry, N. and A. Powell (2014) 'Big Data from the Bottom-Up', Big Data and Society,
	July-September: 1-5.
De Hert, P. and T. Vis (2005) 'Intelligence Led Policing ontleed', Tijdschrift voor
	Criminologie 4, 47, 4: 365 – 376.
De Ruyver, B. (2010) 'Tien jaar politiehervorming: een proeve tot evaluatie van de
	evaluatie', pp. 115-130 in W. Bruggeman, E. Devroe and M. Easton, Evaluatie van
	tien jaar politiehervorming, Antwerpen: Maklu.
De Schutter, O. and J. Ringelheim (2008) 'Ethnic Profiling: A Rising Challenge for
	European Human Rights Law', Modern Law Review 71, 3: 358-384.
Devroe, E. and P. Ponsaers (2014) 'De Pioniersperiode voorbij: Evidence Based beleid en
	praktijk bij de politie in Nederland en België?', Tijdschrift voor de Politie 76, 10:
	20-25.
Farrington, D.P., S.G. Osborn and D.J. West (1978) 'The Persistence of Labelling Effects',
	British Journal of Criminology 18, 3: 277-284.
Farrington, D. (2003) 'Methodological Quality Standards for Evaluation Research',
	The Annals of the American Academy of Political and Social Science 587, 1: 49-68.
Ferguson, A.G. (2014) 'Big Data and Predictive Reasonable Suspicion', University of
	Pennsylvania Law Review 163, 2: 327-410.
Friedman, Kahn and Borning (2014) 'Value Sensitive Design and Information Systems' in
	P. Zhang and D.F. Galetta (eds.) Human-Computer Interaction and Management
	Information Systems, London: Routledge.

Future of Privacy Forum (2015) *Big Data: A Tool for Fighting Discrimination and Empowering Groups*, available at: https://fpf.org/wp-content/uploads/Big-Data-A-Tool-for-Fighting-Discrimination-and-Empowering-Groups-FINAL.pdf [15 November 2015].

Gandy Jr., O.H. (2009) *Coming to Terms With Chance: Engaging Rational Discrimination and Cumulative Disadvantage*, London: Ashgate.

Garland, D. (2001) *The Culture of Control, Crime and Social Order in Contemporary Society*, Chicago: University of Chicago Press.

Gerber, M.S. (2014) 'Predicting Crime Using Twitter and Kernel Density Estimation', *Decision Support Systems* 61: 115-125.

Goffman, E. (1990) *Stigma: Notes on the Management of Spoiled Identity*, London: Penguin Books.

Harcourt, B. (2007) *Against Prediction: Profiling, Policing, and Punishing in an Actuarial Age*, Chicago: University of Chicago Press.

Heck, W. (2014) 'Slimme camera spot afwijkend gedrag van reizigers op Schiphol', NRC *Handelsblad*, 11 september, available at: www.nrc.nl/nieuws/2014/09/11/slimme-camera-spot-afwijkend-gedrag-van-reizigers-op-schiphol.

Hoggard, C. (2015) 'Fresno Police Scanning Social Media to Asses Threat', ABC30 *Action News*, available at: http://abc30.com/news/fresno-police-scanning-social-media-to-assess-threat/525999.

Hunt, P., J. Saunders and J.S. Hollywood (2014) *Evaluation of the Shreveport Predictive Policing Experiment*, Rand Safety and Justice Program, Santa Monica: Rand.

Intrado (2012) *Intrado Arms Agencies with New Weapon to Help Keep Responders and Communities Safe*, available at: www.intrado.com/news/press/2012/intrado-arms-agencies-new-weapon-help-keep-responders-and-communities-safe.

Introna, L.D. (2007) 'Maintaining the Reversibility of Foldings: Making the Ethics (Politics) of Information Technology Visible', *Ethics and Information Technology* 9: 11-25.

Introna, L.D. and H.F. Nissenbaum (2009) *Facial Recognition Technology: A Survey of Policy and Implementation Issues*, Center for Catastrophe Preparedness and Response, New York: New York University.

Jackson, B.A., V.A. Greenfield, A.R. Morral and J.S. Hollywood (2014) 'Police Department Investments in Information Technology Systems', *RAND Research report*, available at: www.rand.org/pubs/research_reports/RR569.html.

Joh, E.E. (2014) 'Policing by Numbers: Big Data and the Fourth Amendment', *Washington Law Review* 89: 35-68.

Johnson, S.D., K.J. Bowers, D.J. Birks and K. Pease (2009) 'Predictive Mapping of Crime by Promap: Accuracy, Units of Analysis and the Environmental Backcloth', pp. 171-198 in D. Weisburd, W. Bernasco and G.J.N. Bruinsma (eds.) *Putting Crime in Its Place*, Dordrecht: Springer.

Johnson, T. (2014) 'Intrado Intrusion, City Council Backs Away from Social Software', *Cascadia Weekly*, Wednesday July 9 2014, available at: www.cascadiaweekly.com/currents/intrado_intrusion.

Jonker, J. and M. van Wely (2015) ICT bij politie een voortdurend drama, available at: www.telegraaf.nl/premium/reportage/24835881/__ICT_bij_politie_ een_voortdurend_drama__.html.

Jussim, L., P. Palumbo, C. Chatman, S. Madon and A. Smith (2003) 'Stigma and Self-Fulfilling Prophecies', pp. 374-418 in T.F. Heatherton, R.E. Kleck, M.R. Hebl and J.G. Hull (eds.) The Social Psychology of Stigma, New York: The Guildford Press.

Kentonline (2013) Predpol Software Which Targets Crime Down to Small Zones Has Slashed North Kent Crime by 6%, available at: www.kentonline.co.uk/kent/news/crime-innorth-kent-slashed-4672.

Kitchin, R. (2013) The Data Revolution: Big Data, Open Data, Data Infrastructures and Their Consequences, London: Sage.

Kitchin, R. (2014) 'Thinking Critically about and Researching Algorithms', The Programmable City Working Paper 5, available at: http://papers.ssrn.com/sol3/Papers.cfm?abstract_id=2515786.

Kranzberg, M. (1986) 'Technology and History: 'Kranzberg's Laws'', Technology and Culture 27, 3: 544-560.

Laney, D. (2001) 3D Data Management: Controlling Data Volume, Velocity and Variety. Gartner, available at: http://blogs.gartner.com/doug-laney/files/2012/01/ad949-3D-Data-Management-Controlling-Data-Volume-Velocity-and-Variety.pdf.

Lerman, J. (2013) 'Big Data and Its Exclusions', Stanford Law Review Online 66: 55-63.

Leun, J.P. van der and M.A.H. van der Woude (2011) 'Ethnic Profiling in The Netherlands? A Reflection on Expanding Preventive Powers, Ethnic Profiling and a Changing Social and Political Context', Policing and Society 21, 4: 444-455.

Loader, I. (1999) 'Consumer Culture and the Commodification of Policing and Security', Sociology 33, 2: 373-392.

Lyon, D. (2001) Surveillance Society: Monitoring Everyday Life, Buckingham: Open University Press.

Lyon, D. (2007) Surveillance Studies: An Overview, Cambridge: Polity Press.

Lyon, D. (2014) 'Surveillance, Snowden, and Big Data: Capacities, Consequences, Critique', Big Data and Society, July-December: 1-13.

Maguire, M. (2000) 'Policing by Risks and Targets: Some Dimensions and Implications of Intelligence-Led Crime Control', Policing and Society 9: 315–336.

Manovich, L. (2011) 'Trending: The Promises and the Challenges of Big Social Data', pp. 460-475 in M.K. Gold (ed.) Debates in the Digital Humanities, Minneapolis: University of Minnesota Press.

Mastrobuoni, G. (2014) Crime Is Terribly Revealing: Information Technology and Police Productivity, Unpublished Paper, available at: www.tinbergen.nl/wp-content/uploads/2015/02/Crime-is-Terribly-Revealing_-Information-Technology.pdf.

Mayer-Schönberger, V. and K. Cukier (2013) Big Data: A Revolution That Will Transform How We Live, Work and Think, London: John Murray Publishers.

McPherson, G. (2015) 'Cambridge Paediatrician's Outrage at Pure Gym System Assuming All Doctors Are Male', *Cambridge News*, March 18 2015, available at: www.cambridge-news.co.uk/Cambridge-paediatrician-8217-s-outrage-Pure-Gym/story-26188693-detail/story.html#ixzz3aVngGRT9 [13 May 2015].

Mitchener-Nissen, T. (2014) 'Failure to Collectively Assess Surveillance-Oriented Security Technologies Will Inevitably Lead to an Absolute Surveillance Society', *Surveillance and Society* 12, 1: 73-88.

Nationale Politie (2015) *Begroting 2016-2020*, available at: www.rijksoverheid.nl/ documenten/begrotingen/2015/09/15/begroting-nationale-politie-2016.

Open Justice Initiative (2009) 'Ethnic Profiling in the European Union: Pervasive, Ineffective and Discriminatory', *Open Society Institute*, available at: www.opensocietyfoundations.org/sites/default/files/profiling_20090526.pdf [30 August 2015].

Open Society Initiative (2013) *Equality under Pressure: The Impact of Ethnic Profiling*, available at: www.opensocietyfoundations.org/sites/default/files/equality-under-pressure-the-impact-of-ethnic-profiling-netherlands-20131128_1.pdf.

Pasquale, F. (2015) *The Black Box Society: The Secret Algorithms that Control Money and Information*, Cambridge, MA: Harvard University Press.

PEN America (2013) *Chilling Effects, NSA Surveillance Drives US Writers to Self-Censor*, New York: PEN American Centre, available at: www.pen.org/sites/default/files/Chilling%20Effects_PEN%20American.pdf [10 April 2015].

Ponsaers, P., E. de Raedt, L. Wondergem and L.G. Moor (eds.) (2015) 'Outsourcing Policing', *Cahiers Politiestudies* 36, Antwerpen: Maklu.

PredPol (2015) *Predictive policing: The Predictive Policing Company*, available at: www.predpol.com [20 November 2015].

Rienks, R. (2015) *Predictive Policing: Kansen voor een veiligere toekomst*, Brave New Books.

Rogaway, P. (2015) 'The Moral Character of Cryptographic Work', *Cryptology ePrint Archive Report 2015/1162*, available at: web.cs.ucdavis.edu/~rogaway/papers/moral-fn.pdf.

Rose, N. (1998) 'Governing Risky Individuals: The Role of Psychiatry in New Regimes of Control', *Psychiatry, Psychology and Law* 5, 2: 177-195.

Schuilenburg, M., R. van Steden and B. Oude Breuil (2014) *Positive Criminology. Reflections on Care, Belonging and Security*, The Hague: Eleven Publishing.

Simon, C. (2014) *'Precob': Polizei will Einbrüche per Software vorhersagen*, Spiegel Online; available at: www.spiegel.de/netzwelt/netzpolitik/einbruch-polizei-testet-precobsoftware- zur-vorhersage-a-1001816.html [21 November 2014].

Skorup, B. (2014) 'Cops Scan Social Media to Help Assess Your 'Threat Rating", *Reuters*, December 12, available at: http://blogs.reuters.com/great-debate/2014/12/12/police-data-mining-looks-through-social-media-assigns-you-a-threat-level/ [15 August 2015].

Tene, O. and J. Polonetsky (2012) 'Privacy in the Age of Big Data: A Time for Big Decisions', *Stanford Law Review* 64: 63-69.

The Guardian (2015) *The Counted: People Killed in the US by the Police*, available at: www.theguardian.com/us-news/ng-interactive/2015/jun/01/about-the-counted [2 September 2015].

Uchida, C.D. (2009) 'Predictive Policing', pp. 3871-3880 in *Encyclopedia of Criminology and Criminal Justice*, Dordrecht: Springer.

UK Statistics Authority (2014) 'Assessment of Compliance with the Code of Practice for Official Statistics', *Assessment Report 268*, available at: www.statisticsauthority.gov.uk/wp-content/uploads/2015/12/images-assessmentreport268statisticsoncrimeinenglandandwale_tcm97-43508-1.pdf.

United Nations Office for Drugs and Crime (UNODC) (2010) 'Handbook on the Crime Prevention Guidelines Making Them Work', *Criminal Justice Handbook Series*, Vienna: UNODC, available at: www.unodc.org/pdf/criminal_justice/Handbook_on_Crime_Prevention_Guidelines_-_Making_them_work.pdf [22 December 2015].

Waller, I. (2006) *Less Law, More Order. The Truth about Reducing Crime*, London: Praegar.

Weber, L. and B. Bowling (2012) *Stop and Search, Police Power in Global Context*, London: Routledge.

Welsh, B.C., D.P. Farrington and S.J. O'Dell (2010) 'Effectiveness of Public Area Surveillance for Crime Prevention: Security Guards, Place Managers and Defensible Space', *Report prepared for the Swedish National Council for Crime Prevention*, available at: www.crim.cam.ac.uk/people/academic_research/david_farrington/survsw.pdf.

White, A. (2014) 'Post-Crisis Policing and Public–Private Partnerships, The Case of Lincolnshire Police and G4S', *British Journal of Criminology* 54, 6: 1002-1022.

Willems, D. and R. Doeleman (2014) 'Predictive Policing – wens of werkelijkheid?', *Het Tijdschrift voor de Politie* 76, 4/5: 39-42.

Winsor, T. (2013) *Home Affairs Committee - Minutes of Evidence*, available at: www.publications.parliament.uk/pa/cm201314/cmselect/cmhaff/c895-i/c89501.htm.

Zarsky, T. (2016) 'The Trouble with Algorithmic Decisions an Analytic Road Map to Examine Efficiency and Fairness in Automated and Opaque Decision Making', *Science, Technology and Human Values* 41, 1: 118-132.

Zedner, L. (2007) 'Pre-Crime and Post-Criminology?', *Theoretical Criminology* 11, 2: 261-281.

NOTES

1   For instance, the UK National Policing Vision (2016) states: "Predictive analysis and real-time access to intelligence and tasking in the field will be available on modern mobile devices. Officers and staff will be provided with intelligence that is easy to use and relevant to their role, location and local tasking."

2   Actually, there is increasing opposition against new surveillance technologies by police officers; in the UK, for instance, an increasing number of police forces is cutting down on their CCTV cameras as they do not feel they are effective: BBC News (2015) The end of the CCTV era?, *BBC News* 15 January 2015. In the course of this study, Belgian police officers also indicated that there was a lot of opposition in their force towards implementing new technologies.

3   Traditionally, the subjects of surveillance discussed in surveillance literature are human beings. However, this does not mean that only humans are being surveilled. Both within and outside surveillance studies, literature can be found on surveillance of animals and nature (Haggerty and Trottier, 2013), of places, locations, and spaces (Koskela 2000; Graham and Wood 2003; Klauser 2008), and of objects (Adey 2004). The term entity is used here to encompass all these categories (a more elaborate discussion can be found in the forthcoming PhD thesis *Taming the Future. A Rhizomatic Analysis of the Consequences of Pre-Emptive Surveillance*).

4   Exceptions include Ferguson (2014) and Joh (2014); however, no European-focused or socioscientific publications were found.

5   This is a summary of a more extensive case study conducted for the WRR.

6   This seems to be in contrast with displacement effects of burglaries identified by the Dutch police in the context of using CAS.

7   Smart video surveillance with behaviour detection software has been implemented at several sites in the US (see AI Insight technology) and is also being trialled in Europe, at Schiphol airport, for example (Heck 2014). The software gives an alarm when it spots suspicious behaviour. Although the intervention itself is still done by humans, the technology has an increasing influence on the decision about what is suspicious behaviour and reasonable suspicion.

8   Neither the PredPol nor the Beware website gives any explanation of how their algorithms work.

9   Data mining learns by example: what a model learns depends on the examples to which it has been exposed. The data that functions as examples is known as training data. Labeling examples is the process by which the training data is separated out into the relevant classifications (Borocas and Selbst 2016).

10   See, for instance, a recent example in Cambridge where a female paediatrician could not use her security passcode to enter the female changing rooms at a gym because anyone with the title of 'doctor' was automatically categorized as male by the algorithm (McPherson 2015).

11   See, for instance, recent instances of ethnic profiling by the police in : violent arrests of teenagers in and students in and violent treatment of the deradicalization expert Montasser Alde'emeh. See Callewaert (2015) 'Amnesty International: Politiek moet zich buigen over

racistische incidenten bij politie', *De WereldMorgen*, available at: www.dewereldmorgen.be/
artikel/2015/12/02/amnesty-international-politiek-moet-zich-buigen-over-racistische-
incidenten-bij-politie.

12   See Surveillance: Citizens and the State – Constitution Committee (www.publications.par-
liament.uk/pa/ld200809/ldselect/ldconst/18/8051403.htm Q568) and *Steel and Morris v.*
ECHR application no. 68416/01 and *Steur v.* ECHR application No. 39657/98.

13   The British newspaper *The Guardian* has started a project known as 'The Counted' to count
the number of people killed by the police and other law enforcement agencies in the United
States since 2015, to monitor their demographics, and to tell the stories of how they died.
The database combines Guardian reporting with verified crowdsourced information to build
a more comprehensive record of such fatalities.

14   In his seminal study of crime control policy in the US and the UK in the 1980s and 1990s,
Garland (2001) showed that the state was not interested in crime reduction per se but "aban-
dons reasoned, instrumental action and retreats into an expressive mode that we might, con-
tinuing the psychoanalytic metaphor, describe as *acting out* – a mode that is concerned not so
much with controlling crime as with expressing the anger and outrage that crime provokes.
It is this predicament and the authorities' deeply ambivalent reactions to it – rather than any
coherent programme or singular strategy – that have shaped crime control and criminal justice in the late modern period." (Garland 2001: 110). For a clear example, see the wide-scale
implementation of CCTV in the in response to the Jamie Bulger murder (Norris and Arm-
strong 1999).

15   It should be noted that knowledge-based and evidence-based here does not refer to evidence
that certain risk factors are more reliable predictors than others but to policies that have been
implemented or piloted and have been shown to work in practice.

PART III

LEGAL PERSPECTIVES ON BIG DATA

6   PREDICTIVE PROFILING AND ITS LEGAL LIMITS: EFFECTIVENESS GONE FOREVER?

Paul De Hert & Hans Lammerant

Societal activities are increasingly mediated by digital technology, leading to new forms of visibility left by their digital traces. The spread of digital technology also gives rise to new forms of cognition, made possible by data analysis techniques that allow sense-making and the steering of governance. 'Big Data' is the new term pointing to the growing availability of data and new data-driven practices. Profiling is one of these new forms of cognition. Although it is not new, profiling is flourishing in the Big Data environment and used on a much wider scale than ever before.

We examine predictive group profiling in the Big Data context as an instrument of governmental control and regulation. We first define profiling by drawing some useful distinctions (section 6.1). We then discuss examples of predictive group profiling from policing (such as parole prediction methods taken from the US) and combatting fraud (the iCOV and SyRI systems in the Netherlands) (section 6.2). Three potential risks of profiling – the negative impact on privacy; social sorting and discrimination; and opaque decision-making – are discussed in section 6.3.

We then turn to the legal framework. Is profiling by governmental agencies adequately framed? Are existing legal checks and balances sufficient to safeguard civil liberties?[1] We discuss the relationship between profiling and the right to privacy (section 6.4) and between profiling and the prohibition on discrimination (section 6.5). The jurisprudence on the right to privacy clearly sets limits to the use of automated and predictive profiling. Profiling and data screening which interfere without distinction with the privacy of large parts of the population are disproportional. Applications need to have some link to concrete fact to be legitimate. An additional role is played by the prohibition of discrimination, which requires strengthening through the development of audit tools and discrimination-aware algorithms. We then discuss current safeguards in Dutch administrative, criminal procedure and data protection law (section 6.6), and witness a trend of weakening safeguards at the very moment when they should be applied with even more rigor. In our conclusion we point to the tension between profiling and legal safeguards. These safeguards remain important and need to be overhauled to make them effective again.

6.1   PROFILING AND BIG DATA: CONCEPTS, DISTINCTIONS AND EVOLUTIONS

Human and automated profiling

It is useful to remind ourselves that profiling is not new and can be done without modern automated and statistical techniques ('human profiling'). Practices of ethnic profiling by police during stops and searches on the street are an example of human profiling, albeit a problematic one.[2]

In general, a profile is a set of characteristics, features and attributes with which a person or a group can be discerned from another person or group. What interests us here is a specific process of differentiating based on the automated processing of data. The form of profiling we have in mind is based on the use of 'Knowledge Discovery in Databases' (KDD), better known as data mining (although this is only the analysis step in the process) (Fayyad et al. 1996). The purpose of KDD is to find useful patterns in data, which can be gathered from different sources. The first stages of the process entail selecting and gathering data and preparing it for analysis. In the actual data mining, data is analysed with the use of algorithms in order to discern patterns. While these patterns reflect correlations in the data, they are no proof of causal relations. A pattern can be an indication of a relevant underlying causal process, but it can also be the result of uninteresting processes or noise. Therefore the final step consists in evaluating these patterns for their relevance. From these selected patterns a profile can be derived. This profile does not consist of 'raw' data or observations, but is a mathematical model of the phenomenon or a reference to the group to discern.

Data mining makes use of new statistical techniques driven more by data than by theory. Traditionally, a hypothesis is formulated first, which is then verified with the data. The emphasis is on clarifying assumptions and using statistical methods to differentiate between significant correlations and correlations that are spurious or cannot be guaranteed to differ from chance. The new data-driven approach, for which the term data mining has become common usage, begins with the data and searches for patterns. Selection is done later as part of the interpretation. This allows discovering unforeseen relations in the data, but also introduces the risk of using correlations and models without understanding the actual process that produced them. Many data mining algorithms are opaque: it is difficult or impossible to determine how the resulting model was built and which correlations were taken into account. We also need to remember that the results are purely probabilistic relations which need verification. In other words, they deliver no proof but only indications for where to look. Whereas the traditional approach uses statistics to determine or measure the veracity or plausibility of a hypothesis, it becomes a discovery method in itself in the data mining approach.

Creating and using a profile: three groups of affected people

What we have described so far is the creation of a profile. It has to be distinguished from the use of profiles in decision-making processes, which consists of applying profiles to datasets and checking which persons, objects or phenomena conform to the profiles, and making decisions based on the result. Profiles can be used to identify people, to attribute specific risks to them, and to act upon them in specific ways. Custers identifies four possible uses of profiling (Custers 2014). First, as a selection instrument to decide which persons or groups deserve more attention to guide controlling efforts.[3] Second, as an instrument in decision-making, where decisions are made based on the profile without further investigation. The space for such use is limited as the data protection framework forbids automated decision-making without further human intervention.[4] A third use of profiling is as a detection instrument, to detect if certain rules have been violated, not who has violated them. Fourth, profiling can be used to evaluate practices and interventions.

The distinction between the creation of a profile and its use is crucial for our legal analysis, as its creation and use happen at different moments and under different circumstances, and make use of different sets of data. To make a profile, data is used from a wide range of people, including citizens who are not suspected of violating any laws. The application of a profile uses only the data of the persons being checked, which can be a large set or just one person. This distinction notwithstanding, profiles are linked to their use. Their envisaged use will define what must be differentiated and thus provide the criteria to discern relevant patterns during the creation of a profile. The purpose also matters when evaluating the legitimacy of profiling.

Three groups are affected by the use of profiling: persons whose data is used to create the profile, persons to whom the profile refers, and persons who are subjected to decision-making based on the profile. These three groups often overlap but are not by definition the same.[5]

Personal and group profiling

Group profiles must be distinguished from personal profiles. A personal profile concerns an individual subject. Through a set of features, this subject can be identified and targeted. An example is device fingerprinting, where a device is recognized by specific technical features such as installed software or an IP number. Face recognition and other forms of biometric profiling also create personal profiles. A group profile concerns a category of people. The data mining process uncovers a range of correlated attributes and links these in a specific pattern that constitutes the category or group profile. While this can be an existing group, in many cases the category is established through the process of profiling itself and has no existence before the creation of the profile (Hildebrandt 2008).

We need to differentiate between distributive and non-distributive group profiles. When all members share the features, the group profile is distributive; the profile gives an exact representation of the features of individual group members. In this case the group profile can be applied to group members as if it is a personal profile. In contrast, a non-distributive profile only represents a statistical relation. Group members do not share all features, but have most of them. Membership represents a correlation between the set of attributes of a member with the attributes of other group members. The difference becomes clear when subjects who accord with a non-distributive profile are treated as if they match a distributive one. An average characteristic or behaviour as represented by the profile is then considered as a characteristic of each group member. The result is stereotyping, which can lead to discrimination (as in the aforementioned ethnic profiling) or normalizing effects on group members (Hildebrandt 2005; Vedder 1999).

Predictive profiling entails the use of profiling to generate predictions. The profile, extracted from data on past behaviour or known cases, is used to infer current or future behaviour or the state of unknown cases. As such, the profile is a probabilistic model. It does not represent actual behaviour or a real state of affairs, but a prediction of this behaviour or state of affairs. Again, treating this probabilistic representation as an exact one can be problematic, as it assumes that nothing changes.

The dual impact of Big Data on profiling

Automated profiling based on data mining is not yet by definition an application of Big Data. Although Big Data is not a precisely defined concept and is often used as a buzzword, it reflects a change in techniques to collect and analyse data. The term originates from developments in database technology, where data became too voluminous to store or analyse on a single computer. Big Data is often characterised by its 3 V's definition (volume, velocity, variety). It has to deal with much larger volumes of data, collected or produced at much higher velocities, and consisting of a much wider variety of, often unstructured, data (Kitchin 2013).

Legally it is irrelevant whether profiling is part of a Big Data application or not. But Big Data magnifies the impact of profiling and puts greater stress on the checks and balances in the legal framework. One important change is that Big Data strengthens the evolution towards a data-driven epistemology, from checking hypotheses to exploring data for correlations (Kitchin 2014). While this was already signalled with the advent of data mining, Big Data creates a new environment in which these techniques become much more powerful.

Another change can be seen in data aggregation and collection methods. Data is aggregated through linking existing data sources and making them inter-operable. Data collection also becomes more sensor-driven, partly through the mediation of digital technology. New types of sensors are entering widespread use, such as

ANPR cameras, or are slowly becoming a technological reality, like smart cameras with face recognition. These changes – from once anonymous train or parking tickets to the more permanent and individualised visibility of behaviour through the use of OV cards and SMS parking – are creating new visibilities. We now look at some concrete examples of profiling in the US and the Netherlands.

6.2   PROFILING IN THE PUBLIC SECTOR: EXAMPLES FROM POLICING AND ADMINISTRATIVE ANTI-FRAUD POLICIES

The advent of profiling as a governmental technique of control is not only due to new technological possibilities, but also fits changing approaches to management and security. Julia Black has written authoritatively on the 'new public risk management' in public administration, where assessments and technologies are used to develop decision-making frameworks to prioritize regulatory activities and deploy resources (Black 2005). A range of other authors, mainly in criminology and police studies, have addressed changes in security policies. Traditional post-crime policing approaches, directed at investigation and the punishment of crime, have been deemed unable to deter crime and have been exchanged for more preventive, pro-active strategies. One of these is intelligence-led policing; its main characteristic is "its insistence to build up intelligence through all kinds of data collection strategies" (Van Brakel and De Hert 2011).

These trends in management and policing interact with technological developments, allowing for much wider data collection, aggregation and analysis. Intelligence-led policing is very open to the growing use of surveillance techniques and leads to a widening net of observation and data collection. Similarly, intelligence-led policing is open to new analytical uses of this data such as predictive and automated profiling. The preventive approach is not only seen in policing strategies, but also in criminal and punitive policy. Again we see the interaction with new technologies, such as the use of profiling techniques for parole decisions in the US (Van Brakel and De Hert 2011).

The interaction of Big Data with intelligence-led policing is equally visible in the growing effort to make data available for law enforcement and security purposes. On the EU level, there has been a steady build-up of European-wide information systems like the SIS II, VIS and Eurodac. The exchange of information between police services has become the norm with the introduction of the principle of availability. Specific legal frameworks concerning information collection and exchange have been set up, e.g. on terrorist financing, the retention of telecommunications data (now annulled by the ECJ), and the ongoing discussion on Passenger Name Records. We now take a closer look at some examples in the US and the Netherlands, first from the security field.

In the US, automated profiling techniques for policing have grown popular under the label of 'predictive policing'. Predictive policing builds on older statistical approaches using crime statistics, but has developed using new data mining techniques and more sources of data. A RAND study on predictive policing gives a good overview of approaches and cases. It found four main methods of predictive profiling in policing: (1) methods for predicting crimes;[6] (2) methods for predicting offenders;[7] (3) methods for predicting perpetrators' identities;[8] and (4) methods for predicting victims of crimes[9] (Perry et al. 2013).

The most widespread forms of predictive policing are type 1 (predicting crimes) and 4 (predicting victims). They aim to uncover crime hotspots, in terms of time and place, where future criminal activity can be expected. Crime statistics are combined with GIS and data sources like traffic data. This predictive profiling of hotspots is used to guide police patrolling and observation. Another example of hotspot profiling reveals which types of shops and branches are most vulnerable to robberies.[10] These methods have been reported to deliver positive results and are becoming general use in the US (Perry et al. 2013).

Although considered much less developed, profiling methods are also entering into use for the criminal profiling of offenders (Perry et al. 2013: 81). The methods for predicting the risk that an individual will offend in the future are mostly based on risk assessments methods. The main challenges for these methods are inter-rater reliability (agreement between raters, a measure of the reliability of this data) and misspecification of the predictive model (Perry et al. 2013). These challenges notwithstanding, parole prediction methods are used in a majority of US states (Harcourt 2005). Previously based on risk assessment methods, they are also now based on software (McCaney 2013). Florida, for example, uses predictive methods to assign juveniles to rehabilitation programs (Perry et al. 2013). Another example, as advanced as it is controversial, is the Chicago police pilot program to create a 'Heat List' – "a rank-order list of potential victims and subjects with the greatest propensity for violence." The Heat List is "generated based on empirical data compared with known associates of the identified person" – that is, on social network analysis (Chicago Police Department 2013). The program is inspired by the work of sociologist Andrew Papachristos, which showed that the majority of homicides occur in a relatively small network within the population. People on the Heat List are contacted and warned not to commit an offence, sometimes to their surprise if they have previously never been in contact with the police (The Verge 2014). Methods to create profiles of likely perpetrators of past crimes are generally not based on automated modelling but on crime analysts combining and querying datasets. They use larger and more diverse sets of data but the modelling itself is not done by algorithms but by human intelligence. Examples include geographical profiling, or trying to locate perpetrators based on the pattern of crimes, and modus operandi similarity analysis (Perry et al. 2013).

Similar methods can be used outside the security context and are now used by the public sector to combat tax and social fraud. A GAO report found the US federal government using a wide range of data mining applications, many but not all using personal data. Typical applications aim to detect fraud or abuse or to improve service or performance (GAO 2004).

A Dutch example is the *Infobox Crimineel en Onverklaarbaar Vermogen* (iCOV), a cooperative structure between the tax and customs authorities, police and public prosecutor to map criminal and unexplained finances, money laundering and fraud constructions and to recover public financial claims. Its tasks include developing indicators and group profiles, which can be based on personal data (Convenant iCOV 2013).

Another Dutch example to combat social fraud is the linking of a wide range of personal information through the SyRI (System Risk Indication) instrument. This system is based on the *Wet structuur uitvoeringsorganisatie werk en inkomen* (SUWI), or the law covering the organisational set-up of government tasks in social insurance and employment. The SyRI system combats social fraud and the abuse of public money, with a range of public authorities pooling their data resources and screening them using risk models. The range of information that can be used is very broad, and includes data on labour, taxes, social security, property registers and debt. Specific sources are selected and a risk model that defines the profile of potential fraud is developed for each project. When approved by the minister, the data goes encrypted to an analysing unit. There the profile is applied to the data and people linked with a potential fraud pattern are flagged. Following analysis, partners receive risk notifications on flagged persons for further action. These are also kept in a register, where people can inquire if they are included.

The SyRI system has a well-developed organisational framework and is said to comply with existing data protection obligations. In terms of proportionality, it is striking that the only limiting factor on the data included for analysis is the risk model or profile of potential fraud. The model has to be developed before the screening of data begins; the system is thus not used without precautions and excludes the unlimited screening of data. However, no suspicion or indications are needed to start a project; nor are factual grounds. The risk models contain general assumptions about indications of fraud, without requiring a concrete problematic based on facts. This has been criticised by the Dutch Data Protection Authority, which insists on preliminary 'evidence' to start the system and the application of the 'Select before you collect' principle. This implies that the link between indicators and possible fraud must be legitimate, and that only those types of data tied to this indicator can be selected. It also implies selecting the persons whose data will be used beforehand and to legitimize this choice (CBP 2014).

6.3   POTENTIAL RISKS OF PROFILING: PRIVACY, SOCIAL SORTING AND DISCRIMINATION, OPAQUE DECISION-MAKING

Profiling techniques can increase efficiency as they allow for more precise targeting and the economizing of efforts in a whole range of areas. Custers describes how prioritizing inspections based on risk models of illegally splitting living space made inspections more effective (Custers 2014). Similarly, guiding policing efforts through predictive policing in the US is generally considered successful (Perry et al. 2013). But it is not without risks, of which we want to highlight three: privacy, social sorting and discrimination, and opaque decision-making.

Firstly, there is a heightened risk of intrusive interferences to privacy due to the heightened surveillance. Profiling is in itself highly intrusive to a wide range of people, especially if it is used routinely. The technical possibilities encourage making a growing amount of data sources available, in terms of both linking existing sources of data and the implementation of new systems soliciting behavioural data. The result is a widening net of data collection and surveillance, which can have a heavy psychological impact. This impact comes not from the data collection itself but from its integration and transformation into knowledge about people (Hildebrandt 2008a). Hildebrandt points to privacy as a public good and its relationship to autonomy and human agency. Profiling can result in information asymmetries threatening such autonomy (Hildebrandt 2008b). This risk affects all people whose data is used to build the profile as well as people to whose data the profile is applied.

Secondly, there is the risk associated with social sorting, or sorting people into categories assigning worth or risk, and stereotyping. The formation of a suspicion, which can legitimize further public intervention, is no longer based on specific facts but on people's characteristics. It thereby threatens the principle of equality and the presumption of innocence and can lead to discrimination (Schermer 2013; Custers 2014; Gandy 2009). Such discrimination can take several forms. It can lead to a high control burden for specific groups who often match the profiles. It can also be hidden discrimination due to the opacity of data mining algorithms.

Thirdly, there are the risks related to opaque decision-making, which plays out on two distinct levels: the application of a profile and the decision-making based on its results. The opacity of data mining techniques can create problems through lack of insight into the veracity of the model. Some data mining techniques result in profiles where it is very unclear which data were most important and which data leads to the flagging of a person. Negative influences on reliability can also result from missing data, bias in the data, or wrong data. This can lead to an accountability risk, when too much responsibility is placed on these techniques. This problem may seem limited, as predictive profiling is mostly used to guide investigative measures and further decisions will be based on their findings. But when predictive profiling is used to legitimize intrusive preventative measures, e.g. based on risk scores, not just the creation of a profile but the whole decision-making process becomes opaque.

Citron (2008) warns how procedural safeguards are imperilled by automation in what she calls the 'automated administrative state'. Involving more humans in the decision-making process will not do, Citron argues, since in practice there is little difference between automated decision-making and non-automated decision-making with human intervention before the decision. People, including state officials, are often fooled by technology or do not possess the ability or information to properly assess the computer-generated suggestion. Too much trust in the results provided by the computer leads to an 'automation bias'. Coding can result in a hidden form of rule-making through programmers' mistakes or interpretations. The construction of a profile can be seen as a similar form of hidden rule-making. Citron shows that procedural safeguards need a major overhaul to remain effective.

6.4   PROFILING AND THE RIGHT TO PRIVACY

The general framework and the problematic proportionality test

Profiling clearly enters the ambit of the fundamental right to privacy. Article 8(1) of the European Convention on Human Rights (ECHR) defines the right to privacy as "the right to respect for his private and family life, his home and his correspondence." Article 8(2) defines when interfering with this right is legitimate.

The first question is if profiling interferes with the right to privacy. Profiling is not in itself a form of data collection, but uses data collected earlier, which we assume took place legally. It means that the data is now in the possession of public authorities, sometimes in the possession of other administrations and collected for other purposes. Whereas data in the US is no longer considered private once it is held by other parties or is public (Solove 2004), the European Court of Human Rights (ECtHR) does not limit private life to the intimate sphere. Even in the public sphere a person's privacy still has a certain protection. The ECtHR pointed out in *P.G. & J.H. v. United Kingdom* that there is "a zone of interaction of a person with others, even in a public context, which may fall within the scope of 'private life'". It also stated that:

> "Private-life considerations may arise, however, once any systematic or permanent record comes into existence of such material from the public domain. It is for this reason that files gathered by security services on a particular individual fall within the scope of Article 8, even where the information has not been gathered by any intrusive or covert method."

This clarifies that the use of data linked to persons is an interference to their private life and needs to be legitimized. Public authorities therefore have a duty to consider the privacy rights of individuals when deciding on the further use of such data. Similar considerations were raised in other case law on the storage (*Leander v. Sweden, Rotaru v. Romania, Amann v. Switzerland*), further retention (*S. and Marper v. United Kingdom*), and diffusion of personal data (*Peck v. United Kingdom, Z. v. Finland, Weber and Saravia v. Germany*). We can conclude that profiling activities by public authorities are to be considered interferences to private life, also when they use data on behaviour in the public sphere (such as mobility data) or data that was earlier handed to public authorities (e.g. in the context of social security or taxation). This concerns both the creation of profiles and the application of profiles to specific persons.

What makes an interference to privacy legitimate? There are three requirements. First, the interference has to be in accordance with the law. There has to be some ground in domestic law for the measure. The ECtHR also looks at the 'quality of the law' or the substantive content, which has "to provide safeguards against arbitrariness" (*P.G. & J.H. v. United Kingdom*). In practice this rather technical requirement has turned out to be an important check on both human and automated profiling. In *Gillan and Quinton* v. *United Kingdom*, the ECtHR held that stop and search powers by law enforcement in the UK violated privacy, because they are "not in accordance with law". Under sections 44-47 of the *Terrorism Act 2000*, police in the UK gained the power to stop and search people without any requirement to first form a reasonable suspicion of unlawful behaviour. The Court held that the extraordinary breadth of power given to the police under the Act lacked appropriate legal safeguards capable of protecting individuals against arbitrary interference. The Court also acknowledged the risks of the discriminatory use of powers against black and Asian persons. Statistics accepted by the Court showed that black and Asian persons were disproportionately affected by police powers in the UK.

The same strict line was also followed in a case concerning digital surveillance, a case that led to *Liberty v. United Kingdom*. Here the ECtHR held that a system of mass surveillance operated by the UK government to spy on all telephone calls, faxes and emails to and from Ireland was in breach of the right to privacy, since relevant domestic law did not indicate with sufficient clarity the scope or manner in which to intercept and examine external communications and did not foresee adequate legal protection against the abuse of power. The law has to organize profiling and data mining powers in such a way that citizens *have an understanding* of the procedure to be followed when selecting for examination, sharing, storing and destroying intercepted material.

Profiling therefore needs a legal basis and legal safeguards need to be provided for the different stages of the process.[11]

Second, the interference has to be for a legal aim, which is relatively easy to fulfil given the broad range of aims listed in article 8(2).

Finally, the interference has to be 'necessary in a democratic society'. The notion of necessity does not involve a strict test of necessity in the sense of 'indispensable'. Nor is it as flexible as 'reasonable' or 'useful'. While it allows for a certain margin of appreciation, which can vary depending on the subject-matter, the scope for interpretation is limited.[12] The interference has to be a response to 'a pressing social need' and has to be 'proportionate to the legitimate aim pursued' (*Leander v. Sweden, Silver v. United Kingdom, Handyside v. United Kingdom*). The proportionality test used to give flesh to the bone of the necessity requirement involves four steps. The measure must be: (1) put in place to ensure a legitimate objective; (2) suitable, i.e. in a causal relation with the policy objective; (3) necessary, i.e. not curtailing rights more than is necessary given alternative options;[13] and (4) proportionate in a strict sense, i.e. even in the absence of a valid alternative, the benefits must outweigh the costs incurred by the infringement of the right.

This framework, including the proportionality test, said to be rooted in German administrative and constitutional law, is well anchored in the working praxis of both European Courts and national courts. But careful analysis of the relevant case law shows that both European and national courts often take a deferential approach towards public security or safety cases in order to leave some discretion to authorities and legislators, and therefore do not always fully assess the third and fourth steps of proportionality, namely the necessity and strict proportionality tests. Judges refrain from assessing choices made by governmental officials. Technically speaking, this is made possible by the lack of any explicit duty to apply the full proportionality test. Nowhere in case law do judges bind themselves to such strict testing. At the European level, the ECtHR in some cases suggests that not choosing the least onerous measure does not necessarily entail a violation of the ECHR or, more bluntly, explicitly rejects the test (Popelier and Van De Heyning 2013; Galetta and De Hert 2014).

Applying the framework: EUCJ data retention (2014) and German Rasterfahndung (2006)
The literature is mostly positive about the privacy case law of the two European Courts. Although the European Convention on Human Rights only mentions the right to privacy and does not mention modern technologies or the need to protect personal data, the ECtHR has opened up the Convention by incorporating most data protection safeguards in its case law. The mere storage of data often triggers the right to privacy; in the ensuing proportionality test, the specific aims of data collection are taken into account. A positive proportionality check for data collection is not automatically carried over to the retention or further use of the data (*S. and Marper v. United Kingdom*), which require separate proportionality considerations. The ECtHR does not oppose using databases containing data of earlier

offenders to investigate future crimes, but the persons affected must be limited and selected according to relevant criteria (*Van der Velden v. the Netherlands*). Retaining data because more data makes the system more useful is considered disproportionate (*S. and Marper v. United Kingdom, M.K. v. France*).

We wish to illustrate the potential effect of the European privacy framework for the practice of profiling with two other court decisions. First is the data retention decision of the European Court of Justice (EUCJ) of 8 April 2014. Directive 2006/24/EC obliged telecommunications and internet service providers to retain traffic, location and related data to identify the user, but not the actual communications, for 6 to 24 months and to allow access to this data by law enforcement agencies for the purpose of investigation, detection and prosecution of serious crimes. The data is not centralised by law enforcement agencies, which can access the data retained by service providers for specific cases. The obligation to retain data is a clear example of the growing surveillance engendered by the preventive approach to security.

The EUCJ bases its analysis on Article 7 of the Charter of Fundamental Rights of the European Union (CFREU), which is almost identical to Article 8(1) ECHR and Article 8 of the Charter. It considers both the retention of data by service providers and the access by law enforcement agencies as distinct interferences with the right to privacy. It points out that retention and subsequent use without informing concerned users "is likely to generate in the minds of the persons concerned the feeling that their private lives are the subject of constant surveillance". The broad retention also entails "an interference with the fundamental rights of practically the entire European population". The EUCJ points out that no differentiation or limitation is made linked to the objective of fighting serious crime. The directive therefore affects persons for whom there is no evidence linking their conduct to serious crime. Similarly, there is no relationship between the retained data and threats to public security. The EUCJ further points to the lack of adequate rules on the access and further use of the data, including criteria to determine the limits of such access and use, procedural rules and conditions, or criteria to limit persons and the retention period to the strictly necessary. The EUCJ therefore declared the directive invalid (EUCJ, C-293/12 - Digital Rights Ireland and Seitlinger and others).

Objections to broad interference – affecting the privacy of people having no connection to the targeted threat or criminal behaviour – pose a particular problem for profiling, especially the creation of profiles and the search for those who fit the profile. The other objections clarify that precise rules on access, use and retention of data are needed in any practice of large-scale profiling.

Another relevant case is the *Rasterfahndung* (data screening) case decided by the German Constitutional Court on 4 April 2006 (ECLI:DE:BVerfG:2006:rs2006 0404.1bvr051802). This decision was induced by the complaint of a Moroccan student against a large-scale data mining operation searching for possible terrorist sleeper cells after the terrorist attacks of 11 September 2001. First a dataset was made of persons fulfilling a set of criteria, which included being of the Muslim faith. In the state of Nordrhein-Westfalen, this dataset included about 11,000 persons, distilled from a set of 5,200,000 people. This dataset was then compared to find suspicious matches with a range of other databases, which contained data concerning between 200,000 and 300,000 people. This screening operation was followed by other investigative measures, but in the end yielded no results. The description lets us suppose that the operation involved the querying of databases, but probably made no use of data mining algorithms.

The German Constitutional Court declared the screening operation unconstitutional. The Court pointed out that the distinct steps of the screening operation were all interferences with the informational self-determination of people against whom no suspicion was present. Such interference could only be made proportional in limited circumstances. More specifically, a concrete danger or threat must be present and this determination must have factual grounds. General assessments of threat are insufficient, as this would lead to unrestricted competence and searches '*ins Blaue hinein*' (fishing expeditions).

These two privacy judgements set clear limits to the use of automated and predictive profiling. In general one can say that the ECtHR has transposed its guidelines on the establishment of safeguards and the minimum safeguards developed in its jurisprudence on secret listening to more modern practices such as profiling.

These practices need to serve a legitimate aim, need to be regulated with enough detail in hard law, and need to meet the proportionality test. Our two examples clarify that activities that interfere without distinction with the privacy of large parts of the population are disproportional and that such activities must in some way be linked to factual grounds. One has to admit, however, that the relevant case law is either very young or scarce, and does not allow stronger or more precise conclusions. Continued scrutiny is thus warranted. Investigative methods evolve together with technological possibilities; old standards can become outdated, even when laid down in the case law of our highest courts. Profiling and Big Data give the police 'something to work with', which might make their actions less discretionary and acceptable in light of existing human rights standards.

Ferguson, for instance, analyses the effects of the growing availability of data on the Fourth Amendment requirement of reasonable suspicion for stop and search interventions. The original 'small data' standard concerned the observable actions of unknown subjects. The facts leading to suspicion had to relate to criminal activity, and not just the person. The availability of more data generally leads to more knowledge about an identified suspect and a resulting prediction feeding into the suspicion. The suspicion becomes less related to facts on actual activity and more related to the person. A suspicion based solely on the person would then allow stopping and searching that individual at any moment without further justification; a link to actual activity thus remains necessary to inform a suspicion (Ferguson 2014). This analysis can be generalized to practices of profiling to guide considerations of proportionality.

The decisions mentioned above show that requiring limitations based on factual grounds is a reasonable approach. The nuanced application of proportionality in the context of profiling requires further development, one which will maintain effective safeguards against the generalised application of intrusive methods as well as methods based on arbitrary or unfounded assumptions.

6.5   PROFILING AND THE PROHIBITION OF DISCRIMINATION

Article 14 ECHR and the 12th Protocol prohibit 'discrimination on any ground such as sex, race, colour, language, religion, political or other opinion, national or social origin, association with a national minority, property, birth or other status' in the enjoyment of any right set forth in the Convention or by law. EU law contains similar non-discrimination principles.

The ECtHR considers discrimination to be "differences in treatment based on an identifiable characteristic, or 'status'" and checks for differences in the treatment of persons "in analogous, or relevantly similar, situations." The difference in treatment is discriminatory if it has "no objective and reasonable justification", if it does not pursue a "legitimate aim" or if there is no "reasonable relationship of proportionality between the means employed and the aim sought to be realised" (*Carson and others v. United Kingdom*). Generally, the principle of non-discrimination requires that comparable situations must not be treated differently and that different situations must not be treated in the same way (EUCJ, *Heinz Huber v. Germany*).

Data mining algorithms search for correlations in data; the resulting profile can make all sorts of characteristics a relevant difference. The non-discrimination principle limits what can be a relevant difference. The protected grounds are characteristics that should not be considered relevant, unless they can be adequately justified. This applies at different stages of the profiling process, from the selection of data to be used in profiling to the application of the profile.

Huber, delivered by the EUCJ, is an innovative judgement on the applicability of the non-discrimination principle in profiling practices.[14] The object of discussion was a database containing the personal details of foreigners applying for residence and its further use by police to fight crime.

The EUCJ concluded, firstly, that this register was not contrary to the law as far as it served the application of the residence legislation, contained only those personal data necessary for that application and granted access to other services which had competences in that field. A comparison with the registration of personal data of nationals in local registers with less personal data was made and the differences were accepted as justified as far as the centralised nature of the register allowed a more effective application of the residence law and it contained only data necessary for that purpose. In other words, the difference in treatment of personal data of foreigners compared with nationals was considered justified as it served legitimate purposes (application of residence legislation) and the difference in treatment was proportionate with that aim. The difference in treatment was objectively reasonably linked with a difference in legal situation, and therefore justified.

The same reasoning led to a different conclusion concerning the use of this register for crime fighting purposes. As the fight against crime involves the prosecution of crimes and offences committed irrespective of the nationality of their perpetrators, this objective cannot justify a difference in treatment between nationals and other EU citizens resident in the member state. A difference in treatment through the processing of personal data with a specific system for foreigners was therefore not justified for this purpose. Again, a comparison was made between foreign EU-citizens and nationals but here the situation of the two groups was too similar to justify a difference in treatment, although the aim was legitimate.

Huber underlines the relevance of the non-discrimination principle for profiling. While the case focused on the government's storage of and access to personal data, all other steps of the profiling process (see section 6.1) must be checked on non-discrimination grounds as well.

Firstly, there is the issue of linking data directly or indirectly to one of the protected grounds when designing profiles. The *Rasterfahndung* decision concerned a profile that included being of the Muslim faith. While the Court approached the case in terms of privacy, and did not make a separate evaluation of the non-discrimination principle, it did point to the risk of stigmatisation. Its general conclusion that such operations need a concrete threat sustained with factual elements also points to the obligation to justify the use of such sensitive criteria.

Secondly, there is a need to apply a non-discrimination test when assessing the results of the profiling process.[15] The application of the profile can result in indirect discrimination, as the 'neutral' application of algorithms leads to an unjustified burden on specific groups. This requires the application of the non-discrimination principle to the results of profiling and active checking of whether they lead to differential treatment that cannot be justified. Differential treatment is not excluded by definition. For example, suspects of terrorism inspired by religious, ethnic or ideological grounds will predominantly be of that religious, ethnic or ideological background, while suspects of social fraud will be recipients of social benefits. Nevertheless, differential treatment requires justification, and we can remind ourselves again of the requirement for a concrete threat sustained by factual grounds set by the German Constitutional Court.

These are just several examples of how profiles and data mining can violate the non-discrimination principle.

In their detailed study of the data mining and profiling process, Barocas and Selbst (2016) found no less than five discriminating mechanisms present at all steps in the process.[16] They include specifying the problem to be solved in ways that affect classes differently, failing to recognize or address statistical biases, reproducing past prejudice, and considering an insufficiently rich set of factors. Even in situations where data miners are extremely careful, there can still be discrimination when using models that, quite unintentionally, pick out proxy variables for protected classes. An additional problem is 'masking', when data miners are able to disguise intentional discrimination as unintentional.

With the exception of such masking, discriminatory data mining, Barocas and Selbst hold, is always unintentional. Evidence in court will be hard to produce, especially since discrimination cannot be legally blocked when there is a 'business necessity' (a US term), a pressing need or a reasonable justification. While both authors propose a range of non-legal solutions (oversampling, making training data and models auditable, pre-screening audits, results-focused balancing), they conclude that law will seldom work and that the market will not inspire costly efforts to do the profiling right, as a lot of Big Data profiling simply becomes ineffective when an absolute interdiction on protected classes or proxy variables is introduced. Other authors are less negative about the effects of anti-discrimination and see a role for specific auditing techniques (to be developed) to uncover hidden biases and for other technological solutions. For instance, the prohibition to discriminate on certain grounds can be modelled into discrimination-aware algorithms (Custers et al. 2013). The legal safeguard must be supported in this area by the development of technical safeguards and their implementation through standards and technical regulations. We return to this below.

Other human rights are affected by profiling, but the right to privacy and the prohibition of discrimination provide the basic safeguards for the problems we identified in our overview of risks. The procedural safeguards provided in Article 6 ECHR will be reviewed in our discussion of Dutch procedural safeguards that apply to profiling for investigative purposes, below.

6.6   ADDITIONAL GUARANTEES IN DUTCH ADMINISTRATIVE, CRIMINAL PROCEDURE AND DATA PROTECTION LAW?

The guarantees offered by the legality and purpose specification principle
While fundamental rights are an important set of checks on governmental powers, other safeguards elaborated in specific areas of law might be relevant as well. We now turn to existing legal safeguards in administrative, criminal procedure and data protection law.

A first safeguard can be found in the legality principle in administrative law: this principle gives flesh to the idea of the rule of law and the need to limit state powers by linking them to competences and purposes. Public authorities and their officials are only allowed to impact on citizens' freedoms when they have a competence to do so provided by law. Public authorities and officials have different roles and are therefore also provided with different competences. Linked to the legality principle is the speciality principle: a law can only be applied in its specific domain and therefore competences can only be used for the purposes provided by this law.

Dutch administrative law embeds this in the prohibition of *détournement de pouvoir* or the prohibition to use competences for other purposes but those for which they were provided. Similarly, in criminal procedure law investigation measures need to be based on law. This requirement not only results from the fundamental rights provisions in the ECHR (see our discussion of the legality requirement in Article 8 ECHR above) but also from 'the principle of procedural legality' found in Article 1 of the Code of Criminal Procedure (CCP) of 1926. Data protection law has its specific application of the legality principle through the purpose limitation principle (personal data may only be collected for specific, explicitly defined and legitimate purposes) and the requirement for legal grounds to process data.

Closer examination reveals that these principles have grey zones that are skilfully used by authorities to operate without detailed legislation. The principle of procedural legality (Article 1 CCP), for example, is interpreted in a restrictive way as covering only those methods of investigation that substantially infringe on fundamental rights. Investigative methods that do not, or do not substantially, breach fundamental rights can always be employed. Article 2 of the Police Act (*Politiewet*) on the task of the police is considered by the courts to provide a sound basis for investigative methods (Van Kempen 2009).

Equally vague is the *Wet bescherming persoonsgegevens* (Wbp), the Dutch Data Protection Act implementing directive 95/46/EC. Article 8 allows the processing of data on the basis of consent (Article 8a) or in order to comply with legal obligations (Article 8c), but then opens the spectre by stating that data processing is also possible when "processing is necessary for the proper performance of a public law duty by the administrative body concerned or by the administrative body to which the data are provided" (Article 8d). Article 9 §1 Wbp adds that "personal data shall not be further processed in a way incompatible with the purposes for which they have been obtained". In other words, in limited circumstances, further processing for another purpose remains possible. These provisions raise important questions about the resilience of the Dutch Data Protection Act (and other similar acts in EU Member States that have identical provisions). Note that Article 9§2 contains provisions to limit the possible abuse of the 'compatibility' clause.[17] The Act on Police Data (*Wet politiegegevens* (Wpg)) contains a similar purpose limitation principle and the grounds for processing, including a specific ground for automated comparison and the combined searching of data.

To the extent that authorities interpret the vagueness in criminal and data protection law to allow profiling, the intensive exploitation of existing data through the use of profiles and data mining will go unnoticed by lawmakers and citizens, since these are considered to be implicit ('compatible') or not 'substantially infringing' powers. This development will leave the automated administrative state largely unchecked by legal rules.

There are signs that this development is already well under way. In the memorandum accompanying the SUWI proposal (see above), the government explained its choice for a broad formulation of purpose in order to allow a range of public authorities to cooperate and act as an integrated public authority. It is thereby silently assumed that this purpose is compatible with the original purpose for which data were collected by participating data providers. SyRI is a framework in which a different group of partners more specifically define the content and purpose of data exchange for each project; this limits the loosening of the principle. SyRI has now become the model for developing a more general legal framework for the exchange of data between public and possibly private partners (Werkgroep Verkenning kaderwet gegevensuitwisseling 2014). In the context of Big Data and the Internet of Things, Moerel and Prins have recently advocated exchanging the purpose limitation principle for a legitimate purpose principle; they point to recent proposals by the European Council to allow further processing even for an incompatible purpose when the legitimate interests of the controller or a third party override the interests of the data subject (Moerel and Prins 2015). In fact we see a similar shift towards a legitimate interest principle in these proposals for cooperation structures, especially when the purpose of data processing is as broadly formulated as the public task of the authorities involved.

Guarantees offered by the proportionality, subsidiarity and necessity principles

A second safeguard is the proportionality principle present in all three legal frameworks. In administrative law the proportionality principle (*evenredigheid*) states that decisions may not affect persons disproportionately, compared to the purpose of the decision. Supervisory and investigative competences may only be used when needed. In criminal procedure law, the proportionality principle is embedded in the conditions, such as the presence of reasonable suspicion, that must be fulfilled before certain investigative measures can be taken. The Dutch Data Protection Act states that personal data shall only be processed when adequate, relevant and not excessive (Article 11). The subsidiarity principle (the purpose cannot be reached with less negative impact) and the necessity principle (the interference is needed to attain the purpose) are linked to the proportionality principle.

In our discussion of the right to privacy (see above), we observed that European and national courts have held back in testing necessity and strict proportionality, thereby allowing some discretion to authorities. Here we focus on the requirement in criminal law that investigative powers can only be used in case of reasonable suspicion that an offence (infraction or crime) has been committed (cf. Article 27 CCP). This is an important safeguard as it prevents, by using a threshold requirement, wide use of the state's far-reaching powers in criminal law. But the rise of supervisory powers other than investigative powers and developments that lower the threshold are thwarting this safeguard. These will be discussed below.

An important distinction in Dutch administrative law is that between supervisory powers (*toezicht*) and investigative powers (*opsporing*). Supervisory powers do not aim to investigate offences but to observe the application of regulations. The use of these powers is not linked to any suspicion. As part of these supervisory powers, officials can demand information or documents. Citizens are obliged to cooperate; refusing to do so is an offence. Supervisory powers are generally part of administrative law and have a proactive or preventive role. In contrast, investigative powers aim to investigate offences with prosecution as their objective. They are used to respond to an offence, to establish the facts and the guilt of the offender. In the traditional view they are linked with a suspicion of guilt for an offence. Investigative powers can be found in both criminal procedure and administrative law, and are exercised under the control of the public prosecutor.

An intermediary position is taken by powers of (repressive) control. These powers are similar to supervisory powers in that they are used without the presence of a suspicion, but with the objective of uncovering offences (e.g. traffic controls). These powers are traditionally included within the legal framework on investigative powers (Borgers 2011).

The distinction between supervisory and investigative powers is important in light of the prohibition of *détournement de pouvoir* as it raises the question of how the subsequent, concurring or overlapping use of different competences is addressed. It turns out that the courts deal leniently with such issues. The use of investigative powers when supervisory powers have uncovered an offence is an obvious, non-problematic response. But questions arise when supervisory powers tied to a specific part of legislation uncover an offence in the ambit of another law. Another problem is the continued use of supervisory powers when investigative powers are employed, or their concurring use. Both have been accepted by the Supreme Court, in the latter case through the procedural rights of investigative measures. The exception is when a competence from one law is used exclusively to obtain the objectives of another law (Borgers 2011).

The link between investigative powers and the condition of reasonable suspicion has been loosened with the introduction of more proactive and preventive investigative measures. With the introduction of a terrorist crime, the condition of reasonable suspicion was lowered to 'indications' of a terrorist crime (Hirsch Ballin 2008; Van Kempen 2009). Article 126gg Sv. regulates the 'exploratory investigation' (*verkennend onderzoek*) that precedes the proper investigation, which considers the presence of crimes or their planning among groups of people. It consists of the collection and analysis of information from police databases or open sources and is not based on a suspicion against a specific person. Exploratory investigations begin based on 'indications following from facts or circumstances'. Mere presumptions are not enough; factual grounds are required. When the exploratory investigation concerns a terrorist crime, Article 126hh Sv. allows summoning the delivery of other databases, including from private data holders. This data can be compared or processed together with other datasets. Article 126gg Sv. still applies.

Articles 126gg and 126hh Sv. regulate data screening operations within the criminal procedure, which may include profiling. Their preliminary character implies that data screening operations remain outside the safeguards of Article 6 ECHR. The main safeguard is that these operations happen under the control of the public prosecutor.

We can conclude that there is a general trend towards allowing data exchange and profiling by loosening existing safeguards in administrative, criminal and data protection law. The *détournement de pouvoir* principle in administrative law was hollowed out much earlier. In criminal procedure we notice the emergence of less stringent conditions to use data-intensive investigative methods in a much earlier phase. In data protection we notice the diminished impact of the purpose limitation principle.

On the one hand, this is done for good reasons. Some of the safeguards were developed for different technological and societal circumstances. The strict application of *détournement de pouvoir* makes good sense for Weberian bureaucratic organisations, but less sense for networked and interconnected organisations sharing tasks. Although the strict application of purpose limitation was logical for isolated databases, the linking of data sources is crucial for the new data-intensive methods.

While successful prevention is clearly beneficial for society, it raises the question of whether attention is now too focussed on loosening safeguards rather than re-inventing or adapting them. In light of the proportionality principle, the negative impacts of heightened surveillance are neglected.

Guarantees offered by procedural safeguards
Procedural safeguards for individuals involved in state procedures are a third category of safeguards. Dutch administrative law contains a duty of care. It obliges the administration to carefully establish and review all relevant factual and legal elements of a case. This includes checking whether advisors have properly carried out the research requested of them. To give them the opportunity to be heard, the administration in certain situations must inform affected parties when preparing a decision. When the authority bases its decision on a technical investigation, the result must be documented in a report to allow later review.

The procedural safeguards offered by Article 6 ECHR play a similar role in criminal procedural law. The procedural rights of a fair trial involve the right of access to a court, an independent and impartial tribunal established by law. It further involves the right to a fair hearing, which includes the right to an adversarial trial, freedom from self-incrimination, and so on. Criminal procedures have extra safeguards such as the assumption of innocence (Harris et al. 2009). Guarantees in criminal procedures apply from the moment a person is charged with a criminal offence; they do not apply to pre-trial investigations or preventive measures preceding a criminal charge. The impact of these rights can be seen in the duty to cooperate with supervisory powers. Once investigative measures are employed, the freedom from self-incrimination comes into play. This also applies to administrative sanctions when these have punitive or deterring objectives (Borgers 2011).

A range of similar safeguards are recognized in data protection law ('data subject rights'): the right to be informed, to access the data, to have it corrected or (when no longer relevant) deleted, and the right to object to processing. Nobody may be subjected to automated decision-making with legal consequences when such decisions are based only on data intended to provide a picture of certain aspects of their personality. Exceptions exist, in which case persons must be allowed to present their views and be informed of the logic on which the automated decision is made. This concurs with the duty of care, which obliges a review of preparatory research and to allow affected persons to be heard.

The SyRI system is an example of how these safeguards are applied to profiling. While the system flags persons linked to suspicious data patterns, this flagging is only guidance for further investigation and does not lead to automatic decisions. Decisions are only taken after investigation and thereby subjected to the whole range of procedural safeguards. Risk notifications are included in a register. People can inquire if they are included in the register, but are not informed directly when they show up in a risk notification.

While profiling is subject to an extensive range of procedural safeguards, Citron warns that these safeguards are imperilled by automation. She points out that automation bias and the opacity of data processing can diminish or eliminate the distinction between automated and computer-assisted decision-making. Exaggerated trust in computers runs counter to the duty of care. EUCJ case C-503/03 between the European Commission and Spain, concerning the refusal of entry into the Schengen area based on flagging in the SIS system, confirms this duty of care. The EUCJ pointed out that such refusal without preliminary verification of whether the person presented an actual danger violated EU law.

Citron points to the need to more effectively implement safeguards. The opacity of automated processes imperils the flow of information to data subjects as well as the proper review of the basis of decisions (in the case of profiling, the flagging of a person as a risk). Proper audit trails, documenting the rules applied and the data considered, should be a required part of the system. Decision-makers should also explain in detail how they relied on computer-generated information, and be trained to critically evaluate such information to combat automation bias. Automated systems should be designed with transparency and accountability as core objectives. Citron advises that code be made available as open source; for profiling, this implies that algorithms and profiles are open to review. As code and algorithms can function as hidden rule-makers, this will provide an alternative means of external scrutiny. For the same reason, Citron advises allowing the public to participate in reviewing the systems. Lastly, she makes a plea for proper testing.

In the case of profiling, this advice can be further specified to require algorithms to be discrimination-aware and to develop auditing and testing protocols for algorithms and profiles (Pedreschi et al. 2013; Romei and Ruggieri 2013). Making algorithms and (risk) profiles open to public review should be a priority. If such transparency facilitates anticipation and avoiding behaviour, the internal auditing and publication of results still remain possible. Protocols to measure or assess the control burden can also be developed and integrated within new technical standards for profiling. Impact assessments foreseen in the draft General Data Protection Regulation can be widened in scope to include aspects such as discrimination.

6.7   CONCLUSION: LEGAL SAFEGUARDS MUST BE OVERHAULED TO MAKE THEM EFFECTIVE AGAIN

We distinguished between the creation of a profile and its application, as they affect different groups of people. We clarified that automated profiling based on data mining is not yet by definition an application of Big Data, but that Big Data magnifies its impact. Profiling in a Big Data context puts greater pressure on the checks and balances in the legal framework.

We then discussed examples of profiling in the US and the Netherlands. Predictive policing, an application of profiling for security purposes, is widely used in the US and is seeing its first applications in the Netherlands. We also presented two Dutch examples of profiling to combat fraud: the iCOV and the SyRI system.

While profiling has clear benefits in guiding efforts and improving efficacy, it comes with several risks. We highlighted three potential risks: the intrusion on privacy, social sorting and discrimination, and opaque decision-making. We therefore reviewed the legal safeguards present in the human rights framework and in Dutch administrative, criminal procedure and data protection law and highlighted the relevant cases. Aware of the potential to discriminate and infringe on privacy, courts insist on proportionality, including clear and detailed rules and requirements such as reasonable indications or suspicious before making larger groups of people the object of governmental actions.

Our review also covered more critical concerns. If courts refrain from testing the necessity and strict proportionality of governmental data mining and use of profiles, these technologies may well go unchecked. If these practices are seen as 'lesser' infringements that do not require detailed regulation, the resilience of the legal framework might similarly be low. Given the opacity of profiles and data mining operations, Barocas and Selbst (2016) point to the difficulty of triggering legal guarantees as well as legal contradictions. There might, for instance, be free speech objections against prohibiting governments and other actors from using certain data when assembling or applying profiles. One paradox we noted concerned the issue of reasonable suspicion and similar thresholds. What will courts do when authorities invoke not facts, but the 'hits' and 'outcomes' of profiling operations to argue that an individual or group of individuals need extra surveillance or investigation? With Ferguson (2014), we believe that the growing availability of data might lead to an erosion of existing standards, rendering police and governmental interventions legitimate because the computer 'said so'.

Our review revealed tensions between the use of profiling as a proactive investigative technique and the legal safeguards in data protection, administrative and criminal law. These tensions have been resolved by loosening legal safeguards.

The *détournement de pouvoir* principle in administrative law was hollowed out much earlier. In criminal procedure we see the emergence of less stringent conditions to use data-intensive investigative methods in a much earlier phase. In data protection we notice the diminished impact of the purpose limitation principle. In considerations of the proportionality principle, the negative impacts of heightened surveillance are neglected.

Human rights jurisprudence on the right to privacy sets clear limits to the use of automated and predictive profiling. It makes clear that profiling and data screening which interfere without distinction with the privacy of large parts of the population are disproportional and that such activities must in some way be linked to concrete and factual elements. On the other hand, the jurisprudence is scarce; drawing strong or precise conclusions remains difficult. While the prohibition of discrimination is a useful legal safeguard, it must be given teeth through the development of audit tools and discrimination-aware algorithms.

Although done for good reasons, the question is whether the focus has not been too much on loosening safeguards rather than adapting them. We concur with Citron that legal safeguards need to be overhauled to make them effective again in the 'automated administrative state'. Transparency and accountability can be designed into profiling practices. This must be backed up with stronger institutional safeguards to allow for independent assessments and rapid feedback into decision-making.

REFERENCES

Barocas, S. and A. Selbst (2016) 'Big Data's Disparate impact', *California Law Review* 104: 1-60 (forthcoming).

Black, J. (2005) 'The Emergence of Risk-Based Regulation and the New Public Risk Management in the United Kingdom', *Public Law* Autumn: 512-549.

Borgers, M.J. (2011) 'De onderzoeksfase: toezicht, controle en opsporing', pp. 455-496 in F.G.H. Kristen, R.M.I. Lamp, J.M.W. Lindeman and M.J.J.P. Luchtman (eds.) *Bijzonder strafrecht. Strafrechtelijke handhaving van sociaal-economisch en fiscaal recht in Nederland*, The Hague: Boom Lemma.

Brakel, R. van and P. De Hert (2011) 'Policing, Surveillance and Law in a Pre-Crime Society: Understanding the Consequences of Technology Based Strategies', *Technology-Led Policing* 20: 165.

Chicago Police Department (2013) *Custom Notifications in Chicago – Pilot Program D13-09*, available at: http://directives.chicagopolice.org/directives-mobile/data/a7a57bf0-13fa59ed-26113-fa63-2e1d9a1obb6ob9ae.html?ownapi=1.

Citron, D.K. (2008) 'Technological Due Process', *Washington University Law Review* 85: 1249-1313.

College Bescherming Persoonsgegevens (2014) *Advies conceptbesluit SyRI*, available at: https://cbpweb.nl/sites/default/files/atoms/files/z2013-00969.pdf.

Custers, B. (2014) 'Risicogericht toezicht, Profiling and Big Data', *Tijdschrift voor Toezicht* 5, 3: 9-16.

Custers, B., T. Calders, T. Zarsky and B. Schermer (2013) 'The Way Forward' in B. Custers, T. Calders, B. Schermer and T. Zarsky (eds.) *Discrimination and Privacy in the Information Society*: 341-57, Berlin/Heidelberg: Springer.

Fayyad, U., G. Piatetsky-Shapiro and P. Smyth (1996) 'From Data Mining to Knowledge Discovery in Databases', *AI Magazine* 17, 3: 37-54.

Federal Trade Commission (2014) *Data Brokers: a Call for Transparency and Accountability*, available at: www.ftc.gov/system/files/documents/reports/data-brokers-call-transparency-accountability-report-federal-trade- commission-may-2014/140527databrokerreport.pdf.

Ferguson, A.G. (2014) 'Big Data and Predictive Reasonable Suspicion', *University of Pennsylvania Law Review* 163: 327.

Galetta, A. and P. De Hert (2014) 'Complementing the Surveillance Law Principles of the ECtHR with Its Environmental Law Principles: An Integrated Technology Approach to a Human Rights Framework for Surveillance', *Utrecht Law Review* 10, 1: 55-75.

Gandy Jr., O.H. (2010) 'Engaging Rational Discrimination: Exploring Reasons for Placing Regulatory Constraints on Decision Support Systems', *Ethics and Information Technology* 12, 1: 29-42.

Harcourt, B.E. (2005) 'Against Prediction: Sentencing, Policing, and Punishing in an Actuarial Age', *University of Chicago Public Law Working Paper* 94.

Harris, D., M. O'Boyle, E. Bates and C. Buckley (2009) *Harris, O'Boyle and Warbrick: Law of the European Convention on Human Rights*, Oxford: Oxford University Press.

Hildebrandt, M. (2008a) 'Defining Profiling: A New Type of Knowledge?' in M. Hildebrandt and S. Gutwirth (eds.) *Profiling the European Citizen*, Dordrecht: Springer Science + Business Media.

Hildebrandt, M. (2008b) 'Profiling and the Rule of Law', *Identity in the Information Society* 1, 1: 55-70.

Hirsch Ballin, M.F.H. (2008) 'Inside View of Dutch Counterterrorism Strategy: Countering Terrorism through Criminal Law and the Presumption of Innocence', *Journal of the Institute of Justice and International Studies* 8: 139-51.

Kempen, P.H. van (2009) 'The Protection of Human Rights in Criminal Law Procedure in The Netherlands', *Electronic Journal of Comparative Law* 13, 2: 37.

Kitchin, R. (2014a) *The Data Revolution: Big Data, Open Data, Data Infrastructures and their Consequences*, London: Sage.

Kitchin, R. (2014b) 'Big Data, New Epistemologies and Paradigm Shifts', *Big Data and Society* 1, 1 DOI: 10.1177/2053951714528481.

McCaney, K. (2013) 'Prisons Turn to Analytics Software for Parole Decisions', GCN, available at: http://gcn.com/articles/2013/11/01/prison-analytics-software.aspx.

Moerel, L. and C. Prins (2015) *Further Processing of Data Based on the Legitimate Interest Ground: The End of Purpose Limitation?*, Tilburg: Tilburg University.

Openbaar Ministerie (2014) *Aanwijzing opsporingsbevoegdheden (2014A009)*, available at: www.om.nl/organisatie/beleidsregels/overzicht-0/opsporing-politie/@86281/aanwijzing-3/.

Pedreschi, D., S. Ruggieri and F. Turini (2013) 'The Discovery of Discrimination', pp. 91-108 in B. Custers, T. Calders, B. Schermer and T. Zarsky (eds.) *Discrimination and Privacy in the Information Society*, Berlin/Heidelberg: Springer.

Perry, W.L. et al. (2013) *Predictive Policing: The Role of Crime Forecasting in Law Enforcement Operations*, Rand Corporation.

Popelier, P. and C. van de Heyning (2013) 'Procedural Rationality: Giving Teeth to the Proportionality Analysis', *European Constitutional Law Review* 9: 230-262.

Romei, A. and S. Ruggieri (2013) 'Discrimination Data Analysis: A Multi-Disciplinary Bibliography, pp. 109-135 in B. Custers, T. Calders, B. Schermer and T. Zarsky (eds.) *Discrimination and Privacy in the Information Society*, Berlin/Heidelberg: Springer.

Schermer, B. (2013) 'Risks of Profiling and the Limits of Data Protection Law, pp. 137-152 in B. Custers, T. Calders, B. Schermer and T. Zarsky (eds.) *Discrimination and Privacy in the Information Society*, Berlin/Heidelberg: Springer.

Senate Committee on Commerce, Science and Transportation (2013) *A Review of the Data Broker Industry: Collection, Use, and Sale of Consumer Data for Marketing Purposes*, available at: www.commerce.senate.gov/public/?a=Files.Serve&File_id=0d2b3642-6221-4888-a631-08f2f255b577.

Solove, D.J. (2004) *The Digital Person: Technology and Privacy in the Information Age*, New York: NYU Press.

United States Government Accountability Office (2004) *Data Mining: Federal Efforts Cover a Wide Range of Uses*, GAO-04-548, available at: www.gao.gov/new.items/ d04548. pdf.

United States Government Accountability Office (2013) *Information Resellers: Consumer Privacy Framework Needs to Reflect Changes in Technology and the Marketplace*, GAO-13-663, available at: www.gao.gov/assets/660/658151.pdf

Vedder, A. (1999) 'KDD: The Challenge to Individualism', *Ethics and Information Technology* 1, 4: 275-281.

The Verge (2014) *The Minority Report: Chicago's New Police Computer Predicts Crimes, But is it Racist?*, available at: www.theverge.com/2014/2/19/5419854/the-minority-report-this-computer-predicts-crime-but-is-it-racist.

Werkgroep Verkenning kaderwet gegevensuitwisseling (2014) *Kennis delen geeft kracht: Naar een betere èn zorgvuldigere gegevensuitwisseling in samenwerkingsverbanden*, available at: http://njb.nl/Uploads/2015/1/blg-442395.pdf.

NOTES

1 An exhaustive analysis of the legal framework within which profiling takes place is not possible in this limited space, but our main question is if this legal framework provides adequate safeguards against the risks mentioned above. The first stage of this analysis is the human rights framework. We then consider Dutch administrative law and criminal procedure.

2 Profiling by police or border control officers during security checks when based on a range of behavioural elements provides a more legitimate example of old fashioned human profiling.

3 Profiling is used in this way in our examples thus far, which is also its main actual use.

4 But Citron (2008) shows how the distinction between automated decision-making and profiling as a decision support tool can become superficial in practice. In our analysis of legal safeguards below, we focus on these uses as they entail the most risk of negative impacts.

5 We implicitly assume that the data and profiling concern persons, but this is not necessarily the case. Profiling can also concern objects, places or other phenomena. For example, profiling can be used in industrial processes to identify defective components or, in the context of customs, to discern ships or containers with a higher risk of illegal imports or places and times with a higher risk for criminal activities.

6 These methods forecast places and times with an increased risk of crime.

7 These methods identify individuals at risk of offending in the future.

8 These techniques are used to create profiles that accurately match likely offenders with specific past crimes.

9 These approaches are used to identify groups or, in some cases, individuals who are likely to become victims of crime.

10 A similar system is in use in: the 'Criminaliteits Anticipatie Systeem' (CAS).

11 But in the Court's reasoning, the expression 'in accordance with law' is compatible with the establishment of national legal regimes to regulate differential privacy interferences. When regulating 'soft' privacy interferences, national law is given greater flexibility and a wider margin of appreciation for remedies used to counter the concerned interference and its negative effects. It is not apparent from the reasoning of the Court how to classify those interferences that imply both monitoring and tracking such as profiling, data mining and Internet monitoring in general. At present, this is an open question in European case law (Galetta and De Hert 2014).

12 The margin of appreciation of the state also depends on factors like the nature and seriousness of the interests at stake and of the interference (*Peck v. United Kingdom, Z. v. Finland, Leander v. Sweden*).

13 A subsidiarity check – whether the legitimate aim could not be obtained through less intrusive and therefore more proportionate means – is found in *Peck v. United Kingdom*.

14 Although it concerned a EU citizen and was based on the prohibition of discrimination on the ground of nationality in EU law, it applied a similar reasoning as the ECtHR.

15 Data mining is sometimes presented as a guarantee against discrimination because its algorithms allow a more objective treatment by excluding human bias (Custers 2014). This view is too optimistic and forgets that such human bias can seep through at all stages of the profil-

ing process, beginning with the selection of data. Data mining algorithms will rather objectively reflect in their results the presence of such human bias in the original data. Therefore one of the main dangers linked with profiling is to make discrimination hidden and as opaque as the functioning of data mining algorithms.

16   Their description is slightly more complex than ours in section 6.1, and distinguishes between: defining 'the target variable', labeling and collecting the 'training data', 'feature selection', and making decisions on the basis of the resulting model.

17   "For the purposes of assessing whether processing is incompatible, as referred to under (1), the responsible party shall in any case take account of the following:

a. the relationship between the purpose of the intended processing and the purpose for which the data have been obtained;

b. the nature of the data concerned;

c. the consequences of the intended processing for the data subject;

d. the manner in which the data have been obtained, and

e. the extent to which appropriate guarantees have been put in place with respect to the data subject".

PART IV

REGULATORY PERSPECTIVES ON BIG DATA

7 THE INDIVIDUAL IN THE BIG DATA ERA: MOVING TOWARDS AN AGENT-BASED PRIVACY PARADIGM

Bart van der Sloot

The current human rights framework in general and the privacy paradigm in particular is based on the individual in a threefold manner: (1) it provides him with a subjective right, (2) to protect his personal interest and (3) the outcome of a court case is determined by balancing the individual against a societal interest. Big Data processes, however, do not revolve around individuals; they focus on large groups and have an impact on society in general. Consequently, the focus on the individual and his interests is becoming increasingly obsolete. To remedy this fact, privacy scholars have suggested to reformulate privacy either as a group right, a societal interest or a precondition for a democratic society. Focusing on other than individual interests obviously has an impact on the way rights and legal claims are attributed, how rules are enforced and how the outcome of legal cases is determined. This contribution discusses the different suggestions that have been put forward and determines in how far they might ameliorate the current privacy paradigm.

7.1 INTRODUCTION

Privacy has been declared dead ever since it was conceived. Already in the sixties of last century, books appeared that proclaimed the end of privacy. Mostly, such eschatological visions point either to the young, who supposedly no longer care about privacy, or to newly emerging technologies, which enable large-scale data collection, whether it be photography, telephone records, data bases, the internet or Big Data. At the same time, scholars have always claimed to 'reinvent' privacy, either by introducing new ways of emphasizing the interests at stake, arguing for a different way of protecting privacy (for example, through commodity rights or through technological regulation) or by introducing new concepts, such as informational privacy and data protection.

Perhaps this is because privacy is about boundaries, boundaries between the private and the public, between the individual and society, between individual autonomy and public rules, etc. Boundaries change over time, and the types of boundaries thought necessary differ per person, per culture and per epoch. Still, what has unified most privacy theories so far is that they focused on the protection of the individual against the collective, of the private against the public. It is exactly this presumption that is wavering in the age of Big Data: it appears to be increasingly difficult to relate the effects of Big Data processes back to individual interests. Increasingly, recourse is taken to the use of metaphors to capture what is at stake in these types of data flows.

The classic metaphor is that of the Panopticon, after the prison model of Bentham, who proposed the design of a prison in which the guard could see the prisoners but the prisoners could not see the guard (Bentham 1791). Foucault suggested that this model is archetypical for current Western society, in which everyone might be watched but is never sure about it (Foucault 1975). This will result in citizens curtailing their behaviour out of precaution, which is also known as the chilling effect. These types of theories do not focus on actual and concrete harm, but on future and hypothetical effects of current surveillance techniques.

Other theories have used metaphors to capture the increased focus on groups and categories in data processing techniques. Those pointing to the Mathew effect argue that Big Data may increase the inequality between groups in society. The use of profiles may have a stigmatizing effect: people living in certain neighbourhoods may have more trouble getting loans, people with a certain ethnic or religious background may be checked and surveilled more often, etc. Others have suggested the metaphor of a Filter Bubble (Pariser 2012), which captures the fear that people will be profiled in a particular category and will get stuck in it because they will only get news, search results and advertisements that fit that profile. These types of theories try to address the fact that the use of data is increasingly moving from the individual to the group.

Reference is also made to environmental protection (Galetta and De Hert 2014). Data is called the new oil (Kuneva 2009) and privacy the canary in the coal mine (Thatcher 2014). Others have likened privacy violations following from Big Data processes to the environmental pollution resulting from the industrial revolution (Hirsch 2014). There are certain similarities between environmental pollution and privacy violations following from Big Data. Both may have an impact on the individual as well as the environment in general. It is not for nothing that environmental laws not only allow claims by specific individuals who have suffered from personal harm, but also facilitate claims regarding damage to the environment as such. Consequently, individual rights and individual interests are complemented by class actions and general interests. With regard to individual impact, it should be noted that it is often very difficult to prove the causal relationship between, for example, air pollution and a specific health condition.

Similarly, Big Data may have an impact on both specific individuals and on the world we live in. Moreover, in individual cases, it is often difficult to determine the direct link between individual harm and Big Data processes. That is why some have argued that, in privacy laws, there should also be room for class actions in the

general interest and that privacy regulators could learn something from the more
relaxed requirements in environmental laws regarding the causality between inci-
dents and individual harm. Finally, the metaphor of Kafka's *The Trial* has often
been proposed (Solove 2008). Here the idea is simply that citizens are unsure why
the government is acting in certain ways and how this might impact them.
The point is not so much that it has a negative impact on them, but simply that
there is no way of finding out whether this is the case and that there are no safeguards against the abuse of power by the government. Again, similarities are
drawn to Big Data processes, which are often vague and incomprehensible to ordinary citizens, even if the outcome of these processes may have a serious impact on
their lives.

What has prompted these theories is that it is increasingly difficult to determine
what is exactly at stake in Big Data processes. Although everyone agrees that,
for example, there is something problematic about the NSA's data collection, it is
hard to point out what that really is, besides mere technical points of whether the
activities were prescribed by law and whether Parliament or even president Obama
knew about them. What impact, for example, has the NSA data collection had on
ordinary American or European citizens? How and in what way did it harm them?
It is also increasingly difficult to focus on individual rights, quite simply because
these large data gathering processes do not revolve around individuals. While the
legal domain focuses on the individual level, on the particular, technical reality
revolves around structural developments and focuses on the general level. Scholars are increasingly trying to develop privacy theories that solve this discrepancy,
by focusing on societal interests, group interests, etc., rather than on individual
interests. This chapter will discuss and evaluate these theories.

Section 7.2 will discuss the original privacy paradigm, which focused on the individual, his/her rights and his/her interests only in part. It will take as an example
the European Convention on Human Rights (ECHR). Section 7.3 will briefly show
that the current paradigm, by contrast, focuses on individual rights and interests
almost exclusively. Section 7.4 will argue why it might prove problematic to maintain this focus because Big Data does not revolve around individuals. The transition between the 'original' and the 'current' paradigm has been discussed in greater
detail in other publications (Van der Sloot 2014a, 2014b, 2014c, 2015a, 2015b, 2016a,
2016b); it is important to stress that the discussion here is idealized and that reality
is far muddier and more complex than a few pages can describe. There is neither a
linear process nor an exact moment in time when the transition from the 'original'
to the 'current' paradigm took place, and it is important to stress that one may still
find elements of the 'original' paradigm in current case law. Still, generally speaking, there has been an enormous change in how cases are approached under the
European Convention on Human Rights. The two idealized models will be con-
trasted in sections 7.2 and 7.3.

After section 7.4, the chapter will continue by discussing the theories that have been proposed to solve this problem. They will be loosely divided in four sections, though there is certainly some overlap. Section 7.5 will focus on theories that argue that privacy is constitutive for societal institutions, such as the healthcare sector, the legal system and journalism. Section 7.6 will discuss the aggregated, group and collective interests that relate to privacy protection. Section 7.7 will discuss theories that focus on potential and future harm, including the chilling effect. Section 7.8 will discuss theories that revolve around the (ethical) evaluation of agents, or potential privacy violators. These theories let go of the requirement of individual harm altogether and instead focus on the moral responsibilities and ethical duties of agents gathering and processing data. Finally, section 7.9 will evaluate these theories and argue that these last theories in particular might prove to be fruitful for privacy protection in the age of Big Data.

7.2   ORIGINAL PARADIGM

The European Convention on Human Rights originally focused on laying down duties and prohibitions for the states who acceded to the Convention. The ECHR provides absolute prohibitions, such as those regarding abuse of power, enacting retrospective legislation, torture and degrading treatment; it lays down rules that may only be curtailed in a state of emergency, such as the right to a fair trial, the right to petition and the right to liberty and security; and it provides conditions under which a number of rights, such as the right to privacy, the right to freedom of expression and freedom of religion, may be curtailed under the rule of law, namely if they are prescribed by law and necessary in a democratic society for the protection of national security or public order, among other things.

The main goal of the Convention was to curtail the actions of governments, to prevent abuse of power and to sanction those states that did not abide by the rules of the ECHR (Robertson 1975-1985). Consequently, its main focus was on the duties of states and only marginally on the subjective rights of individuals. Hence, not only individuals could complain before European institutions, but also states could submit inter-state complaints (Art. 24 original ECHR), and groups as well as non-governmental organizations could invoke the rights under the convention (Art. 25 original ECHR). The main focus was on protecting the general interest of a society, relating to the good and appropriate use of power by the state; this interest could be invoked by everyone, not only by direct victims of practices and laws.

It should also be noted that individuals, groups and legal persons only had the right to submit a case before the European Commission on Human Rights, whose only task it was to declare cases admissible or inadmissible. Cases declared admissible could only be brought before the Court, which did have the authority to assess the substance of the case if either the Commission or a state decided to

pursue them (Art. 48 original ECHR). This allowed them to shift between cases
that addressed only the particular interests of the individual complaint and those
cases that addressed a wider issue, impacting society in general. Individuals did not
have the right to bring a case before the Court, even if their case was declared
admissible by the Commission.

The Convention aimed to protect the general interest by focusing on the integrity
of the rule of law and the democratic process; these guarantees ensured a form of
negative freedom for citizens, groups and legal persons alike. Of all articles contained in the Convention, the rationales of negative obligations for the state and
negative freedom for individuals are most prominent in the right to privacy under
Article 8 ECHR. Already under the Universal Declaration of Human Rights, on
which the ECHR is largely based, it was this provision that was originally plainly
titled 'Freedom from wrongful interference' (UN document: E/HR/3). Likewise
under the Convention, the right to privacy was originally only concerned with
negative liberty, contrasting with other qualified rights in which positive freedoms are implicit, such as a person's freedom to manifest his/her religion or
beliefs (Art. 9 ECHR), freedom of expression (Art. 10 ECHR) and freedom of association with others (Art. 11 ECHR). Likewise, the wording of Article 8 ECHR does not
contain any positive obligation, such as, for example, under Article 2, the obligation to protect the right to life, under Article 5, to inform an arrested person of the
reason for arrest and to bring him or her promptly before a judge, under Article 6,
the obligation to ensure an impartial and effective judicial system, and under Article 3 of the First Protocol, the obligation to hold free elections (Tomlinson 2012: 2).

Finally, the way in which cases should be resolved, according to the Convention
authors, was by assessing the behaviour of the state as such. Hence the absolute
and relative prohibitions in the Convention, and hence the conditions for restricting the qualified rights, such as the right to privacy. Article 8 ECHR holds in paragraph 1 that everyone has the right to private and family life, home and communications. Paragraph 2 specifies the conditions for curtailing this right:

> "There shall be no interference by a public authority with the exercise of this right except
> such as is in accordance with the law and is necessary in a democratic society in the inter-
> ests of national security, public safety or the economic wellbeing of the country, for the
> prevention of disorder or crime, for the protection of health or morals, or for the protec-
> tion of the rights and freedoms of others."

A state, therefore, may curtail the right to privacy if this is prescribed by law, necessary in a democratic society and aimed at one of the goals specified in paragraph 2.

Note that this is a binary test: an infringement is either necessary or it is not, it is
either prescribed by law or it is not and it serves either a legitimate goal or not.
Take as an example the sanctity of one's home: if the police enters a person's house

for a good and legitimate reason, because, for example, they have reason to believe that this person has committed a murder and they want to search this house for a murder weapon, this is necessary for the protection of public order and is, therefore, legitimate. If the police enter a person's home without a legitimate reason, because the person is a famous football player, however, it is not. No balancing of interests takes place; the test is simply whether an infringement is necessary or not.

7.3   CURRENT PARADIGM

These pillars of the original paradigm have undergone significant changes over time. First, the right to complaint has been reduced to natural persons who have suffered as direct or indirect victims of a certain policy or law. Groups are not allowed to complain (only individuals who have all individually suffered from a certain practice are allowed to bundle their complaints); in principle, legal persons are prohibited from invoking the right to privacy (Van der Sloot 2015a); and so far there have only been some 20 inter-state complaints, contrasting sharply with the tens of thousands of individual complaints (Dijk et al 2006: 50). Furthermore, natural persons are only allowed to invoke the right to privacy if they are a victim and have sustained considerable harm.

This means that a number of complaints are principally rejected by the Court. So-called *in abstracto* claims are declared inadmissible in principle. These are claims that regard the mere existence of a law or a policy, without them having any concrete or practical effect on the claimant (Lawlor). *A-priori* claims are rejected as well, as the Court will usually only receive complaints about injury which has already materialized. Claims about future damage will not be considered in principle (Tauira et al.). Hypothetical claims regard damage which might have materialized but about which the claimant is unsure. The Court usually rejects such claims because it is unwilling to provide a ruling on the basis of presumed facts. Applicants must be able to substantiate their claim with concrete facts, not with beliefs and suppositions.

The ECtHR will also not receive an *actio popularis*, a case brought up by a claimant or a group of claimants, to protect not their own interests but those of others or society as a whole. These types of cases are better known as class actions (Asselbourg et al.). Finally, the Court has held that applications are rejected if the injury sustained from a specific privacy violation is not sufficiently serious, even if the matter may fall under the material scope of Article 8 ECHR. For example, a case regarding the gathering and processing of a small amount of ordinary personal data will usually not be declared admissible (see also the *de minimis* rule, Article 35

paragraph 3 (b) ECHR and Trouche, Glass and Murray). Consequently, the right to
complain has been narrowed down to natural persons who have directly and significantly been affected by a certain practice.

Second, Article 8 ECHR seems to have shifted from a right to privacy, laying down
negative obligations for the state and providing protection to the negative freedom
of citizens, to a full-fledged personality right (Van der Sloot 2015c). The element of
positive liberty was adopted quite early in a case from 1976:

> "For numerous Anglo-Saxon and French authors the right to respect for 'private life' is
> the right to privacy, the right to live, as far as one wishes, protected from publicity.
> [H]owever, the right to respect for private life does not end there. It comprises also, to a
> certain degree, the right to establish and to develop relationships with other human
> beings, especially in the emotional field for the development and fulfillment of one's own
> personality" (X. v. Iceland).

Likewise, from very early on, the Court has broken with the strictly limited focus
of the authors of the Convention on negative obligations and has accepted that
states may, under certain circumstances, be under a positive obligation to ensure
respect for the Convention. This has meant an enormously widened material
scope of the right to privacy: it has allowed the European Court of Human Rights
to deal not only with the more traditional privacy violations, such as house
searches, wire-tapping and body cavity searches, but also with the right to develop
one's sexual, relational and minority identity, the right to protect one's reputation
and honour, the right to personal development, the right of foreigners to a legal-
ized stay, the right to property and even work, the right to environmental protection and the right to have a fair and equal chance in custody cases. Consequently,
the right to privacy has shifted from a doctrine prohibiting the state to abuse its
powers, to a right of the individual to develop his/her personality and flourish to
the fullest extent; and with this, it has shifted from a doctrine protecting general
interests to one in which the core focus is on individual interests.

Finally, in most cases, the necessity test has been replaced by a balancing test,
in which the societal and the personal interests involved in a specific privacy violation are balanced and weighed against each other.

> "Establishing that the measure is necessary in a democratic society involves showing that
> the action taken is in response to a pressing social need, and that the interference with the
> rights protected is no greater than is necessary to address that pressing social need. The
> latter requirement is referred to as the test of proportionality. This test requires the Court
> to balance the severity of the restriction placed on the individual against the importance
> of the public interest" (Ovey and White 2002: 209).

The provisions under the European Convention on Human Rights and the right to privacy in particular, therefore, are no longer seen primarily as minimum principles which the state must take into account, but as relative interests of individuals which can always be overridden if a particularly weighty societal interests is at stake.

7.4   BIG DATA

Consequently, the current privacy paradigm focuses largely on the individual, his/her interests and his/her subjective right to protect those individual interests. In the field of privacy, the notion of harm has always been problematic as it is often difficult to substantiate what harm has been caused by a particular violation; what harm, for example, follows from entering a home or eavesdropping on a telephone conversation when neither objects have been stolen nor private information has been disclosed to third parties? Even so, the traditional privacy violations (house searches, telephone taps, etc.) are clearly demarcated in time, place and person, and the effects are, therefore, relatively easy to define. In the current technological environment, with developments such as Big Data, however, the notion of harm is becoming increasingly problematic. An individual is often simply unaware that his or her personal data are gathered by either fellow citizens (e.g., through the use of smart phones), by companies (e.g., by tracking cookies) or by governments (e.g., through covert surveillance). Obviously, people who are unaware of their data being gathered will not invoke their right to privacy in court.

Even if people were aware of these data collections, given the fact that data gathering and processing is currently so widespread and omnipresent and will become even more so in the future, it will quite likely be impossible for them to keep track of every data processing which includes (or might include) their data, to assess whether the data controller abides by the legal standards applicable, and if not, to file a legal complaint. And if individuals go to court to defend their rights, they have to demonstrate a personal interest, i.e. personal harm, which is a particularly problematic notion in Big Data processes: what concrete harm has data gathering by the NSA done to ordinary American or European citizens? This also shows the fundamental tension between the traditional legal and philosophical discourse and the new technological reality: while the traditional discourse focuses on individual rights and individual interests, data processing often affects a structural and societal interest and, in many ways, transcends the individual.

Finally, under the current privacy and data protection regimes, the balancing of interests is the most common way in which to resolve cases. In a concrete matter, the societal interests served with the data gathering, for example, wire-tapping someone's telephone because they are suspected of committing a murder, is weighed against the harm the wire-tapping does to their personal autonomy,

freedom or dignity. However, the balancing of interests becomes increasingly difficult in the age of Big Data, not only because the individual interest involved in a
particular case is hard to substantiate, but also because the societal interest at the
other end is increasingly difficult to specify. It is mostly unclear, for example, in
how far the large data collections by intelligence services have actually prevented
concrete terrorist attacks.

This balance is even more difficult if executed on an individual level, that is,
how the collection of the personal data of this individual (as a non-suspected person) has ameliorated national security. The same holds true for CCTV cameras
hanging on the corners of almost every street in some cities; the problem here is
not that one specific person is being recorded and that data about this identified
individual is gathered, but rather that everyone in that city is being monitored and
controlled. Perhaps more important is the fact that, with some of the large-scale
data collections, what appears to be at stake is not a relative interest, which can be
weighed against other interests, but an absolute interest. For example, the NSA
data collection is so large, has been conducted over such a long time span and
includes data about so many people that it may be said to simply qualify as abuse of
power. Abuse of power is not something that can be legitimated by its instrumentality towards a specific societal interest; it is an absolute minimum condition of
having power.

7.5   CONSTITUTIVE INTERESTS

Many authors have struggled to find an exact definition and description of privacy.
Most authors agree that the value and meaning of privacy differs over cultures,
epochs and persons. Still, the right to privacy is generally linked to underlying values such as human dignity (Benn 1984), individual autonomy (Roessler 2005) or
personal freedom (Mill 1989). This means that, in contrast to those values, the
right to privacy is commonly viewed as an instrumental and not an intrinsic value.
Solove, for example, holds that the problem with theories that ascribe an intrinsic
value to privacy is that they tend to sidestep the difficult task of articulating why
privacy is valued.

> "The difficulty with intrinsic value is that it is often hard to describe it beyond being a
> mere taste. Vanilla ice cream has intrinsic value for many people, but reasons cannot read-
> ily be given why. Individuals like vanilla ice cream, and that is about all that can
> be said. Privacy's value is often more complex than a mere taste, and it can be explained
> and articulated. Although it is possible that some forms of privacy may have intrinsic
> value, many forms of privacy are valuable primarily because of the ends they further"
> (Solove 2008: 84).

Privacy is generally described as an instrumental value, as a relative value (contrasting with absolute values, such as the prohibition of torture) and a personal
value. On this last point, there is a contrast with, among other things, freedom of

speech, which is generally said to be instrumental to individual expression and the possibility of personal development, but also to the search for truth in the marketplace of ideas and to the well-functioning of the press, which, in its turn, may be described as a precondition of a vital democracy.

Because of the points discussed in section 7.4, scholars have increasingly argued that privacy is not only instrumental towards personal values, but also constitutive of general institutions. Constitutiveness, in contrast to instrumentality, signals a necessary relationship: privacy is described as a necessary precondition for societal institutions. An example here is Spiros Simitis, who argued that privacy should be seen as a constitutive element of a democratic society (Simitis 1987). Ruth Gavison, in similar vein, held that:

> "In the absence of consensus concerning many limitations of liberty, and in view of the limits on our capacity to encourage tolerance and acceptance and to overcome prejudice, privacy must be part of our commitment to individual freedom and to a society that is committed to the protection of such freedom. Privacy is also essential to democratic government because it fosters and encourages the moral autonomy of the citizen, a central requirement of a democracy" (Gavison 1980: 455).

Of course, reference can also be made to Habermas, who argues that democracy and human rights are mutually constitutive (Habermas 1994). In these types of theories, privacy is a necessary precondition for democracy, the rule of law or a free and equal society.

Similarly, a connection between privacy and specific institutions is often made. Many of the court cases revolving around mass surveillance by secret services, for example, are initiated not only by civil society organizations protecting the right to privacy in general, but also by professional organizations protecting the specific interests of lawyers and journalists. These organizations point to the fact that both professions can only function properly if a degree of secrecy and confidentiality is guaranteed. Without secrecy between lawyers and clients, clients might not feel free to speak about sensitive issues, which leaves lawyers only partially informed and unable to defend their clients' case. This might undermine the right to a fair trial and, ultimately, the rule of law as such. Similarly, the argument is made that journalists cannot function without a form of secrecy of sources being guaranteed. Sources will not feel free to discuss sensitive matters with journalists or leak secret documents, which might ultimately undermine the position of the press as watchdog or fourth estate. The same might apply to the secrecy of ballot, a quintessential element of democratic elections (Lever 2015). Finally, a similar argument has been made with regard to patient-doctor confidentiality. Anita Allen, for example, holds:

> "First, confidentiality encourages seeking medical care. Individuals will be more inclined to seek medical attention if they believe they can do so on a confidential basis. It is reassuring to believe others will not be told without permission that one is unwell or declining,

has abused illegal drugs, been unfaithful to one's partner, obtained an abortion, or enlarged one's breasts. [...] Second, confidentiality contributes to full and frank disclosures. Individuals seeking care will be more open and honest if they believe the facts and impressions reported to health providers will remain confidential. It may be easier to speak freely about embarrassing symptoms if one believes the content of what one says will not be broadcast to the world at large" (Allen 2011: 112).

The fear is that surveillance in general and certain IT projects in the healthcare sector in particular might undermine the confidentiality required for a well-functioning healthcare sector. Reference is sometimes made to underdeveloped countries, where the fear of others finding out about a certain disease or condition is often greater than the wish to be cured, but also to the United States, where there are many fears about the influence of commercial parties and insurers.

7.6   GROUP AND COLLECTIVE INTERESTS

There are also theories that focus on the connection between individual harm and harm to others. The loss of privacy for one individual may have an impact not only on the privacy of others, but also on other important interests. It is stressed by some that a loss of privacy may undermine social relationships between individuals, which often consist of the very fact that certain information is disclosed between them and not to others. This is called the social value of privacy (Roessler and Mokrosinska 2013). But the loss of privacy for one individual may also have an impact on the privacy of others. This is commonly referred to as the network effect. A classic example is a photograph taken at a rather wild party. Although the central figure in the photograph may consent to posting the picture of him or her at this party on Facebook, it may also reveal others attending the party. This is the case with much information: people's living conditions and the value of their home does not only disclose something about them, but also about their spouse and possibly their children. Perhaps the most poignant example is that of hereditary diseases: data about such diseases might reveal sensitive information not only about a specific person, but also about their direct relatives.

Alternative theories look not only to one specific individual, but to all individuals affected by a specific violation. These theories focus on aggregated harm and primarily aim against the common practice in the legal domain of focusing on the specificities of a case, in combination with the fact that only individual victims can successfully file a complaint. What follows from this approach, according to some scholars, is a situation in which the effects of a certain law or policy are only measured and assessed with regard to its effects on the situation of a specific claimant. In reality, however, the law or policy has an effect on many, sometimes millions of people. In contrast with the individual interest at stake, the general interest, such as that relating to national security, is often assessed at a general and societal level. The question is not how the monitoring of a specific individual (the claimant) has benefited the fight against terrorism, for example, but how the mass surveillance system as such aids this goal. It might be worthwhile, consequently, to assess the negative consequences of a particular law or policy in terms of privacy on a collective level as well.

These theories, though they broaden the scope of individuals being affected, still focus on individual harm. More recent theories have proposed to transcend the focus on the individual when it comes to assessing privacy violations. Generally speaking, this might be done by focusing either on the privacy of a group or on the privacy of larger collectives and the value of privacy for society as a whole. With regard to group privacy (Taylor et al. 2016), there are generally two lines of thinking. First, much in line with the ideas of social privacy, it might be said that groups depend on a form of privacy or secrecy for their existence. Consequently, if the right to privacy is undermined, this might have an effect on the group and its existence. Second, there is an increasing trend to use group profiles not only with regard to crime fighting and the war against terrorism, but also when banks use risk profiles when deciding about loans or health insurers when deciding who to insure, against what price, etc. The fact is that decisions are increasingly made on the basis of these profiles, which might lead to discrimination and stigmatization, as well as loss of privacy. The problem is not so much that this or that specific individual is affected by being put in a certain category, whether rightly or wrongly, but that policies are based on stigmatizing or discriminating group profiles as such, and it has been suggested, therefore, that it might be worthwhile to look into the possibility of granting groups a right as such. Finally, as to the rights of future generations, it is not only a healthy living environment that may be in their best interest, but a good privacy environment may possibly be included in those interests too.

There are also those who have argued that privacy should be regarded as a public good (Fairfield and Engel 2014) or a societal interest (Van der Sloot 2014a) rather than as an individual interest or in addition to it. For example, many of the current privacy violations are taking place on such a large scale and are affecting so many people that this might qualify simply as abuse of power, undermining citizens' trust in the government and in democratic institutions. Others have stressed, in reference to the Panopticon, that the fear following from mass surveillance curtails the scope of their unfettered experimentation and their development, which is detrimental not only to those specific individuals, but also to society as a whole (Richards 2013). When discussing privacy and the common good, Priscilla Regan distinguishes between three types of values.

> "Privacy has value beyond its usefulness in helping the individual maintain his or her dignity or develop personal relationships. Most privacy scholars emphasize that the individual is better off if privacy exists; I argue that society is better off as well when privacy exists. I maintain that privacy serves not just individual interests but also common, public, and collective purposes. If privacy became less important to one individual in one particular context, or even to several individuals in several contexts, it would still be

important as a value because it serves other crucial functions beyond those that it per-
forms for a particular individual. Even if the individual interests in privacy became less
compelling, social interests in privacy might remain. [...] I suggest that three concepts provide bases for discussing a more explicitly social importance for privacy – privacy as a
common value, privacy as a public value, and privacy as a collective value. The first two
concepts are derived from normative theory, while the latter is derived from economic
theory; the styles of analysis, therefore, are different, with the first two being conceptual
and the third more technical" (Regan 1995: 211).

There is a common interest in privacy, Regan suggests, because individuals who
have privacy become more valuable not only to themselves, but also to society as a
whole. Privacy as public value is the idea that privacy is not just valuable in itself,
but is also instrumental towards other values, such as freedom of speech. Finally,
the idea of privacy as a collective value is derived from the economists' concept of
collective or public goods, which are those goods that are defined as indivisible or
non-excludable: not one member of society can enjoy the benefit of a collective
good without others also benefiting. Clean air and national defence, she suggests,
are examples of public or collective goods.

"Currently a number of policies and policy proposals treat privacy as a 'private good' and
allow people to buy back or establish the level of privacy that they wish. For example,
when you subscribe to a magazine, you can indicate that you do not want your name and
information about you incorporated in a mailing list and sold for direct-mail purposes.
Similarly, one policy proposal concerning Caller ID is that individuals be given the ability
to 'block' the display of their numbers. Such examples suggest that you can indeed
'divide' privacy into components and allow people to establish their own privacy level.
But three factors limit the effectiveness of this individual or market-based solution for
privacy: the interests of third-party record holders; the nonvoluntary nature of many
record-keeping relationships; and computer and telecommunication technologies"
(Regan 1995: 228).

7.7   POTENTIAL HARM

There is a third branch of privacy theories that focuses not on actual and concrete
harm at the individual level, but on potential harm. This might be either hypothetical harm or potential future harm. Hypothetical harm can exist when people
might be affected by a certain privacy violation but are unsure about this. The classic example is the potential privacy violation following from the mass surveillance
activities of secret services. As those services usually remain silent about their
practices, victims are often unaware of the fact that they might be affected by these
practices. Normally, people who cannot substantiate their claim that they have
been harmed by a certain practice will not be able to successfully submit a complaint. However, the European Court of Human Rights has stressed that it will
make an exception in these types of cases because it will not accept that the mere
fact that someone is kept unaware of his or her victim-status will result their
remaining powerless to challenge those practices and policies. It has stressed that if
people fit a category specifically mentioned in a law or policy or if people engage in
certain activities which give them reason to believe that they might be subjected to
surveillance activities, this might be enough to accept their victim status (Van der

Sloot 2016a). Besides hypothetical harm, increasing attention is being paid to future harm. This again may be divided into two lines of thought: the one focusing on potential future harm and the other focusing on harm following from self-restraint, also known as the chilling effect. The first category focuses on the possibility that certain harm might occur in the future. Although data, power or techniques may not be abused right now, for example, they may be abused in the future, especially if there are insufficient safeguards. Ultimately, the Second World War hypothesis is applied: imagine that a Nazi-like regime were to seize power; would it not, so the argument goes, be rather simple for such a regime to execute its evil policies if it had access to all the data gathered and stored right now, including racial data? The same argument may be applied to companies such as Facebook and Google, who may do no evil right now but might do so in the future, if their owners or board members change.

There is also increasing attention being paid to future harm in the legal domain, for example, in the proposed General Data Protection Regulation. This will presumably contain rules on privacy impact assessments, which specify that where processing operations present specific risks to the rights and freedoms of data subjects by virtue of their nature, their scope or their purposes, the controller shall carry out an assessment of the impact of the envisaged processing operations on the protection of personal data. This is so when data controllers process privacy-sensitive data. The idea of privacy impact assessments has been borrowed from the domain of environmental law, where such assessments have already been introduced. Such impact assessments may pertain to potential future harm on an individual level or on a societal level and on legal, social or ethical consequences alike.

There is a slight difference with regard to the type of harm that is at the heart of these types of assessments. The Second World War argument stresses that, although there may be no reason now to believe that harm may take place or that power has been abused, you never know for sure. Impact assessments, by contrast, focus on the type of harm that is reasonably foreseeable but ignores the unknown unknowns.

Second, future harm might lie in self-restricting behaviour, that is, when people know that they might be surveilled and possibly punished for their behaviour or face other negative consequences. If people know that confidential information may fall into the hands of third parties, they may feel restrained to experiment freely as they know that they might be confronted with their 'mistakes' in the future. Obviously, this fear also underlies the introduction of the hotly debated right to be forgotten. What proponents of this doctrine argue is that children and adolescents may want to experiment freely in life with hairstyles, alcohol or sex, without them being haunted for the rest of their lives by a certain Facebook tag,

Instagram photo or Youtube video. Not only would this limit their future social, societal and financial perspectives, but they might also choose not to experiment altogether if they know that it is impossible to keep those experiments secret.

This is known in legal terms as the chilling effect, which is also increasingly accepted by the European Court of Human Rights as regards data processing. A good example may be the case of Colon v. the Netherlands, in which the applicant complained that the designation of a security-risk area by the Burgomaster of Amsterdam violated his right to privacy as it enabled a public prosecutor to conduct random searches of people in a large area over an extensive period without this mandate being subject to any judicial review. The government, on the contrary, argued that the designation of a security-risk area or the issuing of a stop-and-search order had not in itself constituted an interference with the applicant's private life or liberty of movement. After the event the applicant complained of, several preventive search operations had been conducted, and in none of them had the applicant been subjected to further attempts to search him. This was, according to the government, enough to show that the likelihood of an interference with the applicant's rights was so minimal that this deprived him of the status of being a victim.

The Court stressed again that, in principle, it did not accept *in abstracto* claims or an *actio popularis*.

> "In principle, it is not sufficient for individual applicants to claim that the mere existence of the legislation violates their rights under the Convention; it is necessary that the law should have been applied to their detriment. Nevertheless, Article 34 entitles individuals to contend that legislation violates their rights by itself, in the absence of an individual measure of implementation, if they run the risk of being directly affected by it; that is, if they are required either to modify their conduct or risk being prosecuted, or if they are members of a class of people who risk being directly affected by the legislation" (Colon v. Netherlands § 60).

It went on to stress that it was:

> "not disposed to doubt that the applicant was engaged in lawful pursuits for which he might reasonably wish to visit the part of Amsterdam city centre designated as a security risk area. This made him liable to be subjected to search orders should these happen to coincide with his visits there. The events of 19 February 2004, followed by the criminal prosecution occasioned by the applicant's refusal to submit to a search, leave no room for doubt on this point. It follows that the applicant can claim to be a 'victim' within the meaning of Article 34 of the Convention and the Government's alternative preliminary objection must be rejected also" (Colon v. Netherlands § 61).

Consequently, the Court accepted that the chilling effect in itself may be enough to meet the victim requirement under the Convention. No concrete harm is required in those instances.

7.8   ABSTRACT TESTS

There is a fourth and final branch of privacy theories that proposes to leave the focus on harm altogether. Scholars have increasingly proposed to move away from classic liberal theories focusing on (individual) harm, because to stay within this paradigm, theories are stretching the notion of harm to the point where it becomes forced and far-fetched. A Second World War scenario is perhaps the most poignant target of such critiques, but the focus on hypothetical and future harm serves the point all the same. The problem with Big Data programmes appears to be not individuals and their interests, but the fact that companies, states or even individuals have certain powers, have access to certain techniques, are in possession of certain types of data, as such. The fourth branch of theories, therefore, suggests not to focus on the 'patient' – the individual being acted upon and potentially violated in his or her privacy – but on the 'agent', the one acting upon the individual and potentially violating his or her privacy.

These types of theories are called agent-based theories. They focus on the behaviour and the character of agents and evaluate them on the basis of either legal or ethical principles. Theories that have been proposed focus, for example, on the existence of power rather than its abuse (real or potential), on the possession of certain data rather than its link to specific individuals, and on the access to certain techniques rather than their actual use or application.

First, with regard to abuse of power, it should be noted that there are certain doctrines in the legal realm that seek to prevent such abuse. Article 18 ECHR, for example, specifies: "The restrictions permitted under this Convention to the said rights and freedoms shall not be applied for any purpose other than those for which they have been prescribed." This is a restriction on abuse of power by states. The curious thing, however, is that the European Court of Human Rights has said that this doctrine can only be invoked by an individual claimant if he or she is curtailed in exercising one or more of his or her individual rights, such as the right to privacy or freedom of expression. The article cannot, however, be invoked independently, to address abuse of power that has had no direct impact on specific individual rights.

It is interesting to see that the Court has made one prominent exception to its strict focus on individual rights and interests: cases that revolve around mass surveillance activities by governmental institutions (see more in detail Van der Sloot 2016a). In such cases, the Court accepts *in abstracto* claims, which revolve around the conduct of states as such, without any harm needing to be demonstrated. Consequently, not only individuals, but also legal persons and civil society organizations may submit a complaint. Because there is no individual harm, the Court cannot determine the outcome of the case by balancing the different interests involved. Rather, it determines whether the surveillance activity was prescribed by law. As these activities are often prescribed by law, the Court has introduced an additional requirement, namely that the law must provide for sufficient safeguards against abuse of power. These safeguards may entail rules on transparency and oversight by either a judge, parliament or an oversight committee. States can be held in violation of the ECHR not only if they have abused their powers, negatively impacting individuals, but also if they have insufficient safeguards in place to prevent such abuse.

In a similar vein, it has been argued that not only the possession of power as such requires certain safeguards, but also the possession of certain types of data. Currently, legal instruments in principle only provide protection to private, privacy-sensitive and personal data: these types of data have a direct link to individuals and can be used to directly affect them. Sensitive data, such as relating to health and sexual or political preferences, are protected to a greater extent because they can be used in a way that has an even greater impact on the individual (Article 8 DPD). In the current technological environment, however, the direct connection of data to an individual is becoming less evident. Data increasingly have a circular life cycle: they may begin as individual data, then be linked to other data so they become sensitive data, then be aggregated and anonymized in a group profile and then a specific individual may finally be linked to the group profile. Consequently, the status of the data and the question of whether they can be linked to an individual at one specific moment is becoming less important. More important is the quality of the data as such, without them necessarily being linked to specific individuals. It has been suggested, therefore, that the sensitivity of the data or dataset itself should be the main determinant for data regulation (Van der Sloot 2015a: footnote 114).

Finally, a similar argument has been made with regard to technology. It has been argued, for example, that it is not so important how a specific technology is used in practice, but rather the capacity of the technology itself. Such theories argue that the core question should be:

> "whether an investigative technique or technology has the capacity to facilitate broad programs of indiscriminate surveillance that raise the specter of a surveillance state if deployment and use of that technology is left to the unfettered discretion of government. We think that the Fourth Amendment and the privacy issues at stake, as we have described them here, suggest taking a different tack. There are a number of ways that the Fourth Amendment status of a surveillance technique or technology could be determined. The most obvious would be for anyone who knows that he or she has been subject to surveillance by a novel technology, or dramatically improved existing technology, to file a civil suit seeking equitable relief or even damages. In such an action, a court would first need to determine whether the technology at issue should be subject to Fourth Amendment regulation. Among the important factors that a court would need to consider are: (1) the inherent scope of a technology's surveillance capabilities, be they narrow or broad; (2) the technology's scale and scalability; and (3) the costs associated with deploying and using the technology. If a court finds that a challenged technology is capable of broad and indiscriminate surveillance by its nature, or is sufficiently inexpensive

and scalable so as to present no practical barrier against its broad and indiscriminate use, then granting law enforcement unfettered access to that technology would violate reasonable expectations of quantitative privacy" (Gray and Citron 2013: 101-102).

Following this line of thinking, access to the technology and the scope and reach of the technology or technical infrastructure become the main points for a regulatory approach.

Two theories have been put forward that try to give such privacy theories an ethical foundation: the republican theory and the virtue ethical theory. Both are agent-based theories that focus on the capacities or the character of the agent as such. Republicanism, in contrast to liberalism, does not view matters as problematic if they affect a specific individual, but it does if an agent possesses power without there being sufficient checks and balances. Roberts, for example, notes that:

> "republicans are concerned about interference, but not interference per se. Concern is reserved for others' capacity to interfere in an agent's choices on an arbitrary basis. The individual who suffers such interference is at the mercy of the agent or agency that has power to interfere. But while such interference will always constitute domination – to a greater or lesser extent, depending on the nature of the interference – a person need not interfere with another's choices in order to exercise dominating control. If an agent or agency has the power to interfere arbitrarily in an individual's choices, freedom is diminished even if the power is never exercised" (Roberts 2014: 6).

What is at the core here is the idea that others should never have the capacity to interfere arbitrarily in another person's choices. This is wrong even without power being actually abused. Virtue theory also proposes to evaluate the ethical conduct of agents such as states, but it goes a step further. It not only stresses that states should not abuse their powers and have sufficient safeguards in place against abuse, but it also provides that states must use their powers in such a way that the lives of citizens are facilitated in their potential to grow on a personal, social or professional level. There is not only a negative obligation to abstain from harming individuals or a positive obligation to prevent harm, but also a positive obligation to help individuals to flourish to an optimum extent (Van der Sloot 2014c).

It should come as no surprise that ethical theories have gained in prominence, given the fact that there is increasing doubt whether legal rules as such, or at least black letter law, could effectively regulate Big Data. Ethical codes, codes of conduct, self-regulation and soft law are more and more proposed as viable alternatives. As has been stressed, many of the problems following from Big Data processes concern general, systemic and societal issues, larger trends that impact society as a whole and potentially have an impact on future generations. These matters are a combination of legal and ethical concerns, and it often proves to be difficult to capture those concerns in legal rules because these questions belong to the political rather than the legal realm.

This ties up with the fact that the enforcement of legal rules is becoming increasingly difficult, because it is increasingly difficult to pinpoint which types of data should be regulated, because it is difficult in Big Data processes to determine who is responsible for what types of data processing activities, because of the territoriality principle, which is difficult to uphold, etc. As the data processing domain is increasingly transnationalizing, this brings with it that different types of norms are endorsed: privacy norms differ largely between different regions and continents. This is why many scholars and privacy advocates have promoted non-legal solutions and codes of conducts, focusing on agreement over underlying ethical principles rather than hard legal rules.

7.9   ANALYSIS

This chapter has argued that the original privacy paradigm focused only partially on the individual, his or her interests and the subjective rights of natural persons. The current privacy paradigm, however, focuses almost exclusively on protecting individual interests; it grants subjective rights to individuals, and the outcome of cases is determined by balancing the individual with the societal interest at stake. This paradigm is wavering because Big Data processes do not revolve around individuals but affect large groups and potentially society as a whole. It is increasingly difficult to link the effects of such processes back to individual interests; it is increasingly difficult for individuals to claim their subjective right in a world where data processing is so endemic; and the balance of interests is difficult to maintain because both the individual and the societal interests at stake are increasingly difficult to capture. This chapter has subsequently discussed several theories that try to find a solution for the discrepancy between the legal domain, which focuses on the individual, and technical reality, which focuses on general and systemic data collection and processing. These have been loosely divided into four categories.

Those theories focusing on the constitutive nature of privacy argue that confidentiality is a necessary precondition for certain societal institutions, such as the medical sector, the legal professions and (investigative) journalism. Those focusing on group and social or societal interests try to reformulate the right to privacy and raise it to a higher level, that is, to an aggregated, a group or a societal level. There are also theories that focus on hypothetical harm, i.e. situations in which people may have been harmed by a certain practice but are unsure of it, on potential future harm, which may be prevented and forestalled through impact assessments, and on chilling effects, the idea that people will restrain their behaviour beforehand if they know that they might be watched or controlled. Finally, there are theories that do not focus on citizens or the person affected by Big Data processes, but on the agent or the one executing the Big Data process. The question is simply whether the agent has power, has access to certain data or is in the position to use certain techniques. If so, certain rules and conditions, checks and balances should be installed.

Each of these theories has appealing facets, but they also have specific downsides. With theories focusing on the constitutionality of privacy towards societal institutions, the downside is twofold. First, the value of privacy is primarily explained in relation to the value of societal institutions, and the value of privacy itself is moved into the background. Second, these theories do not focus on privacy as such but rather on confidentiality. There is an obvious overlap between the two concepts, but privacy is far wider than the mere right to keep things secret.

Theories focusing on group rights and societal interests run into a number of practical problems in terms of granting rights: who should protect the interests at stake and invoke, for example, a group right to privacy? This is problematic because a group formed through group profiles is generally unstable; the group is mostly unaware of the very fact that it is a group; there is no hierarchy or leadership nor a legal representative of the group; and there is no way to determine what is in the interest of the group, as the interests may differ from group member to group member.

Theories focusing on hypothetical and potential future harm have the problem that they tend to become too hypothetical, unrealistic and far-fetched; particularly the Second World War scenario faces this criticism. However, also the chilling effect and future and hypothetical harm are in a way forced attempts to stay within the liberal paradigm, focusing on (individual) harm, while the strength of this approach is waning. In agent-based theories, finally, the concept of privacy is moved into the background and is replaced by a focus on power and safeguards against abuse. It runs the risk, therefore, of no longer being a privacy theory.

Still, the latter type of theories may provide the most fruitful ground for future privacy regulation. In agent-based theories, the focus is no longer on concrete individual interests, but on the general interest of being protected against abuse of power and on the positive obligation of states to use their power to facilitate human flourishing. No balancing of interests takes place, but an intrinsic assessment is applied to evaluate the behaviour, power and actions of states, companies or even citizens, and this requires checks and balances to be in place against abuse of power. An intrinsic assessment could address many of the current privacy and data protection issues, without having to link them back to individual interests. Under an agent-based privacy paradigm, there is no need to attribute privacy claims to natural persons; rather, it facilitates claims in the general interest (class actions) and in abstracto claims. This model has the further advantage of lending itself to non-legal forms of regulation, such as codes of conduct.

It should be stressed that agent-based theories do not require a totally new approach to privacy; rather they resemble in many ways the original privacy paradigm as designed by the authors of the European Convention on Human Rights. It should also be pointed out that the European Court of Human Rights is already willing to relax its focus on individual rights and individual harm when exceptional circumstances apply; in such circumstances, it takes into account chilling effects, future harm, hypothetical harm and *in abstracto* claims. Whether the current paradigm still stands and marginal exceptions are made or whether it is slowly developing into its third phase is still unsure.

What is important, however, is that there are leads in European jurisprudence for national regulators to develop an alternative privacy paradigm that is based on an agent-based instead of a patient-based approach (Van der Sloot 2016a). Obviously, this 'new' or alternative paradigm would need to co-exist with the current paradigm. The current paradigm is very suitable for tackling traditional privacy violations targeting individuals or small groups. The new or alternative paradigm should be installed next to the current paradigm in order to be able to tackle the new privacy challenges following from new technological realities, especially in connection with Big Data.

It has several benefits to let go of the victim requirement, of the notion of harm and of the focus on personal interests. Regulation is now primarily concerned with two phases in which a link with the individual and his or her interests can be made. The first phase is the gathering and storage of personal data. There are numerous data protection rules linked to this moment, for example, the data minimalization principle, the requirement that the data should be correct and up to date, the requirement of a fair and legitimate processing ground and, derived from that, the purpose limitation principle; furthermore, there are rules on storing data safely and confidentially and the obligation to inform data subjects of their data being processed. The second phase is when profiles and correlations drawn from the data analysis process are applied in practice and have an effect on individual citizens. There are rules on automatic decision-making, on fair and non-discriminatory treatment and specific rules regarding redlining, bank loans and health insurance. This approach has three disadvantages that an agent-based approach may tackle:

1. The material demarcation of the right to privacy and data protection is linked to personal interests, namely when private, privacy-sensitive or personal data are processed. However, increasing use is made of metadata, group data and aggregated data; in principle, these types of data fall outside the scope of privacy and data protection laws because they do not identify a particular individual. Still, they can be used to significantly affect a person's life, and even metadata can give a detailed picture of someone's life. Aggregated and non-personal data may also be linked to other data and datasets at a later stage and thus

become personal or even sensitive data. This focus on personal data, consequently, is no longer working in Big Data processes. Letting go of the focus on
the individual, an agent-based approach could shift the focus from the question whether data identify a certain person to the question whether possession
of data gives an entity a certain type of power. This would allow the inclusion
of non-personal data, metadata and group data alike.

2. As has already been stressed several times in this chapter, the focus of current
regulations is primarily on effects on the individual, whereas Big Data processes often have an effect on society as such and on societal institutions.
An agent-based approach to privacy regulation would take into account these
broader and more abstract interests as well.

3. The current regulations focus on the moment when personal data are gathered
and the moment when the use of data processing has an effect on concrete
individuals. The phase in between, however, when data are analyzed and
aggregated, and when algorithms search for patterns and statistical correlations
are signalled, is mostly left out of the equation, partly because the individual
element and interest is mostly absent from this phase. Data analysis tends to
revolve around large quantities of aggregated data, and the group profiles gathered usually depend on characteristics that apply to many persons, for
example, 'people using felt under their chair legs are more prone to paying
their debts than those who do not', and the statistical correlations usually use
categories with a high n. This phase, however, is becoming increasingly important because, in reality, this is where the most substantial decisions are made
and conclusions are drawn. An agent-based approach to privacy regulation
could install a number of rules, such as on the transparency of the process,
rules on which algorithms may be used, how datasets may be integrated, what
kind of methodology is used for the research, etc.

There are also some other, more practical advantages of the agent-based approach:

4. An agent-based approach could focus on ethical choices that are made by
agents as such, without actual, hypothetical or future individual harm needing
to be in play. Referring to the previous point, if a bank chooses to use a profile
based on race, whether directly or indirectly through redlining, this could be
addressed as such because it is an ethically wrong decision and a wrong way to
use power. Similarly, if the police primarily gather data around neighbourhoods with a high number of immigrants, it would be wrong for them to draw
general conclusions from this data because it is biased. An agent-based theory
may also include positive rules on the use of power: that it should be used in a
way that promotes the human flourishing of citizens.

5. Currently, citizens are often unaware of the very fact that their data are gathered; it is virtually impossible for ordinary citizens to assess all data-processing
initiatives, to check whether they contain any of their personal data, whether
the processing of personal data is conducted fairly and legitimately and, if not,

to go to court and find redress; it may be difficult to substantiate individual harm. An agent-based privacy approach would allow for class actions on behalf of specific individuals, groups or society as a whole.

6. Currently, there is a problem in the enforcement of legal instruments that mostly consist of hard rules and black letter law. This has three disadvantages: First, these types of rules tend to become more outdated more quickly than general duties of care. Second, black letter laws can be circumvented more easily because their scope and definition is often more precise than soft law rules. Third, there are enormous differences between black letter laws in different countries and continents, and companies can locate their headquarters in places with the least regulatory burden. The agent-based approach to privacy regulation would allow for an additional focus on soft law, general ethical rules and general duties of care.

REFERENCES

Allen, A.L. (2011) *Unpopular Privacy: What Must We Hide*, Oxford: Oxford University Press.

Andrejevic, M. (2014) 'The Big Data Divide', *International Journal of Communication* 8.

Benn, S.I. (1984) 'Privacy, Freedom, and Respect for Persons', pp. 223-244 in F. Schoeman (ed.) *Philosophical Dimensions of Privacy: an Anthology*, Cambridge: Cambridge University Press.

Bentham, J. (1971) *Panopticon; or the Inspection-House*, Dublin.

Bollier, D. (2010) 'The Promise and Peril of Big Data', available at: www.emc.com/collateral/analyst-reports/10334-ar-promise-peril-of-big-data.pdf.

Boyd, D. and K. Crawford (2011) 'Six Provocations for Big Data', available at: http://papers.ssrn.com/sol3/papers.cfm?abstract_id=1926431.

Busch, L. (2014) 'A Dozen Ways to Get Lost in Translation: Inherent Challenges in Large Scale Data Sets', *International Journal of Communication* 8.

Craig T. and M.E. Ludloff (2011) *Privacy and Big Data: The Players, Regulators and Stakeholders*, Sebastopol: O'Reilly Media.

Crawford, K. and J. Schultz (2014) 'Big Data and Due Process: Toward a Framework to Redress Predictive Privacy Harms', *Boston College Law Review* 55, 93.

Custers, B. et al. (eds.) (2013) *Discrimination and Privacy in the Information Society: Effects of Data Mining and Profiling Large Databases*, Berlin: Springer.

Davis, D. and D. Patterson (2012) 'Ethics of Big Data: Balancing Risk and Innovation', available at: www.commit-nl.nl/sites/default/files/Ethics%20of%20Big%20Data_0.pdf.

Dijk, P. van, F. van Hoof, A. van Rijk and L. Zwaak (eds.) (2006) 'Theory and Practice of the European Convention on Human Rights',pp. 50 in *Intersentia*, Antwerpen.

Driscoll, K. and S. Walker (2014) 'Working Within a Black Box: Transparency in the Collection and Production of Big Twitter Data', *International Journal of Communication* 8.

Dusseault, P.-L. (2013) 'Privacy and Social Media in the Age of Big Data: Report of the Standing Committee on Access to Information, Privacy and Ethics', available at: www.parl.gc.ca/content/hoc/Committee/411/ETHI/Reports/RP6094136/ethirp05/ethirp05-e.pdf.

Fairfield, J. and C. Engel (2014) *Privacy as Public Good*, available at: http://papers.ssrn.com/sol3/papers.cfm?abstract_id=2418445.

Feinberg, J. (1984) *Harm to Others*, New York: Oxford University Press.

Fletcher, G. P. (1979) 'Privacy as Legality', in *Liberty and the Rule of Law*, College Station, Texas A&M University Press.

Foucault, M. (1975) *Surveiller et punir: naissance de la prison*, Paris: Gallimard.

Galetta, A. and P. De Hert (2014) 'Complementing the Surveillance Law Principles of the
ECtHR with Its Environmental Law Principles: An Integrated Technology
Approach to a Human Rights Framework for Surveillance', *Utrecht Law
Review* 10, 1.

Gavison, R. (1980) 'Privacy and the Limits of Law', *Yale Law Journal* 89.

Goffman, E. (1959) *The Presentation of Self in Everyday Life*, Garden City: Doubleday and
Company.

Gray, D. and D. Citron (2013) 'The Right to Quantitative Privacy', *Minnesota Law Review*
98, 62.

Habermas, J. (1994) 'Über den internen Zusammenhang zwischen Rechtsstaat und
Demokratie' in U.K. Preuß (ed.) *Zum Begriff der Verfassung, Die Ordnung des
Politischen*, Frankfurt am Main.

Hirsch, D. (2014) 'The Glass House Effect: Big Data, The New Oil and The Power of
Analogy', *Maine Law Review* 66: 373-396.

Hoofnagle, C.J. (2013) 'How the Fair Credit Reporting Act Regulates Big Data', available at:
http://papers.ssrn.com/sol3/papers.cfm?abstract_id=2432955.

International Working Group on Data Protection in Telecommunications (2014) 'Working
Paper on Big Data and Privacy, Privacy Principles under Pressure in the Age of Big
Data Analytics', 55th Meeting 5-6 May, Skopje.

Kitchin, R. (2014) *The Data Revolution: Big Data, Data Infrastructures and Their
Consequences*, Los Angeles: Sage.

Kuneva, M. (2009) 'Keynote Speech, Roundtable on Online Data Collection, Targeting and
Profiling', available at: http://europa.eu/rapid/press-
release_SPEECH-09-156_en.htm.

Lever, A. (2015) 'Privacy and Democracy: What the Secret Ballot Reveals', *Law, Culture and
Humanities* 11, 2.

McAfee, A. and E. Brynjolfsson (2012) 'Big Data: The Management Revolution: Exploiting
Vast New Flows of Information Can Radically Improve Your Company's
Performance. But First You'll Have to Change Your Decision Making Culture',
Harvard Business Review October.

Mill, J.S. (1989) *On Liberty' and Other Writings*, Cambridge: Cambridge University Press.

Mayer-Schönberger, V. and K. Cukier (2013) *Big Data: A Revolution That Will Transform
How We Live, Work and Think*, Boston: Houghton Mifflin Harcourt.

Pariser, E. (2012) *The Filter Bubble: What the Internet Is Hiding From You*, London: Penguin
Books.

Payton, T.M. and T. Claypoole (2014) *Privacy in the Age of Big Data: Recognizing Threats,
Defending Your Rights, and Protecting Your Family*, Plymouth: Rowman and
Littlefield.

Ovey, C and R.C.A White (2002) *The European Convention on Human Rights*, Oxford:
Oxford University Press.

Richards, N.M. (2013) 'The Dangers of Surveillance', *Harvard Law Review*, available at:
http://harvardlawreview.org/2013/05/the-dangers-of-surveillance/.

Richards, N.M. and J.H. King (2014a) 'Three Paradoxes of Big Data', *66 Stanford Law Review* online 44.

Richards, N.M. and J.H. King (2014b) 'Big Data Ethics', *Wake Forest Law Review* 49.

Puschmann, C. and J. Burgess (2014) 'Metaphors of Big Data', *International Journal of Communication* 8.

Regan, P.M. (1995) *Legislating Privacy: Technology, Social Values and Public Policy*, Chapel Hill: University of North Carolina Press.

Roberts, A. (2014) 'A Republican Account of the Value of Privacy', *European Journal of Political Theory* 14, 3: 320-344.

Robertson, G. (ed.) (1985) *Collected Edition of the 'Travaux Préparatoires' of the European Convention on Human Rights/Council of Europe = Recueil des travaux préparatoires de la Convention européenne des droits de l'homme / Conseil de l'Europe*, The Hague: Martinus Nijhoff.

Roessler, B. (2005) *The Value of Privacy*, Cambridge: Polity.

Roessler, B. and D. Mokrosinska (2013) 'Privacy and Social Interaction', *Philosophy Social Criticism* 39, 8.

Roessler, B. and D. Mokrosinska (eds.) (2015) 'Social Dimensions of Privacy: Interdisciplinary Perspectives', Cambridge: Cambridge University Press.

Rubinstein, I. (2012) *Big Data: The End of Privacy or a New Beginning?*, NYU School of Law, Public Law Research Paper 12-56.

Simitis, S. (1987) 'Reviewing Privacy in an Information Society', *University of Pennsylvania Law Review* 135, 3.

Sloot, B. van der (2014a) *Privacy in the Post-NSA Era: Time for a Fundamental Revision?*, JIPITEC, 1.

Sloot, B. van der (2014b) 'Do Data Protection Rules Protect the Individual and Should They? An Assessment of the Proposed General Data Protection Regulation', *International Data Privacy Law*, 4.

Sloot, B. van der (2014c) 'Privacy as Human Flourishing: Could a Shift towards Virtue Ethics Strengthen Privacy Protection in the Age of Big Data?', JIPITEC 3.

Sloot, B. van der (2015a) 'Do Privacy and Data Protection Rules Apply to Legal Persons and Should They? A Proposal for a Two-Tiered System', *Computer Law and Security Review* 1.

Sloot, B. van der (2015b) 'How to Assess Privacy Violations in the Age Of Big Data? Analysing the Three Different Tests Developed by the ECtHR and Adding for a Fourth One', *Information and Communication Technology Law* 1.

Sloot, B. van der (2015c) 'Privacy as Personality Right: Why the ECtHR's Focus on Ulterior Interests Might Prove Indispensable in the Age of 'Big Data'', *Utrecht Journal of International and European Law* 80.

Sloot, B. van der (2016a) 'Is the Human Rights Framework Still Fit for the Big Data Era? A Discussion of the ECtHR's Case Law on Privacy Violations Arising from Surveillance Activities' in S. Gutwirth et al. (eds.) *Data Protection on the Move, Law, Governance and Technology*, Series 24.

Sloot, B. van der (2016b) 'Privacy as Virtue: Searching for a New Privacy Paradigm in the Age of Big Data' in *Passau Conference book* (forthcoming).

Solove, D. (2008) *Understanding Privacy*, Cambridge: Harvard University Press.

Stevenson, D.D. and N.J. Wagoner (2014) 'Bargaining in the Shadow of Big Data', *Florida Law Review* 66, 5.

Taylor, L.L. Floridi and B. van der Sloot (eds.) (2016) *Group Privacy*, Springer (forthcoming).

Tene, O. and J. Polonetsky (2013) 'Big Data for All: Privacy and User Control in the Age of Analytics', *Northwestern Journal of Technology and Intellectual Property* 11, 5: 239-273.

Thatcher, J. (2014) 'Big Data, Big Questions. Living on Fumes: Digital Footprints, Data Fumes, and the Limitations of Spatial Big Data', *International Journal of Communication* 8: 1765-1783.

Tomlinson, H. (2012) 'Positive Obligations under the European Convention on Human Rights', available at: http://bit.ly/17U9TDa.

Legal documents and case law

Charter of Fundamental Rights of the European Union (2000/C 364/01).

Convention for the Protection of Human Rights and Fundamental Freedoms, Rome, 4.XI. 1950.

Directive 95/46/EC of the European Parliament and of the Council of 24 October 1995 on the Protection of Individuals with Regard to the Processing of Personal Data and on the Free Movement of Such Data, *Official Journal L 281 , 23/11/1995 P. 0031-0050*.

ECmHR, Glass v. The United Kingdom, Application no. 28485/95, 16 October 1996.

ECmHR, Tauira and Others v. France, Application no. 28204/95, 4 December 1995.

ECmHR, Trouche v. France, Application no. 19867/92, 1 September 1993.

ECmHR, X. v. Iceland, Application no. 6825/74, 18 May 1976.

ECtHR, Asselbourg and 78 Others and Greenpeace Association-Luxembourg v. Luxembourg, application no. 29121/95, 29 June 1999.

ECtHR, Colon v. The Netherlands, Application no. 49458/06, 15 May 2012.

ECtHR, Lawlor v. the United Kingdom, Application no. 12763/87, 14 July 1988.

ECtHR, Murray v. The United Kingdom, Application no. 14310/88, 10 December 1991.

General Data Protection Regulation, available at: http://ec.europa.eu/justice/data-protection/document/review2012/com_2012_11_en.pdf.

8 PRIVACY PROTECTION IN THE ERA OF 'BIG DATA': REGULATORY CHALLENGES AND SOCIAL ASSESSMENTS

Colin J. Bennett & Robin M. Bayley

It is commonly assumed that the phenomenal and rapid expansion in the capacities of computing technology has entailed fundamental and qualitative changes in the 'volume, variety and velocity' of data processing (US Executive Office of the President 2014). We are told that we live in a 'data-driven society', in which ubiquitous data collection from a bewildering variety of observational technologies is fundamentally changing organizational life and human values in revolutionary ways. As the US Executive Office of the President concluded in a recent report (2014: 54):

> "Whether born analog or digital, data is being reused and combined with other data in ways never before thought possible, including for uses that go beyond the intent motivating initial collection. The potential future value of data is driving a digital land grab, shifting the priorities of organizations to collect and harness as much data as possible. Companies are now constantly looking at what kind of data they have and what data they need in order to maximize their market position. In a world where the cost of data storage has plummeted and future innovation remains unpredictable, the logic of collecting as much data as possible is strong."

For all the hype around the 'Big Data revolution', we have to remember that the last fifty years have ushered in numerous claims about the revolutionary nature and potential of new technologies. If we can be persuaded that revolutions are occurring, we can also be persuaded to jump on board for fear of losing economic advantage or social esteem. 'Revolutions' don't just emerge, they are constructed. And more often than not, these claims make simplistic assumptions about the trajectories of technological development, and gloss over complex social, political and economic assumptions. The messy, contradictory and ambiguous character of technological change is quite often simplified in the rush to encapsulate the present and extrapolate the future within a catchy phrase.

'Big Data' is a socio-technical phenomenon that rests on a good deal of mythology (Boyd and Crawford 2012). It is not a precise scientific concept, but a highly contested idea that means different things depending on who is talking about it. There is not, and will never be, any consensus on what 'Big Data' means, nor on how its processing differs from the data analytical techniques of the past. There is no clear threshold at which point 'data' becomes 'Big Data'. It is a highly fashionable, and, therefore, inherently suspect idea that encompasses a complex array of technologies, practices and interests. 'Big Data' in and of itself means nothing and signifies nothing in the absence of a wider understanding of the organizations that are conducting the analysis, and an assessment of those organizations' wider interests and motives.

The fundamental epistemology of Big Data is inductive, where data analysis is conducted without the benefit of a guiding hypothesis. The data itself, according to Mayer-Schönberger and Cukier, reveals the patterns; the human reasoning and judgment about causation comes afterwards (2013: ch. 4). Deductive methods, according to these authors, constrain the power of the data to find patterns that would not otherwise be discovered. They offer several illustrations (2013: 55):

> "No longer do we necessarily require a valid substantive hypothesis about a phenomenon to begin to understand the world. Thus, we don't have to develop a notion about what terms people search for when and where the flu spreads. We don't need to have an inkling of how airlines price their tickets. We don't need to care about the culinary tastes of Walmart shoppers. Instead we can subject Big Data to correlation analysis and let it tell us what search queries are the best proxies for the flu, whether an airfare is likely to soar, or what anxious families want to nibble on during a storm. In place of the hypothesis-driven approach, we can use a data-driven one. Our results may be less biased and more accurate, and we will almost certainly get them much faster."

These arguments are, of course, controversial, and raise a host of epistemological questions that are beyond the scope of this article. They raise the possibilities of 'spurious correlations' and about whether the data are reliable and valid proxies for the phenomena in question. They also rest on some questionable deterministic assumptions about the power of technology.

Mayer-Schönberger and Cukier also recognize that there is a 'dark side to Big Data' which poses significant challenges to conventional legal instruments of privacy protection (2013: 170). Big Data is a surveillance tool, and magnifies the capacity of organizations to monitor individuals' lives, to erode anonymity and to discriminate on the basis of gender, race, age, location and other factors. Big Data analytics using secret algorithms can lead to automatic and discriminatory judgments with widespread implications for the types of people most likely to engage in certain more risky behaviours (Pasquale 2015). The 'social-sorting' of the population using new technologies has been a theme in the surveillance literature for some time (Gandy 1993, 2009; Lyon 2003). These new tools permit a surveillance of the population in ways that were unimaginable a few years ago.

For instance, Big Data correlations have learned that workers with longer commutes quit their jobs sooner. Is it then fair to turn away job applicants with longer commutes? And what if those applicants tend to be disproportionately from minority populations (Robinson and Yu 2014)? And is it appropriate for a company to assign you a credit score based on where you live, and inferences about the creditworthiness of your neighbours (National Consumer Law Center 2014)? And is it acceptable for political parties to draw conclusions about how you might vote, on the basis of analysis of Facebook friends, Twitter followers and other evidence of the 'social graph'? (Bennett 2013).

In the United States, in particular, 'Big Data' leads to scoring practices, which are compiled based on financial, demographic, ethnic, racial, health, social, consumer and other data to characterize individuals or predict behaviours like spending, health, fraud, academic performance or employability. Scores can be correct, or they can be inaccurate or misleading, but they are rarely transparent. Persons affected may not be aware of the existence of the score itself, its uses and the underlying sources (World Privacy Forum 2014). Citizens are generally unable to challenge the score, determine how the score is constructed, correct the data on which it is based or opt out of being scored altogether.

The use of predictive analytics based on our online connections and activities can also inhibit freedom of association, and chill our online interactions. As the Electronic Information Privacy Center (EPIC) has stated:

> "The use of our associations in predictive analytics to make decisions that have a negative impact on individuals directly inhibits freedom of association. It chills online interaction and participation when those very acts and the associations they reveal could be used to deny an individual a job or flag an individual for additional screening at an airport because of the determination of an opaque algorithm, that may consider a person's race, nationality, or political views" (EPIC 2014).

Where, then, do these trends leave personal information rights and the many policy instruments that have been designed to protect those rights? This chapter addresses three central questions about the protection of privacy in this new environment. First, what are the problems involved with the current information privacy or data protection model with regard to the regulation of Big Data? Some have claimed that the traditional privacy protection model, based on notice and consent, is now obsolete and counter-productive, and have insisted that the focus of regulation should shift to the 'accountable' uses of personal data (Mundie 2014). We engage in this debate and attempt to provide a more focused assessment of the key issues.

This second section of the chapter builds upon this analysis to consider whether privacy impact assessments (PIAs) and the methodology that underpins them can remedy the perceived weakness of existing regulatory models. A considerable literature already exists on PIAs and on their development and implementation in different countries (Wright and De Hert 2012). They are now institutionalized under many data protection regimes and will become, in some contexts, mandatory under the new EU General Data Protection Regulation (GDPR) (EU 2012). In the main, however, these methodologies were developed before the challenges posed by Big Data analytics and tend not to incorporate assessments of the broader discriminatory impacts of these practices.

Do existing PIA methodologies need to be revised to enable the evaluation of risk in the context of Big Data? What tools might be developed to assess the broader social risks of excessive surveillance and categorical discrimination? We address proposals for Surveillance Impact Assessments (Wright and Raab 2012), and for more unified ethical frameworks, developed to guide data scientists (IAF 2014, 2015). The paper questions whether the integration of existing PIA methodologies into a broader ethical frame is a critical condition for the mitigation of individual and social risks in this new era of Big Data analytics.

Thirdly, and finally, what other regulatory solutions have been proposed, both now and in the past, that could offer ways to allow the promise of Big Data analytics, and at the same time, to protect individual privacy rights? Is it really necessary to give up on the central tenet of privacy protection law and philosophy in order to permit Big Data analytics to realize their potential? We do not think so. On the contrary, we argue that the current debate tends to rest on a false dichotomy and a fundamental misunderstanding about the theory of information privacy that developed 40 years ago, and the data protection policies that it generated (Bennett 1992).

8.1   INFORMATION PRIVACY AND THE FAIR INFORMATION PRINCIPLES

Contemporary data protection regimes in Europe and elsewhere have been based on a principle that the individual should have some control over the collection, use and disclosure of personal data that relates to him or her. That theory was developed in the 1960s in the United States and was later refined by other countries (Bennett 1992). According to the theory of 'information privacy', regardless of technology and regardless of organization, individuals have a right to a modicum of control over the information that circulates about them. It is the theory that underpins the set of 'fair information principles' that structure international norms and national statutes, the world over. Those principles give rights to individuals (data subjects) and impose responsibilities on organizations (data controllers). The codification varies according to different national administrative and legal traditions, but the underlying premises remain consistent. Whether national policy is framed in terms of 'privacy' or as 'data protection', there has been, and continues to be, a remarkable consensus on basic legal principles (Bennett 1992; Bennett and Raab 2006).

Privacy protection, therefore, is not a result or a condition but a dynamic process of
finding appropriate balances between privacy and multiple competing interests.
The appropriate balance cannot be struck by legislating in advance those types of
personal data that might never be captured or processed. Rather, the balance is
struck around the principle of relevance to an explicit and legitimate purpose. The
personal data required within any one organizational context are governed by a set
of social norms about what might be an appropriate intrusion (Nissenbaum 2010).
Those shifting norms then guide 'reasonable expectations of privacy' in different
organizational settings. Public and private organizations are expected, indeed
mandated, only to collect and process personal data related to a legitimate purpose.
The data may not be used for a different purpose without the individual's knowledge and consent, or unless there is a separate statutory justification.

It is also worth pointing out, that these simple principles are overwhelmingly supported by national and comparative public opinion surveys (e.g., Zureik et al.
2010). Privacy opinion polls have a long, and controversial, history. Their methodologies and their usefulness have varied dramatically. However, there is a common
theme that runs through them. The mass public can generally draw a line between
legitimate and illegitimate requests for personal data. Most people know how to
apply a 'none of your business' test. The line will vary over time, and according to a
host of demographic and cultural variables. Concerns about privacy also permeate
the business world. A recent survey of businesses in Belgium, France, Germany,
the Netherlands and the UK revealed that concerns over customer information and
compliance with privacy rules are the biggest challenges businesses face when
implementing Big Data strategies (Xerox 2015).

All privacy protection laws, therefore, are based on the transparent communication of the purposes for which personal data will be processed. This transparency
establishes a relationship of *trust* that personal data will not be re-used, repurposed and disclosed to other organizations. This principle is at the heart of the
theory of information privacy and reinforces powerful social norms. It also gov-
erns both the processing of personal data *and* its collection and capture.

8.2   BIG DATA AND THE CHALLENGES TO FAIR INFORMATION PRINCIPLES

There are three general and overlapping aspects of what we will call the 'Fair Information Principles' model that, critics argue, are fundamentally challenged by
Big Data and its implications. The first relates to the definition of personally identifiable information (PII) itself. Regulation in this area is triggered by the capture
and processing of data that, in some way, relates to an identifiable individual
(Schwartz and Solove 2011). The line between what is personal and non-personal
data is increasingly difficult to draw for several reasons.

Personal data can more easily be re-identified from the combination of data elements which, on their own, say little or nothing of about any one particular person. Our online tracks are tied to smartphones or personal computers through Unique Devise Identifiers (UDIDs), IP addresses, 'fingerprinting' and other means. Given how closely these personal communication devices are associated with the individuals who use them, information linked to these devices is, to all intents and purposes, linked to individuals. The sophistication of contemporary re-identification science gives a false sense that data can ever be stripped of identifying markers (Ohm 2010). Big Data can increase the risk of re-identification, and in some cases, inadvertently re-identify large swaths of de-identified data all at once.

The problem is magnified in the context of the Internet of Things, where inferences about our behaviours and actions can more easily be drawn from the capture of data from objects in our possession – our phones, cars, household appliances and so on. Generally speaking, ordinary people go about their lives in complete ignorance of the technical identifiers that are attached to these devices and constantly emit information about their personal lives. Furthermore, decisions about the individual are increasingly made on the basis of inferences that are drawn about the categorical group to which we are presumed to belong. The world of Big Data feeds off this growing ambiguity about what is, and what is not, personally identifiable information (The New Transparency 2014: 71-85).

A second, and related, challenge is to the principle of 'data minimization'. Organizations are required to limit the collection of personal data to that which is necessary to achieve their legitimate purposes and to delete that which does not conform to those purposes. The business model of Big Data is antithetical to these principles. Rather, it incentivizes the direct and indirect capture and retention of any data, by any technical means. Whereas it was once cheaper to delete information than to retain it, the obverse is now the case (Mayer-Schönberger 2011). "Data minimization is simply no longer the market norm" (Tene and Polonetsky 2013: 260).

The final challenge relates to the central tenet of the FIPS model, a clear definition and transparent communication about the purposes to which personal data are being processed. Some have argued that Big Data analytics require that presumption to be discarded, or at least fundamentally rewritten. The inductive power of analytics presumes that new purposes will and should be found for personal data, if the promise of the technology is to be realized. Mayer-Schönberger and Cukier (2013: 173) are emphatic on this point: "In the era of Big Data, however, when much of data's value is in secondary uses that may have been unimagined when the data was collected, such a mechanism to ensure privacy is no longer suitable." In the

words of the US President's Council of Advisors for Science and Technology:
"The notice and consent is defeated by exactly the positive benefits that Big Data
enables: new, non-obvious, unexpectedly powerful uses of data" (2014: 36).

Scott Taylor of Hewlett Packard, and a key participant in the Information Accountability Foundation, has likened the process of Big Data analytics to a chemical reaction (Taylor 2014). Just as something new, and in some cases unpredictable, is
created from the reaction of two chemicals, the same is true for Big Data. And just
as one would not prevent the collection of certain chemicals because they have a
chance, in reaction with others, to cause an explosion, he argues that we should
not prevent the capture and processing of personal data, because it might, when
applied, have adverse consequences for individuals, groups and for society as
a whole.

According to this position, there is no category of data that is *a priori* 'none of your
business'. The promise of Big Data, we are told, assumes further uses for purposes
not originally conceived. Craig Mundie, one of the members of the President's
Council (2014), insists that we should "focus on data use, not data collection."
He adds a familiar argument that there is already so much personal data 'out there'
that it cannot be retrieved, and it is practically impossible to provide notice and
seek consent for every conceivable use. Mundie, and others, envision a revision of
the privacy framework that permits almost unlimited collection, in return for
stronger accountability mechanisms that govern uses and disclosures. The argument broadly comports with a more long-standing effort to reorient privacy protection away from notice and consent, and towards an emphasis on accountability
of organizational practices (Weitzner 2008; Center for Information Policy Leadership 2009).

Against this more 'pragmatic' approach to privacy regulation, certain privacy
advocates have weighed in to defend traditional interpretations of the privacy
principles. Hoofnagle (2014), for instance, warns that "use-regulation advocates are
actually arguing for a broad deregulation of information privacy." It amounts to the
following: "1) Data companies can collect anything they want and analyse it however they please; 2) They are liable only for misuses of data, which businesses
define themselves, narrowly; 3) If pressed, they can argue that use restrictions are
unconstitutional censorship; and 4) Companies can purposely engage in those
misuses, and only be liable when it causes concrete injury." Privacy pragmatism
masks a 'radical deregulatory agenda', according to Hoofnagle: "A regime that only
pays attention to use erects a Potemkin Village of privacy. From a distance, it looks
sound. But living within it we will find no shelter from the sun or rain." The Electronic Privacy Information Center (EPIC 2014) also warned of huge dangers posed

by data breaches and of the failure of organizations to adequately safeguard the personal data under their control, when those data are increasingly stored in larger and larger data repositories.

Central to any resolution of these questions in Europe is the interpretation and enforcement of the new General Data Protection Regulation (GDPR). Indeed, and as has been pointed out on numerous occasions, individual consent is just one possible legal ground for legitimate processing of personal data under the GDPR. Others expressed in Article 6 (1) include: if

> "processing is necessary for the purposes of the legitimate interests pursued by a controller, except where such interests are overridden by the interests or fundamental rights and freedoms of the data subject which require protection of personal data, in particular where the data subject is a child. This shall not apply to processing carried out by public authorities in the performance of their tasks."

This provision was amended by Parliament in March 2014 to read:

> "processing is necessary for the purposes of the legitimate interests pursued by the controller or, in case of disclosure, by the third party to whom the data is disclosed, and which meet the reasonable expectations of the data subject based on his or her relationship with the controller, except where such interests are overridden by the interests or fundamental rights and freedoms of the data subject which require protection of personal data. This shall not apply to processing carried out by public authorities in the performance of their tasks" (Text adopted by Parliament, March 12, 2014).

The balance struck in the last condition, therefore, speaks directly to the processing of Big Data, and is a matter that will require regulation in different contexts according to judgments about 'legitimate interests'. DPAs, therefore, might very well intervene to make those judgments and reach more finely grained judgments about how the interests in data processing beyond the initial purpose of the collection, might best be communicated to establish 'reasonable expectations' and to promote the relationship of trust between the controller and the data subject in particular contexts.

These provisions also need to be regarded in relation to the other provisions. The GDPR contains a more accurate and faithful expression of the various policy instruments that currently comprise the 'governance of privacy' than was the case for the original 1995 Directive (Bennett and Raab 2006). It is rooted in the traditions of European data protection law, but it also borrows from policy innovations first introduced in countries outside Europe. These include: the provisions in Article 23 for 'data protection by design and by default'; the provisions for breach notification in Article 31; the encouragement of Codes of Conduct and certification in Articles 38 and 39; and the rules for Data Protection Impact Assessments in Article 33. Each of these instruments has been pioneered outside Europe, and each is now embraced within this new body of European law.

It seems that the legitimate processing of personal data, therefore, will not just be determined by what consumers consent to. It is, more generally, structured by a context in which there is more pro-active assessment of risk and demonstration of accountability. While Big Data does certainly pose challenges for the transparent communication of legitimate purposes and for the securing of consumer rights, its regulation will depend greatly on the application of these other instruments, and particularly on the use of Data Protection (Privacy) Impact Assessments.

8.3   BIG DATA AND PRIVACY IMPACT ASSESSMENTS

Privacy Impact Assessments (PIAs), called Data Protection Impact Assessments (DPIAs) under the GDPR, have been in existence for at least 20 years. They were initially introduced in countries like New Zealand and Canada, and then gradually spread to other English-speaking systems like Australia and the United States. Since then, PIAs have been spreading around the advanced industrial world as a result of: legislative requirements; policy guidance by central government agencies; recommendations by privacy and data protection commissioners; and recognition by organizations that PIAs can expose and mitigate privacy risks, avoid adverse publicity, save money, develop an organizational culture sensitive to privacy, build trust and assist with legal compliance (Wright and De Hert 2012). The British Information Commissioner's Office was the first European DPA to develop guidance as to how PIAs should be conducted (ICO 2007).

PIAs have been advocated to mitigate a range of organizational risks: vulnerabilities to organizational systems and assets; threats from malicious attacks; negative media publicity; loss of consumer confidence; infringement of laws; financial losses; dilution of brand, reputation and image; and so on (Wright and De Hert 2012: 14-15). They also arguably produce many positive benefits in their engagements with customers, stakeholders, regulators and others. They may also operate as a learning experience for the organization and its employees about what personal data the organization has, why it was collected, how it is stored and to whom it will be communicated (Wright and de Hart 2012: 16-17). The prospective analysis of privacy impacts is now regarded as one critical element of good privacy management and governance.

Crucially, therefore, PIAs need to offer an identification of privacy risks *before* systems and programmes are put in place. PIAs are only valuable if they have, and are perceived to have, the potential to alter proposed initiatives in order to mitigate privacy risks. They also have to consider privacy risks in a wider framework, which takes into account the broader set of community values and expectations about privacy. PIAs should also be more than the end-product or statement.

They refer to an entire process and appear to be more effective when they are part of a system of incentives, sanctions and review, and/or where they are embedded in existing project workflows or quality assurance processes (Warren et al. 2008).

However, PIAs vary across a number of dimensions: the levels of prescription, the application, the circumstances that might trigger PIAs, the breadth of the PIA exercise, the agents who conduct PIAs, the timing, the process of review and approval and the level of public accountability and transparency. In most jurisdictions where law or policy require or highly recommend that PIAs be conducted, an official PIA template, format or other tool to describe how they should be conducted, is provided. However, there is no simple formula for the conduct of a PIA. Each PIA should be dictated by the specific institutional, technological and programmatic context of the initiative in question. Any PIA needs to be sensitive to a number or crucial variables: the size of the organization; the sensitivity of the personal data; the forms of risk; and the intrusiveness of the technology (Warren et al. 2008).

There are several examples of guidance on how PIAs should be conducted. The UK ICO, for example, offers a helpful set of screening questions to determine whether, and what of kind of, PIA is needed. A PIA assessment template then involves a six-step process: 1) identify the need for a PIA; 2) describe the information flows and determine who should be consulted in that process; 3) identify privacy and related risks; 4) identify the privacy solutions; 5) sign off and record the PIA outcomes; and 6) integrate the PIA outcomes back into the project plan (ICO 2014a).

The current reality, however, is that PIA methodologies are overwhelmingly driven by the black letter of the law, and DPAs often cannot legally advise or require organizations to go beyond those explicit legal requirements. Many PIAs are simply legal compliance checks, are not published and certainly are not conducted with broad input from relevant stakeholders. Where they are conducted in a mechanical fashion for the purposes of satisfying a legislative or bureaucratic requirement, they are often regarded as exercises in legitimation rather than risk assessment (Warren et al. 2008).

Under Section 34 of the GDPR, Data Protection Impact Assessments are expected:

> "Where processing operations present specific risks to the rights and freedoms of data subjects by virtue of their nature, their scope or their purposes, the controller or the processor acting on the controller's behalf shall carry out an assessment of the impact of the envisaged processing operations on the protection of personal data."

The Regulation then goes on to spell out where those specific risks might arise:

a. a systematic and extensive evaluation of personal aspects relating to a natural person or for analysing or predicting in particular the natural person's economic situation, location, health, personal preferences, reliability or behaviour, which is based on automated processing and on which measures are based that produce legal effects concerning the individual or significantly affect the individual;
b. information on sex life, health, race and ethnic origin or for the provision of health care, epidemiological researches, or surveys of mental or infectious diseases, where the data are processed for taking measures or decisions regarding specific individuals on a large scale;
c. monitoring publicly accessible areas, especially when using optic-electronic devices (video surveillance) on a large scale;
d. personal data in large scale filing systems on children, genetic data or biometric data;
e. other processing operations for which the consultation of the supervisory authority is required pursuant to point (b) of Article 34(2).

The assessment is supposed to contain:

> "at least a general description of the envisaged processing operations, an assessment of the risks to the rights and freedoms of data subjects, the measures envisaged to address the risks, safeguards, security measures and mechanisms to ensure the protection of personal data and to demonstrate compliance with this Regulation, taking into account the rights and legitimate interests of data subjects and other persons concerned."

The data controller is also expected to seek the views of data subjects or their representatives, at least where it does not harm commercial interests. Controversially, however, these provisions do not apply to public authorities or where the processing results from a legal obligation.

It should be noted that these provisions will be affected by delegated acts adopted by the Commission. They have also been extensively amended and fleshed out by Parliament, which gives more explicit guidance on how the DPIA should be conducted throughout the entire lifecycle of the data processing operation. How these requirements will appear in the final version, after current negotiations between Parliament and the Council of Ministers are concluded, is still unknown.

To the extent that PIAs are seen by data controllers as valuable tools that can mitigate financial and reputational risk, then they are likely to be seen as such when personal data is being repurposed in a Big Data environment. To the extent that the assessment is framed in broader terms than data protection, then the larger issues related to discrimination and social sorting may then be addressed. In their paper on *Big Data and Data Protection*, the UK Information Commissioner's Office

(2014b: 13) stress that PIAs should play a crucial role in assessing the impact of Big Data projects on individuals and weigh those implications against the supposed benefits to society. The justifications for PIAs in the Big Data environment seem as compelling as ever.

However, there are also some extraordinary challenges. First, how does an organization assess the expected benefits when the analytical process is essentially an inductive 'fishing expedition' within the data? Big Data analytics tend to be premised upon very vague assertions about the rewards to society, business and consumers. And whereas privacy professionals now have a familiar set of tools for assessing privacy risk, it is not clear how they assess and prioritize a project's potential rewards when the benefits are often so speculative (Polonetsky and Tene 2013). Furthermore, how can PIAs be conducted when multiple organizations and data sources may be involved in a Big Data project, where lines of accountability may become very blurred? PIAs should ideally be transparent. Yet Big Data analytics often rely on the application of secret and proprietary algorithms, the understanding and assessment of which is necessary for the overall consideration of privacy risk.

Though PIAs are often necessary, they are not sufficient to address the broader set of risks in a Big Data environment. In this light, two further sets of tools have been proposed.

8.4   BIG DATA AND SURVEILLANCE IMPACT ASSESSMENTS

According to David Lyon, surveillance is "any collection and processing of personal data, whether identifiable or not, for the purposes of influencing or managing those whose data have been garnered" (Lyon 2001: 2). Surveillance is not simply about large organizations using sophisticated technology; it is also something that individuals increasingly engage in. It is good and bad, top-down and bottom-up, and directed to humans, non-humans and spaces (The New Transparency 2014). It is conceived as a broad mode of governance, rather than a narrow policy problem that can adequately be addressed by passing privacy laws. If privacy can never be the antidote to surveillance (Stalder 2002), then it follows that PIAs can never adequately address the broad range of social problems that surveillance brings in its wake (Cas 2015).

In this vein, Charles Raab and David Wright (2012) have introduced the concept of the 'Surveillance Impact Assessment' (SIA) to respond to the critique that PIAs are too narrowly focused on individual privacy. In common with current usage, they adopt a quite broad definition of surveillance to embrace the systematic capture of personal data beyond that collected through visual means. In addition to 'watching', surveillance is conducted through listening, locating, detecting, dataveillance, as well as through the combination of those practices in 'assemblages' (2012: 370-372). Raab and Wright conceptualize four nested concentric circles of an SIA. The conventional PIA, focused on individual privacy, falls in the innermost circle (PIA1). PIA2 adds other impacts on an individual's relationships, positions and freedoms. The third stage (PIA3) adds the impact on groups and categories. The fourth (outermost) ring of the circle (PIA4) adds the broader impacts on society and the political system. The model is intended to be cumulative. Under this framework, privacy progressively assumes the character of a social or collective good (Regan 1992) as one extends the analysis to the outer limits of the circle.

How could this framework assist with the analysis of Big Data analytics? A concrete illustration might assist. Take the example of the practice of credit-scoring, based on neighbourhood characteristics such as crime rates, property values, and so on (World Privacy Forum 2014). The impact of such a score on the individual's ability to get a loan would be regulated under the Fair Credit Reporting Act (FCRA) in the United States, but it would only apply to those aspects of the scoring system that were affected by an individual's credit report. This law, like other data protection acts, regulates the sources of legitimate personal data and offers limited recourse to access and correct erroneous reports. A PIA1 would thus be confined to ensuring that the provisions of the law are appropriately considered when the credit-scoring system was put in place. At the next stage (PIA2), the impact of your credit score on your immediate social network would be analysed. That could include neighbours in an immediate geographical sense, but also friends, family and other individuals with whom one regularly associates, online or offline. At the third stage (PIA3), the analysis would expand to the effect of categories of individuals and groups. If you are the kind of person with a bad credit score, then inferences might be drawn about the credit-worthiness of similar people with a similar profile. And at the final stage (PIA4), one would consider the general workings of society: social and community relations, democratic rights, political participation, the impact on the criminal justice system and so on.

Wright, Friedewald and Gellert (2015) followed up this analysis with an attempt to develop a more explicit SIA methodology and tested it on four separate 'smart' surveillance systems. Their project organized a series of scenario-based workshops to which different stakeholders were invited to inform the project (SAPIENT) about the different drivers for surveillance technologies, the current legal rules on transparency and consent, the relative vulnerability of individuals, the possibilities of resistance and the variety of potential solutions. These authors also point out the limitations of existing PIA methodologies and, therefore, seek a methodology that addresses wider privacy rights than just data protection, as well as other fundamental human rights and ethical values (p. 50). They too are insistent that the SIA should be conceived as a process, culminating in a published report that documents that process.

They then outline a twenty-step process in three phases (p. 51):

Phase I: Preparation
1. Determine whether an SIA is necessary.
2. Develop terms of reference for the surveillance assessment team.
3. Prepare a scoping report (What is the scope of the surveillance system?).
4. Check compliance with legislation.
5. Identify key stakeholders.

Phase II: Risk identification and analysis
6. Initiate stakeholder consultation.
7. Identify risk criteria.
8. Identify primary assets and feared events (What could happen if the surveillance system is implemented?).
9. Analyse the scope of feared events.
10. Analyse the impact of feared events.
11. Identify supporting assets.
12. Identify threats and analyse vulnerabilities.
13. Identify threat sources and analyse capabilities.
14. Create a risk map (for prioritizing risks for treatment).

Phase III: Risk treatment and recommendations
15. Risk treatment identification and planning.
16. Prepare an SIA report.
17. Record the implementation of the report's recommendations.
18. Publish the SIA report.
19. Audit the SIA.
20. If necessary, update the SIA.

In the interest of keeping the process relatively simple, this methodology has obviously been framed in quite high-level principles. They are also aware that overly complex and lengthy guidelines can scare away potential users. It is also obvious that, once the assessment goes beyond legal compliance, more subjective evaluations of risk inevitably enter the analysis. Those subjective assessments require consultations with a wide range of stakeholders, including the general public. It follows that the assessment has to explain the technology and the practice in a way that is understandable to the layman.

Both SIA methodologies reviewed here are probably more geared to public sector surveillance systems and to projects that have some defined technical and institutional parameters. Much of the appeal of Big Data analytics is that there are often no parameters. As noted above, organizations are invited to 'fish around' in the data until they find interesting correlations. Often there is no 'project' as such, and, therefore, no obvious starting-point at which an SIA could begin nor an end-point at which it could be published. These realities only reinforce the broad conclusion that any risk assessment should be conceived as a process rather than as an end-product.

8.5   BIG DATA, ACCOUNTABLE PRIVACY GOVERNANCE AND ETHICAL IMPACT ASSESSMENTS

Under the auspices of the Information Accountability Foundation (IAF), certain privacy experts from the private sector have also been thinking about how to reconcile the promise of Big Data analysis with traditional privacy principles. The project is a work in progress (Information Accountability Foundation 2014, 2015) but is worthy of comment. Unlike PIAs and SIAs, these assessments, it should be stated at the outset, are explicitly motivated by the question of how to analyse Big Data ethically.

This project builds upon earlier work by Martin Abrams and his colleagues to generate methods to encourage and measure organizational accountability (Center for Information Policy Leadership 2009). Decision-making about the ethics of Big Data analysis, therefore, is inextricably connected to whether or not the organization has an effective privacy management framework in place. Logically, if overall privacy governance is done well within a company (and the project is focused mainly on the private sector), then it will have the systems (management and technical) in place to assess the risks and put the necessary safeguards in place. In Canada, the privacy commissioners have offered explicit advice about the various elements of good privacy governance (OPC 2012). One of the ways in which organizations might mitigate risk, therefore, is to ensure that privacy is an integral part of an organization's commitments and governance structure.

The IAF's project on Big Data conceives of four integrated steps: A Unified Ethical Frame; An Interrogation Framework; An Enforcement Discussion; and Industry Interrogation Models. Only drafts of the first two elements are currently available for comment. The idea is that the project will begin with an analysis of the larger ethical considerations and progressively drill down to more practical guidance for industry.

Part A of this project conceives a 'Unified Ethical Frame' designed to ensure a "balanced ethical approach to Big Data" (IAF 2015: 7). The paper identifies five core values: beneficial, progressive, sustainable, respectful and fair. The paper suggests an ethical review that goes way beyond data protection, privacy and surveillance. The ambition is to produce a framework that also embraces the individual rights and interests addressed in common declarations of fundamental rights such as the United Nations Charter of Fundamental Rights, including values such as health, education, and opportunity and benefits from technology, which are advanced by the data processing. It is also intended to encompass corporate interests in innovation and in return on investment.

These values then inform the Interrogation Framework designed to be used when "Big Data projects reach key milestones and decision points" (IAF 2015: 3), meaning at the concept, discovery, application and review phases. The framework yields a worksheet designed to alert organizations to the key questions that need to be addressed at each stage to determine if the project is beneficial, progressive, sustainable, respectful and fair. This is explicitly an 'Interrogation Framework' rather than a more rigid set of guidelines. It is designed as a prompt that might be adapted for different companies and for different purposes. The key is that organizations have to be accountable and that they are able to demonstrate to regulators "that they have, effectively and with integrity, identified the full range of individual interests, and balanced those interests with other societal concerns" (2015: 5). Clearly, the value of these tools will only be properly judged when these higher-level instruments are applied to more specific industry applications.

8.6 CONCLUSIONS

The debate about Big Data and the protection of privacy is often framed in terms of a transatlantic clash of fundamental values between US beliefs in innovation and the free flow of information, and the European philosophy that data protection is a 'fundamental right'. These stark contrasts are fundamentally misleading and often based on serious misunderstandings of law on both sides of the Atlantic (Kuner 2014). They also, of course, ignore the startling contemporary fact that there are now more countries outside Europe with data protection law than within Europe (Greenleaf 2015). Those fault lines do not, and should not, structure the appropriate discourse for the debate in the rest of the world.

Aside from technical solutions, is there a way to reconcile Big Data analytics with traditional information privacy principles? And what role might PIAs play in that process? We will conclude with two separate attempts to grapple with these questions.

One approach is offered by Tene and Polonetsky (2013). These authors regard the information privacy principles not as a rigid framework but as a:

> "set of levers that must be adjusted to adapt to varying business and technological conditions. Indeed, the ingenuity of the FIPPs is manifest in their flexibility, which has made them resilient to momentous change – some principles retract while others expand depending on the circumstances. In the context of Big Data this means relaxing data minimization and consent requirements while emphasizing transparency, access, and accuracy" (p. 242).

They propose a set of solutions that de-emphasize the role of individuals at the point at which personal data is captured. They concede the fundamental weaknesses of a notification and consent model that relies on opting into, or out of, data processing practices based on the non-reading of complex and legalistic privacy policies. Rather, they want to shift emphasis to the empowerment of individuals, allowing them to engage with the benefits of Big Data for their own particular usage. As a "quid pro quo for looser data collection and minimization restrictions, organizations should be prepared to share the wealth created by individuals' data with those individuals." Individuals would then have access to 'their data' and would be able to make more useful choices about how to live their lives. They contend that the 'featurization' of Big Data could unleash more applications and create a market for such end-user innovations. A model would be the smart-grid applications designed to allow users to monitor their energy usage and make more intelligent decisions about their appliance usage and about energy consumption.

They concede that this call for greater transparency is not new. It is just that the mechanisms (requirements for the transparent notification of purposes, and individual access and correction rights) have not succeeded as regulatory tools. The entire 'app economy' is now, however, premised on individuals being able to access their own personal data to make intelligent choices about consumption, finance, health, and so on. It can, and should, be leveraged to provide individuals with access to their data in 'usable' format and thus render the Big Data 'ecosystem' more transparent. To this end, they propose that organizations reveal not only the existence of their databases but also the criteria (not necessarily the algorithms) used in their decision-making processes, subject to protection of trade secrets and intellectual property. In this way, individuals could scrutinize not only the accuracy of the data but also the reasonableness of the inferences drawn from that data (2013: 270-71). For Tene and Polonetsky, the problem is not 'Big Data' per se, but 'secret Big Data'.

A second approach is offered by the Center for Information Policy Leadership (2013), which formed the basis for the development of the IAF's Unified Ethical Framework, cited above. This 2013 paper sought to explain in a little more detail how Big Data analysis is actually conducted with a view to offering practical and effective privacy guidance. The paper insists that there is a crucial distinction between knowledge discovery and application. The former comprises acquisition, pre-processing, integration, analysis and interpretation. In each of these phases, algorithms perform a variety of classificatory, associational and sequential tasks (p. 10). It is only in the application phase, they argue, that insights about individuals might be enabled. For the most part, the knowledge discovery phase "does not involve analysis of a particular individual's data (which may be de-identified or pseudonymised) and does not result in decisions about him or her" (p. 14). Because the individual is implicated but not affected by the first phase, different protections are warranted.

Privacy rules for Big Data, therefore, need to: 1) recognize and reflect the two-phased nature of analytic processes; 2) provide guidance for companies about how to establish that their use of data for knowledge discovery is a 'legitimate business purpose' (under the GDPR); 3) rely upon fair information principles but apply them in a manner appropriate to the processing of Big Data for analytics; 4) emphasize the need to establish accountability through an internal privacy programme; 5) take into account that analytics may be an iterative process using data from a variety of sources; 6) reinforce the importance of appropriate data security measures; and 7) foster interoperability across diverse jurisdictions. Like Tene and Polonetsky, the fair information principles are regarded as 'a cornerstone for guidance' rather than as a rigid set of regulatory requirements. In this light, notions of consent for the collection of data can, and should, be flexible, and assessed in the light of the ways in which those data are used.

Are such distinctions possible, however? Many legal regimes have abandoned the attempt to distinguish between 'collection' and 'use'. Those separate steps were a feature of regulations in the 1980s and are expressed as separate principles in the OECD Guidelines of 1981 (OECD 1981). However, it is not a distinction that features prominently in contemporary European law, which has favoured one undifferentiated concept of 'data processing' (EU 1995). Furthermore, the emphasis on individual control as *the* central tenet of data protection law may also be misplaced. In many countries outside the United States, privacy regulation is underpinned by the assumption that personal data processing requires more proactive oversight through specialized data protection authorities (DPAs). This recognition goes back to the beginning of the modern data protection movement (Simitis 1978).

In conclusion, we agree with Kerr and Earle when they conclude that "the nexus between Big Data and privacy is not a simple story about how to tweak existing data protection regimes in order to 'make ends meet'; Big Data raises a number of foundational issues" (Kerr and Earle 2013). Though the model has always been under stress, it has yet been able to adapt and embrace the regulation and management of an enormous range of new technologies and practices. As the UK ICO concludes: "The basic data protection principles (…) are still fit for purpose (…) Big Data is not a game that is played under different rules"(ICO 2014b: 41).

Moreover, it is also crucial to regard the governance of privacy as embracing a package of different regulatory, self-regulatory and technological policy instruments (Bennett and Raab 2006), with both proactive and reactive elements. In this light, the development and application of broader, surveillance and ethical assessment tools can obviously play a central role in ensuring that Big Data analysis is conducted with appropriate regard for privacy and other values. However, data controllers and data regulators also need to pay heed to prior advice (e.g., Warren et al. 2008; Wright and de Hert 2012) about how PIAs should be conducted within existing privacy regimes. Privacy assessment tools need to: genuinely conduct a prospective identification of privacy risks *before* the data is analysed, involving all relevant employees and consulting with key stakeholders; assess the impacts in terms *broader* than those of legal compliance; be *process-oriented* rather than output-oriented; and use a *systematic* methodology. The challenges posed by these new analytical processes are real, to be sure. But organizations are less likely to face legal, financial and reputational damage if they seriously heed existing advice about how accountable organizations should identify and mitigate risks and implement effective privacy management within their organizations.

REFERENCES

Bennett, C.J. (1992) *Regulating Privacy: Data Protection and Public Policy in Europe and the United States*, Ithaca: Cornell University Press.

Bennet, C.J. (2013) 'The Politics of Privacy and the Privacy of Politics: Parties, Elections and Voter Surveillance in Western Democracies', *First Monday* 18, 8, available at: http://firstmonday.org/ojs/index.php/fm/article/view/4789 [5 August 2013].

Bennett, C.J. and C. Raab (2006) *The Governance of Privacy: Policy Instruments in Global Perspective*, Cambridge: MIT Press.

Boyd, D. and K. Crawford (2012) 'Critical Questions for Big Data', *Information, Communication and Society* 15: 662-667.

Cas, J. et al. (2015) 'Social and Economic Costs of Surveillance', pp. 211-258 in D. Wright and R. Kreissl (eds.) *Surveillance in Europe*, New York: Routledge.

Center for Information Policy Leadership (2009) 'Data Protection Accountability: The Essential Elements', available at: www.huntonfiles.com/files/webupload/ CIPL_Galway_Accountability_Paper.pdf [October 2009].

Center for Information Policy Leadership (2013) 'Big Data and Analytics: Seeking Foundations for Effective Privacy Guidance', Discussion Document, available at: www.hunton.com/files/Uploads/Documents/News_files/ big_Data_and_Analytics_February_2013.pdf [February 2013].

Electronic Information Center (EPIC) (2014) 'Comments to the Office of Science and Technology Policy on 'Big data and the Future of Privacy', available at: https://epic.org/privacy/big-data/ [4 April 2014].

European Union (1995) *Directive 95/46/EC of the European Parliament and of the Council on the Protection of Individuals with regard to the Processing of Personal Data and on the Free Movement of Such Data*, Brussels: OJ, no. L281, 24, October.

European Union (EU) (2012) Proposal for a Regulation of the European Union and the Council on the *Protection of Individuals with Respect to the Processing of Personal Data and on the Free Movement of Such Data (General Data Protection Regulation)*, Published January 25, available at: http://eur-lex.europa.eu/legal-content/en/ALL/?uri=CELEX:52012PC0011.

Gandy, O.H. (1993) *The Panoptic Sort: A Political Economy of Personal Information*, Boulder: Westview.

Gandy, O.H. (2009) *Coming to Terms with Chance: Engaging Rational Discrimination and Cumulative Disadvantage*, Aldershot: Ashgate.

Greenleaf, Graham. (2015) 'Global Data Privacy Laws 2015: 109 Countries, with European Laws Now in a Minority', *Privacy Laws and Business International Report* 133: 14-17.

Hoofnagle, Ch. (2014) 'The Potemkinism of Privacy Pragmatism', *Slate*, available at: www.slate.com/articles/technology/future_tense/2014/09/data_use_ regulation_the_libertarian_push_behind_a_new_take_on_privacy.2.html [2 September 2014].

Information Accountability Foundation (2014) 'A Unified Ethical Frame for Big Data
Analysis', Draft, available at: http://informationaccountability.org/wp-content/
uploads/IAF-Unified-Ethical-Frame-v1-08-October-2014.pdf [8 October 2014].

Information Accountability Foundation (2015) 'IAF big data Ethics Initiative Interrogation
Framework,' (Draft March 18) available at: http://
informationaccountability.org/wp-content/uploads/IAF-big-Data-Ethics-
Initiative-Draft-Part-B-Final-03-03-2015.pdf.

Information Commissioner's Office UK (2007) *Privacy Impact Assessment Handbook*,
Wilmslow: ICO.

Information Commissioner's Office UK 2007 (2014a) *Conducting Privacy Impact
Assessments: Code of Practice*, Wilmslow: ICO, available at: https://ico.org.uk/
media/for-organisations/documents/1595/pia-code-of-practice.pdf.

Information Commissioner's Office UK 2007 (2014b) *Big Data and Data Protection*,
Wilmslow: ICO, available at: https://ico.org.uk/media/for-organisations/
documents/1541/big-data-and-data-protection.pdf.

Kerr, I. and J. Earle (2013) 'Prediction, Pre-Emption, Presumption: How Big Data Threatens
Big Picture Privacy', *Stanford Law Review* 66, available at:
www.stanfordlawreview.org/online/privacy-and-big-data/prediction-
preemption-presumption.

Kuner, C. (2014) 'EU and US Data Privacy Rights: Six Degrees of Separation', available at:
http://concurringopinions.com/archives/2014/06/eu-and-us-data-privacy-
rights-six-degrees-of-separation.html.

Lyon, D. (2001) *Surveillance Society: Monitoring Everyday Life*, Buckingham: Open
University Press.

Lyon, D. (2003) *Surveillance as Social Sorting: Privacy, Risk and Digital Discrimination*,
London: Routledge.

Mayer-Schönberger, V. (2011) *Delete: The Virtue of Forgetting in the Digital Age*, Princeton:
Princeton University Press.

Mayer-Schönberger, V. and K. Cukier (2013) *Big Data: A Revolution that Will Transform
How We Live, Work and Think*, New York: Houghton, Mifflin, Harcourt.

Mundie, C. (2014) 'Privacy Pragmatism: Focus on Data Use, Not on Data Collection,'
Foreign Affairs, March/April.

National Consumer Law Center (2014) *Big Data: A Big Disappointment for Scoring
Consumer Credit Risk*, Boston: NCLC, available at: www.nclc.org/images/pdf/pr-
reports/report-big-data.pdf.

The New Transparency Project (2014) *Transparent Lives: Surveillance in Canada*, Athabasca:
Athabasca University Press.

Nissenbaum, H. (2010) *Privacy in Context*, Palo Alto: Stanford University Press.

Office of the Privacy Commissioner Canada (OPC); Office of the Information and Privacy
Commissioner of Alberta; Office of the Information and Privacy Commissioner of
BC (2012) *Getting Accountability Right with a Privacy Management Program*,
available at: www.priv.gc.ca/information/guide/2012/gl_acc_201204_e.asp
[April 2012].

Ohm, P. (2010) 'Broken Promises of Privacy: Responding to the Surprising Failure of Anonymization,' UCLA Law Review 57: 1701.

Organization for Economic Cooperation and Development (OECD) (1981) *Guidelines for the Protection of Personal Information and Transborder Data Flows*, Paris: OECD, available at: www.oecd.org/document/18/0,3343,en_2649_34255_1815186_1_1_1_1,00.html.

Pasquale, F. (2015) *The Black Box Society: The Secret Algorithms that Control Money and Information*, Cambridge: Harvard University Press.

Polonetsky, J. and O. Tene (2013) 'Privacy and Big Data: Making Ends Meet,' 66 *Stanford Law Review Online* 25, available at: www.stanfordlawreview.org/online/privacy-and-big-data/privacy-and-big-data.

Raab, Chr.D. and D. Wright (2012) 'Surveillance: Extending the Limits of Privacy Impact Assessment' in D. Wright and P. De Hert, *Privacy Impact Assessments*, Dordrecht: Springer.

Regan, P. (1995) *Legislating Privacy: Technology, Social Values and Public Policy*, Chapel Hill: University of North Carolina Press.

Robinson, D. and H. Yu (2014) *Civil Rights, Big Data and your Algorithmic Future*, Leadership Conference on Civil and Human Rights, available at: https://bigdata.fairness.io/wp-content/uploads/2014/11/Civil_Rights_big_Data_and_Our_Algorithmic-Future_v1.1.pdf.

Schwartz, P.M. and D.J. Solove (2011) 'The PII Problem: Privacy and a New Concept of Personally Identifiable Information', *New York University Law Review* 86: 1814, available at: http://scholarship.law.berkeley.edu/facpubs/1638.

Simitis, Sp. (1978) 'Reviewing Privacy in the Information Society', *University of Pennsylvania Law Review* 135: 707-746.

Stalder, F. (2002) 'Privacy is not the Antidote to Surveillance', *Surveillance and Society* 1: 120-124.

Taylor, S. (2014) 'Conference Highlights, International Data Protection Commissioner Conference, Mauritius, available at: www.privacylaws.com/Int_enews_October14_4.

Tene, O. and J. Polonetsky (2013) 'Big Data for All: Privacy and User Control in the Age of Analytics', *North-Western Journal of Technology and Intellectual Property* 11, 5: 239-273.

United States, Executive Office of the President (2014) *Big Data: Seizing Opportunities, Preserving Values*, The White House, May.

United States President's Council of Advisors on Science and Technology (2014) *Big Data and Privacy: A Technological Perspective*, The White House, May 1, available at: www.whitehouse.gov/bigdata.

Warren, A., C.J. Bennett, R. Clarke, A. Charlesworth and R.M. Bayley (2008) 'Privacy Impact Assessments: International Experience as a Basis for UK Guidance', *Computer Law and Security Report* 24: 233-242.

Weitzner, D.J. et al. (2008) 'Information Accountability,' *Communications of the ACM* 51, 6: 84, June.

World Privacy Forum (2014) *The Scoring of America: How Secret Consumer Scores Threaten Your Privacy and Your Future*, available at: www.worldprivacyforum.org/wp-content/uploads/2014/04/ WPF_Scoring_of_America_April2014_fs.pdf.

Wright, D. and P. De Hert (eds.) (2012) *Privacy Impact Assessments*, Dordrecht: Springer.

Wright, D., M. Friedewald and R. Gellert (2015) 'Developing and Testing a Surveillance Assessment Impact Methodology', *International Data Privacy Law* 5, 1.

Xerox Corporation (2015) *Big Data in Western Europe Today*, available at: www.xerox.co.uk/services/campaigns/xerox-forrester-report-2015/ engb.html&CMP=EMC-XEROX-BIG-DATA-DOWNLOAD-REPORT-2015-UK.

Zureik, E., L. Harling Stalker, E. Smith, D. Lyon and Y.E. Chan (2010) *Surveillance, Privacy and the Globalization of Personal Information*, Montreal: McGill-Queens University Press.

PART V

INTERNATIONAL PERSPECTIVES ON BIG DATA

9 FROM COLLECTION TO USE IN PRIVACY REGULATION? A FORWARD-LOOKING COMPARISON OF EUROPEAN AND US FRAMEWORKS FOR PERSONAL DATA PROCESSING

Joris van Hoboken

9.1 INTRODUCTION

How are we to ensure respect for information privacy in the 21st century? Answering this question, some have put forward the argument that regulation should focus on the use of data instead of its initial collection (Mundie 2014; White House 2014a; White House 2014b; Cate et al. 2014; Landau 2015; World Economic Forum 2013). The main argument for this shift tends to be pragmatic, namely that the collection of personal data has become the normal state of affairs. As a result, focusing the regulation of personal data-driven processes by limiting the collection of data (data minimization) is no longer feasible and desirable. Regulation should focus on issues arising from the actual use of personal data instead.

The arguments for use regulation tend to involve two specific elements. First, the existing mechanisms for establishing the *legitimacy* of personal data collection and further use (in view of information privacy) need to move away from a negotiation at the time of collection, in terms of specified, legitimate purposes, towards a focus on data use and management practices. Second, a use-based approach could provide the *flexibility of re-use of data* across contexts, which is argued to be required to extract the optimal value from data analytics. Cate et al. (2014) argue:

> "The evolution of data collection and data use necessitates an evolving system of information privacy protection. A revised approach should shift responsibility away from individuals and toward data collectors and data users, who should be held accountable for how they manage data rather than whether they obtain individual consent. In addition, a revised approach should focus more on data use than on data collection because the context in which personal information will be used and the value it will hold are often unclear at the time of collection" (Cate et al. 2014).

The resulting debate about regulatory flexibility for Big Data analytics may be one of the core data privacy debates of our time. On one side of the debate are those that propose more flexibility for the further processing of personal data for new unanticipated purposes (at the moment of collection) in view of the opportunities of data analytics. For example, the German Member of the European Parliament Voss recently argued: "there is one necessary condition for enabling innovation to flourish: allowing data to be processed without a pre-determined purpose" (Voss and Padova 2015).

On the other side of this debate about information privacy principles are those that remain committed to the basic principle that data processing purposes and their legitimacy should be established from the moment of collection of personal data. Other authors have questioned the European focus on data minimization in view of its minimal impact in practice but have argued for different regulatory solutions. As Koops (2014) argues:

> "the Data Protection Directive has done little to prevent the development of massive databases or the advent of the Big Data era, and it is folly to think that the GDPR will fare better in preventing 'unnecessary' data processing. Who in his right mind can look at the world out there and claim that a principle of data minimisation exists?".

Koops (2013) argues that, in a world of data analytics, regulation should increasingly focus on decision transparency to be able to guarantee due process and fair treatment of individuals.

This article will look at the position advocating use-based regulation as an alternative for restrictions on collection, from a transatlantic comparative legal and policy perspective. It will first look at the legal question about the position of the related principles of purpose limitation, data minimization and the question regarding the legitimacy of personal data processing in the European and US privacy regimes and make an assessment of the impact of existing regulatory frameworks on industry and government practices. On this basis, it will explore the viability and consequences of a possible shift towards a focus on the use of personal data in the information society. It will put this discussion in the context of current developments in Europe and in the United States. While focusing mostly on the commercial context, the article will also discuss collection and use from a government perspective, including the question of constitutional rights to information privacy and their consequences for collection and use in privacy law and policy.

The following two main questions will be specifically addressed. First, what is the current position of data minimization (and restrictions on the collection of personal data) in existing legal frameworks for data privacy, in Europe and in the US? As a considerable divide can exist between privacy law in the books and privacy law in practice, this question will be answered with reference to the impact of data minimization in practice. Specific reference will be made to legal developments affecting the central position of collection in the regulation of personal data processing, including the debate about the adoption of a new EU General Data Protection Regulation. Second, what are the rationales underlying a focus on collection and to what extent do these rationales remain valid? This also involves the question whether the regulation of the use of personal data can be considered as an alternative for the regulation of the collection of personal data.

For the purposes of this article, collection is broadly defined as whether a particular entity has access to or control over (personal) data for any potential use. Purpose limitation is understood as the principle that personal data must be processed for specified, explicit and legitimate purposes and not further processed in ways that are incompatible with those purposes. Data minimization is understood as the principle that the processing of personal data, including its collection, should be kept at a necessary minimum. Use of personal data is defined as any kind of use of personal data by a particular entity, including the transfer of data to third parties.

9.2   COLLECTION AND USE IN EUROPE

The primary legal data privacy instrument in Europe is the Data Protection Directive (95/46/EC, DPD), which harmonized data privacy legislation in the Member States. The dual aim of the DPD was to protect "the fundamental rights and freedoms of natural persons, and in particular their right to privacy with respect to the processing of personal data", while ensuring that such protection would "neither restrict nor prohibit the free flow of personal data between Member States" (Article 1 DPD). Proposals to replace the DPD with a General Data Protection Regulation (GDPR) have been debated at the EU level since 2012 (European Commission 2012, European Parliament 2014, Council 2015)[1] and were *de facto* adopted in December 2015.[2]

The DPD and its implementations in the Member States exist against the backdrop of fundamental right protection of data privacy at the EU level and within the Council of Europe and the international context. Article 8 of the European Convention on Human Rights (ECHR) includes protection of data privacy. Notably, the scope of the right to private life of Article 8 is wide, but not all personal data processing is covered (FRA 2014). Article 8 ECHR not only applies to interferences by public authorities but also entails positive obligations on public authorities to ensure respect for the protection in horizontal relations, which the DPD can be considered to effectuate. The Council of Europe Convention for the Protection of Individuals with regard to Automatic Processing of Personal Data (Convention 108) adopted in 1981, is the first regional framework for the processing of personal data and applies to all personal data processing in the public and private sector, including for law enforcement and national security.

Since the Lisbon Treaty entered into force in 2009, the EU data privacy regime in the DPD has been further anchored at the fundamental rights level in the EU Charter (Fuster 2014). The EU Charter contains a separate binding right to the protection of personal data (Article 8), alongside the protection of private life, family life and correspondence (Article 7). Article 8 of the Charter on the 'Protection of personal data' provides protection for personal data processing, including collection, and stipulates that:

1. Everyone has the right to the protection of personal data concerning him or her.
2. Such data must be processed fairly for specified purposes and on the basis of the consent of the person concerned or some other legitimate basis laid down by law. Everyone has the right of access to data which has been collected concerning him or her, and the right to have it rectified.
3. Compliance with these rules shall be subject to control by an independent authority.

The DPD applies to the processing of personal data in the private sector as well as the public sector, with certain exceptions, including the processing of personal data by law enforcement and national security agencies.[3] Personal data is defined broadly as "any information relating to an identified or identifiable natural person ('data subject')", where "an identifiable person is one who can be identified, directly or indirectly, in particular by reference to an identification number or to one or more factors specific to his physical, physiological, mental, economic, cultural or social identity" (Article 2(a) DPD). The DPD imposes a set of interlinked obligations on the processing of personal data by data controllers, i.e. the entity "which alone or jointly with others determines the purposes and means of the processing of personal data" (Article 2 DPD). Basically, any operation one could perform on data, including collection, storage, organization and disclosure or transfer to third parties falls within the definition of processing. The DPD also applies to personal data that have been made public. In view of freedom of expression, Member States are required to adopt exceptions and derogations to the "processing of personal data carried out solely for journalistic purposes or the purpose of artistic or literary expression only if they are necessary to reconcile the right to privacy with the rules governing freedom of expression" (Article 9).

Data minimization, i.e. keeping the processing of personal data at a necessary minimum, is a core principle of the existing European legal data protection framework. It follows from a combination of the principle of purpose limitation and the requirement of a legitimate ground. With respect to purpose limitation, Article 6 DPD provides that personal data can only be "collected for specified, explicit and legitimate purposes and not further processed in a way incompatible with those purposes." It also requires that the personal data should be "adequate, relevant and not excessive in relation to the purposes for which they are collected and/or further processed", "accurate and, where necessary, kept up to date" and "kept in a form which permits identification of data subjects for no longer than is necessary for the purposes for which the data were collected or for which they are further processed." Recital 28 provides that the purposes "must be determined at the time of collection of the data."

The DPD does not contain the assessment criteria whether further processing is incompatible with the purposes for which the data were collected. Member States have developed these criteria in specific national legal provisions, including "the relationship between the purposes for which the data have been collected and the purposes of further processing", "the context in which the data have been collected and the reasonable expectations of the data subjects as to their further use", "the nature of the data and the impact of the further processing on the data subjects" and the "the safeguards applied by the controller to ensure fair processing and to prevent any undue impact on the data subjects" (Article 29 Working Party 2013a: 23-27).

There are exceptions to the principle that data should only be processed for compatible purposes. First, Article 13 DPD stipulates that Member States can provide for exceptions to the further processing of personal data, including for law enforcement and national security. Typically, lawful access regimes in the Member States do provide for such exceptions. Second, an exception applies to the "further processing for historical, statistical or scientific purposes." Such processing may take place as long as 'appropriate safeguards' are implemented. Recital 29 of the DPD specifically provides that these safeguards must "rule out the use of the data in support of measures or decisions regarding any particular individual."

In practice, it appears that the exception for statistical and scientific purposes is used for data mining by commercial entities and the development of group profiles (Article 5.3.2 Dutch Code of Conduct Financial Industry 2010). As these group profiles tend to be used to support subsequent decision making regarding data subjects, this raises questions about the interpretation and enforcement of this recital in current legal practice. The GDPR provides for more flexibility with respect to the further processing of personal data for historical, scientific and statistical purposes. Recital 29 of the DPD, which the EDPS still recommended to include in the text of the GDPR, has been deleted from all official versions of the current text (EDPS 2015). On the question of the status of group profiles, the GDPR provides an ambiguous answer. Article 20(1) of the GDPR could be read in a way that it covers the processing of group profiles, but the rest of Article 20 suggests otherwise, and the scope of the GDPR generally remains restricted to the processing of personal data, thus leaving the larger issue of profiling unaddressed (Koops 2014: 257-8).

The strength of the data minimization principle depends on which data processing purposes, to be stipulated by the data controller at the time of collection, can be considered legitimate. This question is answered in general terms in Article 7 DPD, which lists six possible legitimate grounds for the processing of personal data.

Four of these grounds are framed in terms of whether the processing is 'necessary' for a generally accepted purpose for the processing of personal data. This includes that the processing should be necessary for "the performance of a contract to which the data subject is a party" (sub b), which is a primary ground for data processing in the private sector. For the public sector it provides the legitimate grounds that the processing is "necessary for compliance with a legal obligation to which the controller is subject" (sub c) or "necessary for the performance of a task carried out in the public interest or in the exercise of official authority vested in the controller or in a third party to whom the data are disclosed" (sub e). In addition, data processing is legitimate if it "is necessary in order to protect the vital interests of the data subject" (sub d).

There are two additional legitimate grounds of a somewhat different nature. Article 7 (f) provides for a balancing test, requiring that the processing:

> "is necessary for the purposes of the legitimate interests pursued by the controller or by the third party or parties to whom the data are disclosed, except where such interests are overridden by the interests for fundamental rights and freedoms of the data subject [protected by the DPD]."

The balancing test in Article 7(f) provides particular flexibility in practice for the private sector. It does not require controllers to conduct the balancing in a transparent manner, making it hard to challenge for data subjects (Bits of Freedom 2012).

Article 7(a) provides for the legitimate ground that "the data subject has unambiguously given his consent", which is increasingly portrayed as the primary legitimate ground for the processing of personal data. In early data privacy laws in Europe, the consent of the data subject played a more limited role (Kosta 2013: 383-384; Fuster 2014: 137). The DPD and even more so the proposals for the GDPR, however, placed increased emphasis on consent, connecting to the understanding of data privacy as control over one's personal data (Westin 1970; European Commission 2012). The new fundamental right to the protection of personal data in the EU Charter (Article 8) also gives consent a central role (Fuster 2014: 204).

Still, the function of consent remains limited to the legitimate ground test. The other requirements in the DPD or the GDPR are not dependent on the consent of the data subject, including that personal data are only processed fairly, transparently, for compatible specific explicit purposes, stipulated from the time of collection, that controllers respect data subject's rights to access, correction and deletion, all of which are subject to oversight by the Data Protection Authorities.

To summarize the above and its consequences for the regulation of the collection of personal data, the DPD regulates the processing of personal data from the moment of collection, but it does not regulate collection in the sense that it strictly prevents the collection of personal data. Except for the processing of sensitive data, the DPD does not prohibit personal data collection and further processing, but places it under many flexible general conditions, many of which are procedural.

Thus, the general DPD regime for the processing of personal data can best be characterized as 'yes, you can collect and process personal data as long as.' In sum, we may have to answer Koops's remarks about data minimization cited in the introduction with the conclusion that the current European model was never designed to prevent the 'development of massive databases or the advent of the Big Data era' (Koops 2014). It merely aimed to put some reasonable conditions on the collection and processing of personal data, including that they are collected for acceptable purposes. This does not mean that there is no data minimization principle. It just means that this principle does not stand in the way of legally permissible large-scale personal data processing activities.

To illustrate this, a data controller can easily maximize the amount of personal data it can legally collect and use by stipulating a large variety of data processing purposes that it is ready to defend as legitimate on the basis of Article 7 DPD. For data-intensive services or organizations, this would amount to a long list of data processing purposes, ranging from specific legal requirements to monitoring of fraud and abuse, monetization and the offering of specific personalized service features. It would indeed be a stretch, therefore, to argue that a *strict* principle of data minimization exists in the current regime. Clearly, the available legitimate grounds can flexibly cover a large range of reasonable processing purposes that private and public sector data controllers tend to be involved in.

The DPD regulates the use of personal data by requiring that the further use that is made of personal data is compatible with the specific, explicit and legitimate purposes for which the data were collected. As mentioned, the further use of personal data for historical, statistical or scientific purposes is not generally considered incompatible and permitted as long as appropriate safeguards have been applied. Another specific example of use regulation in the DPD is the provision on automated decision-making in Article 15. This provision reads as a prohibition of decisions with regard to data subjects that are solely based on processing of personal data that produce legal effects or significantly affect her or him. The DPD further gives data subjects the right to obtain "knowledge of the logic involved in any automatic processing of data" in such uses of personal data. The GDPR text on protection against profiling in Article 20, discussed above, is based on Article 15 DPD.

The legislative documents relating to the GDPR showed a general willingness to relax the existing restrictions on the further use of personal data once they have been collected. The EC proposal explicitly includes the principle that personal data be "limited to the minimum necessary in relation to the purposes for which they are processed" (Article 5(c), replacing the 'not excessive' language from the DPD in Article 6 (European Commission 2012). Some might conclude from this that the EC aims to strengthen the data minimization principle, but whether this is the case depends on the interpretation of necessity and legitimate purpose. More importantly, the EC proposes that processing for incompatible purposes would be allowed in the future, outside of the existing exceptions, as long as consent would be obtained or the incompatible processing could be based on another legitimate ground for processing (European Commission 2012, Article 6(4)). As noted by the EDPS, this proposal would open up "broad possibilities for re-use of personal data in particular in the public sector" and would blur the distinction between the cumulative requirements of purpose limitation and legitimate ground for processing of personal data (EDPS 2012: 123). It also places the requirement that "purposes should be explicit and legitimate and determined at the time of the collection of the data" in a new light (European Commission 2012, Recital 30). The European Parliament proposes to delete the proposed Article 6(4), staying closer to the current regime (European Parliament 2014).

The Council's General Agreement went a step further than the Commission in relaxing restrictions on incompatible use. It proposed that "further processing for incompatible purposes on grounds of legitimate interests of the controller or a third party shall be lawful if these interests override the interests of the data subject" (Council 2015, Article 6(4)). Moerel and Prins argue in favour of these proposals by the Council and conclude that it is "the only feasible way to guarantee a future-proof mechanism" (Moerel and Prins 2015). The EDPS (EDPS 2015), the Article 29 Working Party (Article 29 Working Party 2015a) and a large coalition of civil society organizations (McNamee 2015) warned against the further erosion of purpose limitation and the use of this balancing test to sanction uses of data incompatible with the purposes for which they were collected.

The Dutch Government anticipated this possible relaxation of purpose limitation in its exploratory proposals for a Framework Act for data-driven collaborations in the public sector. This Framework Act aims to provide the necessary legal basis for collaboration between different entities to exchange personal data, even if the resulting exchange would be incompatible with the purposes for which the respective agencies had collected them (Kaderwet 2015: 12). A specific use that the law would facilitate is combining data sets to develop risk profiles and apply these to the respective data sets. In addition, it would override confidentiality requirements and other provisions in specific public sector data processing regulations limiting the sharing of personal data with other entities, including private parties. As the exploratory report states:

> "With respect to disclosure for such collaborations, the confidentiality requirements in these sectorial laws focus on 'no, unless'. A framework act could tilt this paradigm to 'yes, unless'" (Rapport Verkenning Kaderwet 2014: 34).

Notably, without the changes to the possibility of further processing for incompatible purposes, as included in the EC proposal and the Council's General Agreement, this proposed regime in the Netherlands would be incompatible with European Law.

The ongoing enforcement actions of national data protection authorities with respect to Facebook and Google can help to illustrate the current regime for the private sector in Europe. When we review the available documents, it becomes clear that for purpose limitation to function as a meaningful check on personal data processing activities, it is essential that controllers be specific enough about their actual data processing purposes. Otherwise, it is impossible for regulators to make an assessment of the legitimate ground as well as the restriction on further processing for incompatible purposes. However, not unlike many other data controllers, Google and Facebook communicate about their purposes for the processing of personal data in vague general terms and appear to formulate those purposes in a way to optimize their legal space for the combination and further use of data, once collected. Consider the conclusion form a recent study from the University of Leuven for the Belgian Privacy Commission with respect to Facebook:

> "Overall, Facebook's revised [Data Use Policy] signals the company's data use practices in a more prominent way. In this regard, Facebook seems to have taken an important step forward. However, the uses of data are still only communicated on a general and abstract level. Much of the [Data Use Policy] consists of hypothetical and vague language rather than clear statements regarding the actual use of data" (Van Alsenoy et al. 2015: 10).

With respect to Google, the Dutch Data Protection Authority explains in its 2013 report that it "has distinguished four actual purposes, and ascertained that these are so vague or broad that during the collection process they cannot provide any framework against which it can be tested whether the data are necessary for that purpose or not." At the end of 2014, the Dutch DPA decided to impose a cease and desist order on Google, partly based on the following conclusion:

> "Google acts in breach of Article 7 of the Dutch Data Protection Act, which proscribes that personal data are collected for specific and legitimate purposes, because the evaluated purpose specifications in the Google Privacy Policy and the newly mentioned purpose by

Google of 'the provision of the Google Service' are not well defined and insufficiently specific and because Google does not have a legitimate ground for the processing of the personal data for the assessed four purposes" (Dutch Data Protection Authority 2014).

In other words, even after enforcement pressure, Google and Facebook have not yet been willing to disclose specific enough information about their processing purposes for purpose limitation to fulfil its designated role. Notably, these data controllers do not choose the strategy of formulating a long list of purposes, as discussed above, but a more problematic strategy of formulating a small set of vague broad purposes, shielding their specific data use practices from a thorough legitimacy assessment by data subjects and regulators. In other words, the purpose limitation principle may already have to be taken with a grain of salt in practice. This may partly be explained by the lack of enforcement powers and capacity, which the GDPR revisions aimed to address. At the same time, however, the GDPR could provide more flexibility to the changing and reformulation of purposes, as discussed above, making the impact of the GDPR on these practices difficult to assess.

To conclude this section on collection and use in the European data privacy context, it is worth discussing the case of mandatory retention of electronic communication data. This phenomenon exists on the interface of private and public sector personal data collection practices and raises particularly interesting questions with respect to the question of collection and use in data privacy regulation. Specifically, the recent judgment of the Court of Justice of the European Union (CJEU) in *Digital Rights Ireland*, in which it struck down the Data Retention Directive (DRD), provides some guidance on the position of collection and use in an assessment related to the fundamental rights to private life and the protection of personal data (CJEU 2014). More generally, this judgement illustrates the significance of the EU Charter for the protection of data privacy in the European legal order.

Data retention fits in a wider trend in which governments optimize their ability to exercise power and control on the basis of private sector data (Prins et al. 2011: 96-97). In the Netherlands, for instance, a series of laws have been put in place that facilitate access by law enforcement authorities to any type of data held in the private sector.[4] These laws build on the exception to purpose limitation in Article 13 DPD, making it possible that data collected for the purpose of providing a commercial service end up being used in criminal investigations. Dutch criminal procedural law provides for lawful access by law enforcement to almost any kind of personal data held by others if the data are relevant to an ongoing investigation. Only in cases of sensitive data is there a need for a check by a judicial authority (Van Hoboken 2006).

Agencies other than law enforcement, such as the Dutch Tax Administration, have considerable data collection powers as well, as illustrated most recently in the debate over lawful bulk collection of data of an automated parking service, SMS Parking (Court of Appeals Den Bosch 2014). Once collected by the Dutch Tax office, these data also become available to Dutch law enforcement and intelligence agencies (Martijn 2014). Recent proposals for a new Dutch law for the intelligence agencies provide for broadened powers to gather data from private and public sector entities, including bulk and direct access (Ministerie van Binnenlandse Zaken 2015, Artikel 22). Finally and unfortunately, the shadow of government access to private sector data does not limit itself to national borders. Internationally operating companies can be approached by government agencies abroad to access data of individuals residing elsewhere, regardless of legal process and substantive requirements in their proper jurisdictions (see Van Hoboken et al. 2013).

The DRD went one step further than laws facilitating mere government access, by requiring that electronic communications traffic and location data would continue to be stored, even if the data were no longer necessary for private sector purposes, for a period between 6 and 24 months. The basic rationale of data retention is that data should be retained to ensure their availability to public authorities, in case the respective data should be relevant to a future investigation. Thus, data retention legitimizes collection in view of *potential* future use, putting additional stress on the purpose limitation principle.

The CJEU invalidated the DRD in its *Digital Rights Ireland* judgment because of its incompatibility with the Charter.[5] The CJEU established that the directive's retention obligation amounted to a wide-ranging and particularly serious interference with Articles 7 and 8 of the Charter. The CJEU did not consider the essence of the rights affected as the directive did not apply to communications content (Article 7 Charter) and imposed obligations to implement measures "against accidental or unlawful destruction, accidental loss or alteration of the data" (Article 8 Charter).[6] The CJEU subsequently concluded that the "retention of data for the purpose of allowing the competent national authorities to have possible access to those data, as required by Directive 2006/24, genuinely satisfies an objective of general interest"(par. 44).

The Court's invalidation of the Directive was the result of its application of a strict proportionality test, in which it observed a general lack of limitations, exceptions and possible safeguards in the DRD. The CJEU noted specifically how the directive affected 'all persons using electronic communications services' and applied 'even to persons for whom there is no evidence capable of suggesting that their conduct might have a link, even an indirect or remote one, with serious crime' (par. 58).

In addition, it signalled that it would expect a much more granular legitimation for the retention of the relevant data in terms of its likely possible use, noting that the directive did:

> "not require any relationship between the data whose retention is provided for and a threat to public security and, in particular, it is not restricted to a retention in relation (i) to data pertaining to a particular time period and/or a particular geographical zone and/or to a circle of particular persons likely to be involved, in one way or another, in a serious crime, or (ii) to persons who could, for other reasons, contribute, by the retention of their data, to the prevention, detection or prosecution of serious offences" (par 59).

These considerations place any general data retention mandate (regarding personal data that is particularly revealing with respect to the private life of individuals) in a suspect light, as such general data retention laws precisely follow the logic that they allow these links to be established after the potentially useful data has been collected. What is at issue, therefore, in the Court's perspective on the fundamental rights to privacy and the protection of personal data, is the mere collection and retention of the data.[7]

9.3   COLLECTION AND USE IN THE UNITED STATES

US privacy law is a fairly complicated area of legal doctrine, consisting of a combination of specific privacy torts, sectoral and state level data privacy laws for the private sector as well as a number of public sector related privacy laws, including the Privacy Act and legal rules relating to government access to data and communications. In contrast to the European omnibus data privacy law model, US data privacy law is characterized by a sectoral approach to legislating modern data privacy issues (including through self-regulation) as well as the adoption of information privacy law at the State level. An initial omnibus bill for the public and private sector was introduced in 1974, but not adopted (Schwartz 2009: 910-913). Instead, Congress adopted the federal Privacy Act for the public sector and a series of sectoral laws for the private sector, including the Fair Credit Reporting Act (FCRA) of 1970, the Family Educational Rights and Privacy Act of 1974, the Right to Financial Privacy Act of 1978 and the Video Privacy Protection Act of 1988. Discussions to adopt some form of omnibus protection of information privacy remain ongoing – most recently a Consumer Privacy Bill of Rights was proposed by the White House – but have been unsuccessful until now.

In comparison with Europe, whose approach is often characterized in the US as an approach seeing privacy as a fundamental right, relevance of constitutional privacy safeguards in the US is relatively limited. The US Constitution does not recognize a general fundamental right to private life or a right to protection of one's personal data, but several provisions in the US Bill of Rights protect certain elements of a more fundamental right to privacy. US legal doctrine generally does not recognize the existence of positive state obligations to protect or establish horizontal effect of constitutionally protected rights of individuals.

The First Amendment can entail protection of certain personal data against government collection, if such collection would interfere with the First Amendment's protection of freedom of speech and freedom of association (Strandburg 2008; Solove 2010). The Fourth Amendment protects against unreasonable searches and seizures, requiring the issue of a warrant on probable cause. Arguably, this is a stricter requirement than the flexible proportionality test required by Article 8 ECHR or the EU Charter.

A reason for increased attention to the implications of the First Amendment for government surveillance is that the Fourth Amendment provides only a weak check on government data collection practices. The protection of the Fourth Amendment against government surveillance is limited in several respects by the case law of the US Supreme Court, most notably by the so-called third-party doctrine. Under an aggressive interpretation of this doctrine, individuals generally do not enjoy the protection of the Fourth Amendment for information held by or turned over to third parties. In a world of Big Data and comprehensive sets of personal data relating to all aspects of social and economic life, the doctrine severely restricts the Fourth Amendment's impact on the US government's personal data collection practices. Although this strict interpretation of the third-party doctrine is still widely defended in US scholarship (see e.g., Kerr 2009), a growing body of legal scholarship and judicial opinions, Justice Sotomayor's concurrence in *US v. Jones* in particular, points towards a more nuanced answer to the question of reasonable expectations of privacy in records held by third parties (Strandburg 2011; Baer 2014).

If we take a look at the third-party doctrine from the perspective of the collection versus use debate, a number of observations can be made. First, the third-party doctrine entails an interpretation of the Fourth Amendment's focusing almost exclusively on the (initial) collection of data as the relevant issue. Once data has been disclosed to third parties, Fourth Amendment protection is no longer applicable, on the rationale that it implies consent (Kerr 2009: 565). In the face of such reasoning, the idea that collection of data should no longer be the law's focus in protecting the right to privacy is unpersuasive. If anything, a continued adherence to the third-party doctrine means that collection of one's data by a third party is precisely something to worry about because collection implies the loss of constitutional protection. The alternative to such protection is for the US legislature to adopt statutory protections that afford privacy protections against unrestrained government collection. Such statutory protections do exist for some specific categories of information held by third parties. Examples are the Right to Financial Privacy Act adopted in response to *Miller* and the Pen Register and Trap and Trace Devices Statute adopted in response to *Smith*.

In the consumer privacy context, the Federal Trade Commission has used its authority with respect to unfair and deceptive business practices to develop an increasingly robust information privacy doctrine at the federal level (Solove and Hartzog 2014). The FTC has been the dominant federal agency involved in addressing privacy issues in the online context through self-regulatory initiatives and has authority to oversee and enforce an increasing number of privacy regulations. Indeed, the FTC has become the *de facto* Data Protection Authority in the US for the consumer privacy context (Solove and Hartzog 2014): first, it has applied the unfair and deceptive business practices to personal data collection and use. Second, it has recommended various versions of the Fair Information Practices to shape self-regulatory initiatives to address privacy issues in different sectors of commerce, including online advertising and data brokerage. Finally, it has enforced statutory laws, including the FCRA, the Safe Harbor Agreement with the EU, and the Children's Online Privacy Protection Act (COPPA).

In its self-regulation initiatives, the FTC has been influenced by the framework of Fair Information Practice Principles, notice and choice in particular, but it has not strongly endorsed a collection limitation or purpose specification and limitation principle.[8] A set of five Fair Information Practice Principles (FIPPs) were first proposed in the 1970s by the Department of Health Education and Welfare and included the principle that: "there must be a way for a person to prevent information about the person that was obtained for one purpose from being used or made available for other purposes without the person's consent" (US Department of Health 1973). An international version of the FIPPs was developed in the OECD context and consisted of eight principles, including the 'collection limitation principle' and the 'purpose specification principle'. These principles do not appear in recent FTC recommendations, such as the slimmed-down set of four FIPPs for online privacy (Strandburg 2014: 6-8), with only the two core principles (notice and choice) having implications for data collection and use:

1.   Notice: Websites would be required to provide consumers clear and conspicuous notice of their information practices, including what information they collect, how they collect it (e.g., directly or through non-obvious means such as cookies), how they use it, how they provide Choice, Access, and Security to consumers, whether they disclose the information collected to other entities, and whether other entities are collecting information through the site.

2. Choice: Websites would be required to offer consumers choices as to how their personal identifying information is used beyond the use for which the information was provided (e.g., to consummate a transaction). Such choice would encompass both internal secondary uses (such as marketing back to consumers) and external secondary uses (such as disclosing data to other entities).

FTC privacy doctrine does provide some regulatory tools to prevent data from being used for new unexpected purposes. In this regard, the establishment of the notice principle (in self-regulation in combination with statutory and Safe Harbor requirements on privacy policies and notification) has had positive synergies with the FTC's deception standard. Once the practice of privacy policies was established, the deception standard allowed the FTC to take action against misrepresentations about the use of data. Furthermore, the FTC's doctrine of deception has moved beyond policing broken promises. It now also includes "a general theory of deception in obtaining personal information and deception due to insufficient notice of privacy-invasive activities" (Solove and Hartzog 2014: 627-638).

Notwithstanding the progress the FTC has made in establishing a more robust data privacy regime in the US, filling the large legal gaps left by sectoral statutory law, the notice and choice regime of privacy self-management has been widely criticized for being ineffective, for overburdening individuals and for being a procedural sidestep on substantive questions about the legitimacy of personal data processing (see e.g., Solove 2013; Barocas and Nissenbaum 2014). In practice, the choice principle is a weak form of consent with respect to personal data processing and is generally satisfied by giving some opt-outs or a simple 'take it or leave it' option. As Grimmelmann has summarized recently, pointing to more general issues with respect to terms of service and contract law:

> "Any attempt to empower consumers – think 'notice and choice' in privacy law – ends up tossing a few more shovelfuls of disclosure onto the contractual dung heap. Now consumers have 'notice' of the practice regulators want them to know about. But their 'choice' is emptier than ever" (Grimmelmann 2015).

There remains a large area of data collection and use untouched by the doctrines and laws mentioned above, including data collected and used in the absence of interactions with data subjects in commercial relations. This largely unregulated area of personal data processing can be illustrated with a short discussion of the phenomenon of data brokers and the attempts of the FTC to impose some checks and balances on this multibillion dollar industry involved in the collection, profiling and sale of personal data (FTC 2014). Data brokers, such as the Acxiom company, collect personal data from a variety of sources, including government records, publicly available sources, including (new) media, and commercial sources of data (including other data brokers). Acxiom reportedly has 3,000 data segments for nearly every US consumer (FTC 2014: 6). Data brokers sell their data for use in (personalized) marketing as well as for profiling and risk assessment in the private and public sector. Outside specific areas of activity regulated by the FCRA, the collection and use of this information mostly remains a matter of contractual agreements between data sources, data brokers and further users, with minimal levels of transparency and accountability towards data subjects and society more generally.

As the FTC mentions in its study, there are but few laws that regulate the use of certain public records by data brokers, such as state laws that restrict the use of voter registration records for commercial or non-election-related purposes (FTC 2014: 12). Additionally, use restrictions are sometimes made part of contractual agreements by government sources of data:

> "[C]ertain federal or state laws or agencies require a written agreement affirming that the data broker will only use the data for a specified purpose. Sources may also prohibit data brokers from reusing or reselling the data without permission; decoding or reverse engineering the data; illegally or illicitly using the data; and using the data in violation of the FCRA, Gramm-Leach-Bliley Act (GLBA), HIPAA, or Children's Online Privacy Protection Act (COPPA)" (FTC 2014).

The Fair Credit Reporting Act has been mentioned as an example of use-based regulations of personal data; it regulates certain uses of consumer credit information by Credit Reporting Agencies (CRAs). Specifically, the FCRA establishes data protection standards for the issuing of consumer credit reports, i.e. personal data that is collected and combined to evaluate credit, insurance or employment eligibility. It imposes transparency obligations and data subject rights of access and correction and requires that CRAs "follow reasonable procedures to assure maximum possible accuracy of the information concerning the individual about whom the report relates" (15 U.S.C. § 1681e, (b)). The FCRA also contains obligations to suppress certain information from consumer reports and requires that CRAs take measures to ensure that information from credit reports is not used for purposes other than the purposes for which it was requested. When CRAs comply with the FCRA's safeguards, they are shielded from liability.

When taken as an example of use-based regulation, the FCRA cannot be considered a resounding success. Hoofnagle concludes that

> "[c]onsumer reporting shows us that while use-based regulations of Big Data provided more transparency and due process, they did not create adequate accountability. Indeed, despite the interventions of the FCRA, consumer reporting agencies (CRAs) remain notoriously unresponsive and unaccountable bureaucracies" (Hoofnagle 2013).

The FCRA singles out a set of data usage in the data broker industry for stricter regulation. Unsurprisingly, the particular scope of the FCRA is contested and the subject of active litigation. Recently, the US Supreme Court has granted certiorari in a case in which a people search engine *Spokeo* was confronted with a class action law suit alleging violation of the FCRA.[9] The case, which currently revolves around the initial question of standing in information privacy laws like the FCRA, also illustrates the issues that arise from singling out the use of certain information by certain actors for stricter regulation. Spokeo disputes that it can be considered a CRA and warns visitors to its website that "none of the information offered by Spokeo is to be considered for purposes of determining any entity or person's eligibility for credit, insurance, employment, or for any other purposes covered under FCRA" (Spokeo 2014).

Finally, a use-based regulatory approach through statutory laws may run into First Amendment troubles. Several lawsuits have argued, unsuccessfully until now, that the FCRA imposes restrictions on the use of data in violation of the First Amendment or that use restrictions on data could be ignored on the basis of the First Amendment (Hoofnagle 2014). These interpretations of the First Amendment typically follow a line of argument presented by Bambauer as 'data is speech'. Not only 'traditional forms of communication (utterances, journals, movies, and the like)' should be protected, but also the gathering and processing of data more generally because of the First Amendment aims to protect against interferences with the creation of knowledge (Bambauer 2013).

In sum, US law provides for less strict collection limitation in comparison to the European framework in the commercial sphere. It has a number of sectoral laws that regulate certain uses of personal data, such as the FCRA, but these approaches have their limitations. Notably, US law does not legally require a legitimate basis for the processing of personal data. FTC privacy doctrine in combination with privacy policy requirements provides some check on the use of personal data for new purposes through the notice and choice framework. This check, which advocates of use-based regulations of personal data consider outdated in a world of Big Data, is already inapplicable to a mature multibillion dollar industry, which provides a good chunk of the data collection and analytics machinery to a world relying on Big Data. Within this industry, use regulation does play a role, but primarily through contractual agreements between data sources and users, including provisions that existing statutory use limitations will be respected downstream.

9.4   FROM COLLECTION TO USE?

The classic informational self-determination rationale for information privacy regulation is that the collection of personal data enables the exercise of power and can have chilling effects on individual freedom and behaviour, effects which should not only be assessed in terms of the impact on specific individuals but also in view of the values of pluralism and democratic self-governance.[10] This rationale, which is specifically tied to the collection of personal data, is widely accepted in European data privacy jurisprudence and affirmed in fundamental rights case law, including the famous census decision of the German Constitutional Court (BVerfG 65, 1

1983) and the Court of Justice of the EU (Digital Rights Ireland par. 28). Individuals may be worried about the collection of data about them and about the purposes for which these data would be used. Personal data, once collected, could be used in ways that are unfair or make their lives more difficult.

While recognizing that there are legitimate reasons for organizations to collect and use data, data privacy law aims to provide the legal conditions for a negotiation to take place on the question whether the collection of certain data for certain purposes is indeed legitimate and restricts the use of data for other, incompatible purposes. In the European context, this question of legitimacy involves either the existence of informed consent or a proportionality test in view of the fundamental right to privacy and the protection of personal data. In the US context, legitimacy is generally not dependent on a legal test as stipulated in the DPD, and in the consumer privacy context the emphasis has been placed on notice and a weak form of consent, i.e. choice.

As a political project, data privacy law and policy has been centrally concerned with shoring up public trust in the way organizations process personal data (as well as trust in information technologies and services), focusing in particular on the foreseeability of data-processing outcomes (Bygrave 2002: 107-112). This foreseeability, which is also a requirement for interferences with fundamental rights in the European context, is specifically promoted through the principles of purpose specification and limitation. The argument for use regulation generally implies that this negotiation on legitimacy would no longer take place at the moment of collection in terms of purposes in a way that restricts the further use of the data collected. When the question of legitimacy shifts to the question whether some defendable use could be made of personal data in the future, however, much personal data collection easily becomes legitimate in a world of Big Data. It is hard to see how such a framework will provide for the foreseeability of data processing in a similar manner. It would put oil on the slippery slope of data collection and unpredictable further use instead.

As discussed with reference to data retention in Europe and the third-party doctrine in the US, a specific rationale for considering the mere collection of data by organizations as a fundamental privacy issue is that collection in the private sector implies the possible collection and use by government agencies for purposes of law enforcement and national security. Data privacy rules typically provide for exceptions to the principle of purpose limitation for such government collection purposes. It does not matter for which purposes the data was collected in the private sector context. When a law enforcement agency fulfils the statutory requirements for collecting the relevant data, government access can generally take place. This places data collection by other organizations in a particular light that cannot be undone by use-based regulations. In fact, the Snowden revelations have made people and organizations more acutely aware of this reality than ever. In fact, certain industry players are adopting encryption schemes that prevent certain forms of government access from taking place. This shows that increasing trust by limiting data collection through technical means is a viable strategy for the private sector, in the absence of better safeguards against government collection (Van Hoboken and Rubinstein 2014).

In a way, it almost appears as if the advocates of use-based regulation (as an alternative to the regulation of collection of personal data) believe that the concerns of individuals with respect to mere collection will miraculously disappear and that European constitutional judges will eventually overturn their reasoning about data collection and fundamental rights. Considering the increased importance of personal data processing in all facets of society and the increased benefits as well as risks for data subjects, this seems both an unreasonable expectation as well as an undesirable way forward. Instead, it seems more reasonable to expect that more guarantees will be needed instead of less, to ensure the respect for information privacy and the continued trust in information technologies in a world in which any piece of data that is collected can end up being used for any purpose. In sum, to the extent that the advocacy of use regulation can be characterized as a deregulatory agenda (Hoofnagle 2014), such advocacy is unconvincing.

The criticism of the notice and choice requirement by use-based regulation advocates can be considered in this light as well. The argument that notice and choice puts unrealistic and undue burdens on individuals is actually quite convincing. But what conclusions should be drawn from this criticism? First and foremost, the conclusion would be that notice and choice is, for the most part, not a convincing mechanism for determining the *legitimacy* of data processing activities and that alternatives for establishing this legitimacy are needed. Nissenbaum's theory of privacy as contextual integrity is centrally concerned with establishing such an alternative, in which consent plays a much more limited normative role. Instead, objective information privacy norms should be derived from context-depended values, norms and expectations with respect to personal information flows (Nissenbaum 2009). In this theory, privacy:

> "is a right to live in a world in which our expectations about the flow of personal information are, for the most part, met; expectations that are shaped not only by force of habit and convention but a general confidence in the mutual support these flows accord to key organizing principles of social life, including moral and political ones" (Nissenbaum 2009: 231).

European data protection law, although increasingly preoccupied with informed consent as the primary legitimate ground, entails a theory of legitimate grounds that allows substantive, objective assessments of legitimacy to take place.

The debate about collection and use also illustrates a fundamental tension at the basis of privacy and data protection laws, i.e. the tension between privacy as a right to be let alone, on the one hand, and privacy as the fair data-driven treatment of individuals, on the other. The tension can be illustrated with a simple small data example. Article 41 of the Dutch Data Protection Act gives individuals the right to object to the processing of their personal data for marketing purposes. A paradoxical situation emerges for people requesting the deletion of their data from a specific organization. Instead of their request leading to deletion from the marketer's databases, their data now ends up being lawfully included in the marketer's objectors file (Court of Appeals Amsterdam 2011). This file will help ensure the person will no longer receive marketing messages. But from the perspective of privacy as a right to be let alone, this solution is unsatisfactory as it would require the marketer to stop processing the person's data altogether.

A more general version of this tension emerges when one recognizes that the fair data-driven treatment of individuals may have to involve the processing of additional data to ensure that no undue or unfair treatment takes place. In their discussion of Big Data and discrimination, Barocas and Selbst explain that protection against undue discrimination in data mining may sometimes necessitate the collection of more data (Barocas and Selbst, forthcoming). Van der Sloot has argued for data *minimum*mization (instead of minimization), proposing that a minimum of data is collected, stored and clustered, in particular metadata establishing the context of the data, to ensure fair personal data processing through knowledge discovery (Van der Sloot 2011). Interestingly, these arguments seem to imply that purpose specification and limitation would be more important than ever because the legitimacy of such additional data collection in view of fair treatment of data subjects can be much more easily established if the data is only and specifically used for the promised beneficial purposes.

Within boundaries, it is appropriate that data privacy laws allow for the collection and use of additional data to ensure fair data-driven treatment. At some point, however, the argument for more and richer data for a better world will cease to be convincing. For instance, it would be hard to accept the bulk collection of large troves of personal data simply to ensure that no innocent people are convicted of crimes. While some Big Data enthusiasts may embrace the value of bad and messy data (Hoofnagle 2013: 5), this can hardly mean that data privacy law should simply allow the processing of incorrect data, undoing the principle of information quality in data privacy altogether.

The collection and use debate may be best summarized as being about establishing new frameworks for determining the legitimacy of large data processing infrastructures. Considering the historical role of data protection law, it is also about establishing new frameworks for achieving general societal acceptance for personal data processing taking place in the private and public sector. The use-based regulation approach would not only radically shift the balance between competing legal principles underlying the right to privacy as a right to be let alone towards the fair and legitimate processing of personal data. In the process, it would also erode the legitimacy assessment currently in place for the processing of personal data, applicable from the moment of collection. What would take centre stage are requirements for data security, transparency and enforcement of any measures the data controller has taken to ensure the data is only used in the ways it has considered legitimate. What would be left out are legitimate political, social and moral concerns about the ways in which the collection of personal data shapes and affects people's lives from the moment of collection.

The discussion of European data protection law and the GDPR proposals show that some shift in this direction is not unlikely. Specifically, the GDPR, as adopted, is likely to end up providing more flexibility for the re-use of data for purposes incompatible with the purposes established at the time of collection. This remains controversial and problematic in view of the continued Commission's assertions that the GDPR would not undermine the level of protection established by the DPD (MacNamee 2015). A complete reorientation of European data protection to regulating use seems unlikely, however, for a number of reasons. First, as discussed at the beginning of this section, concerns about the collection of personal data remain at the heart of the fundamental right to privacy in European constitutions and the EU Charter. A strong reorientation would make data protection rules incompatible with the fundamental rights framework, creating constitutional turbulence for decades to come. Second, the omnibus character of European data protection law and its hostility towards exceptions has a strong political and institutional link with the project of European integration (Schwartz 2009). It is unlikely, therefore, that essential areas of data processing activities (collection) will be deregulated at the European level.

A use-based regulatory approach to data privacy is more easily compatible with US privacy law. US law already contains various examples of use-based regulation and lacks a general principle of collection limitation, but there are some hurdles. First, use-based regulation would no longer apply the principle of notice and choice at the moment of collection as the primary assessment for establishing legitimacy of data processing in the consumer privacy context. Considering the deep-rooted ideological attachment to the idea of privacy self-management, this transformation could prove to be a difficult and long process. Second, US constitutional law continues to entail the principle, although increasingly controversial, that data collected by third parties generally loses its fourth amendment protection in view of government collection. From a European perspective, the absence of a comprehensive regulatory framework for the activities of data brokers can easily serve as an example of what not to like in use-based regulation. Under US law, data brokers can collect, combine, analyse and sell their data largely without any transparency and accountability. Use regulation exists, but mostly as a form of contractual agreements between the sources of data and their subsequent users.

It appears fair to assert that underlying use-based regulation advocacy is the belief that the commercial and societal value present in large data collections is too great to continue restricting the lifecycle of personal data. What the proliferation of data analytics in almost every aspect of society means, however, is that there is more rather than less at stake for people than in the 1970s, when these principles were adopted in the face of mounting public pressure and privacy concerns. And much is at stake from the moment of collection, including the abuse of data, data ending in the wrong hands, old and new unpredictable forms of unfair treatment and discrimination and a general exacerbation of power imbalances. In other words, the real challenge is not to weaken existing protections but to find new ones that give new interpretations to the right to privacy in the digital age.

An ongoing orientation of data privacy law as being concerned with establishing restrictions on the collection of data, including the principle of purpose limitation functioning from the moment of collection, does not imply that use-based regulation does not deserve the attention of scholars and regulators. It simply means this should not be seen as an alternative, but rather as a complementary regulatory strategy to ensure fairness and justice in Big Data analytics. Both sides of the debate about collection or use regulation should be able to agree that the challenges of data analytics for the effective protection of data privacy are substantial. Amongst the most challenging may be the fact that the personal data of others may be as significant as one's own data due to predictive analysis and uses (Barocas and Nissenbaum 2014). A convincing answer to this challenge, however, still needs to be developed.

9.5   CONCLUSION

This article has looked at the collection versus use debate from a comparative perspective. Specifically, it has looked at the question of the current and future position of the principle in data privacy law that personal data should only be collected and further processed for specified and legitimate purposes, established at the time of collection of the data. And it has looked at the question whether use-based regulation can be seen as an alternative for regulation focused on limiting data processing from the moment of collection of personal data, considering the rationales for such regulatory approaches.

Ultimately, the collection versus use debate centres on the question of how to establish legitimacy for the processing of personal data. As the frameworks for establishing such legitimacy in Europe and the US are different in various regards, the use versus collection debate plays out differently in these legal contexts. In general, the European framework is characterized by regulation of all personal data processing from the moment of collection of personal data. The US framework is primarily focused on addressing specific (perhaps the most egregious) data privacy issues, while leaving much to other than legal mechanisms. These differences notwithstanding, the article concludes that there are significant hurdles to refocusing data privacy law towards use-based regulation on both sides of the Atlantic. In Europe, the existing fundamental rights framework is one of these hurdles as well as the omnibus approach to data privacy regulation. In the US, the ideological attachment to notice and choice, a weak form of consent, as well as the third-party doctrine, stand in the way of the radical reorientation proposed by use-based regulation advocates. In addition, the existing experiences with use-based regulation in the US context can hardly be described as a resounding success.

At the core of the debate about collection and use-based approaches to data privacy is an inherent tension between different legal interpretations of the right to privacy, with the right to privacy as a right to be let alone, on the one hand, and the right to the fair processing of personal data, on the other. Data privacy law will have to come to grips with this inherent tension and find ways to respect both rights without undoing either one of them. The most productive way to address this tension would be to see use-based regulation not as an alternative to regulation of collection, but as a complimentary regulatory strategy that can help address some of the new challenges to privacy inherent in the possibilities of large-scale data analytics.

REFERENCES

Alsenoy, B. van et al. (2015) 'From Social Media Service to Advertising Network, a Critical Analysis of Facebook's Revised Policies and Terms', Draft study, commissioned by the Belgian Privacy Commission 31 March 2015, available at: www.law.kuleuven.be/icri/en/news/item/facebooks-revised-policies-and-terms-v1-2.pdf.

Article 29 Working Party (2013a) 'Opinion on Purpose Limitation', Brussels.

Article 29 Working Party (2013b) 'Statement on Big Data', Brussels.

Article 29 Working Party (2015a) 'Press Release on Chapter II of the Draft Regulation for the March JHA Council', Brussels.

Article 29 Working Party (2015b) 'Opinion on the Draft Regulation in View of the Trilogue, Press Release', Brussels.

Baer, M.H. (2014) 'Secrecy, Intimacy, and Workable Rules: Justice Sotomayor Stakes Out the Middle Ground in United States v. Jones', *The Yale Law Journal* 123: 393.

Bambauer, J. (2013) 'Is Data Speech', *Stanford Law Review* 66, 1: 57.

Barocas, S. and H. Nissenbaum (2014) 'Big Data's End Run around Procedural Privacy Protections', *Communications of the* ACM 57, 11: 31-33.

Barocas, S. and A.D. Selbst, 'Big Data's Disparate Impact', *California Law Review* 104, (forthcoming).

Bennett, C.J. (1992) *Data Protection and Public Policy in Europe and the United States*, Ithaca and London: Cornell University Press.

Bits of Freedom (2012) 'A Loophole in Data Processing', available at: www.bof.nl/live/wp-content/uploads/20121211_onderzoek_legitimate-interests-def.pdf [11 December 2012].

Bundesverfassungsgericht (1983) BVerfG 65, 1 (*Volkszählung*).

Bygrave, L. (2002) *Data Protection Law: Approaching its Rationale, Logic and Limits*, Information Law Series 10, The Hague: Kluwer Law.

Cate, F.H. et al. (2014) 'Data Protection Principles for the 21st Century, Revising the 1980 OECD Guidelines', available at: https://ico.org.uk/media/for-organisations/documents/1541/big-data-and-data-protection.pdf.

Cate, F.H. and V. Mayer-Schönberger (2013) 'Notice and Consent in a World of Big Data', *International Data Privacy Law* 3, 2.

CJEU 8 April 2014, Joined Cases C-293/12 and C-594/12 (*Digital Rights Ireland*).

Convention for the Protection of Individuals with Regard to Automatic Processing of Personal Data (Convention 108) adopted in 1981, Council of Europe, Strasbourg.

Council Directive 95/46/EC of 24 October 1995 on the Protection of Individuals with Regard to the Processing of Personal Data and on the Free Movement of Such Data.

Council of the European Union (2015) Council General Approach to the General Data Protection Regulation, as Included in Interinstitutional File 10391/15, 2012/011 (COD), Brussels, 8 July 2015, available at: www.statewatch.org/news/2015/jul/eu-council-dp-reg-trilogue-10391-15.pdf.

Court of Appeals Amsterdam 15 February 2011, ECLI:NL: GHAMS: 2011: BQ4006.

Court of Appeals Den Bosch 19 August 2014, ECLI: NL: GHSHE: 2014: 2803.

Dutch Code of Conduct Financial Industry (2010) 'Gedragscode Verwerking Persoonsgegevens Financiële Instellingen', approved by the Dutch Data Protection Authority on 13 April 2010, *Staatscourant* 6429, 26 April.

Dutch Data Protection Authority (2013) 'Investigation into the Combining of Personal Data by Google', *Report of Definitive Findings*, November: z2013-00194.

Dutch Data Protection Authority (2014) 'Cease and Desist Decision with Respect to Google', The Hague, available at: https://cbpweb.nl/sites/default/files/atoms/files/last_onder_dwangsom_google_privacyvoorwaarden.pdf [17 November 2014].

Dutch Ministry of Security and Justice (2014a) *Brief aan de Tweede Kamer over Verkenning kaderwet gegevensuitwisseling*, 19 December, The Hague.

Dutch Ministry of Security and Justice (2014b) *Rapport Werkgroep Verkenning Kaderwet Gegevensuitwisseling*, 19 December, The Hague.

European Commission (2012) *Proposal for a Regulation of the European Parliament and of the Council on the Protection of Individuals with Regard to the Processing of Personal Data and on the Free Movement of Such Data* (General Data Protection Regulation) COM 11 final.

European Data Protection Supervisor (2012) *Opinion of the European Data Protection Supervisor on the Data Protection Reform Package*, Brussels, 7 March.

European Data Protection Supervisor (2015) 'Europe's Big Opportunity, EDPS Recommendations on the EU's Options for Data Protection Reform', *Opinion* 3/2015, 27 July.

European Parliament (2014) *Legislative Resolution on the General Data Protection Regulation*, COM(2012) 0011 – C7-0025/2012, Strasbourg, 12 March 2014.

Fair Credit Reporting Act, consolidated text available at: www.consumer.ftc.gov/sites/default/files/articles/pdf/pdf-0111-fair-credit-reporting-act.pdf.

Federal Trade Commission (2014) *Data Brokers, a Call for Transparency and Accountability*, May.

Fundamental Rights Agency (2014) 'Handbook on European Data Protection Law', available at: http://fra.europa.eu/sites/default/files/fra-2014-handbook-data-protection-law_en.pdf.

Gellman, B. (2015) 'Fair Information Practices, Version 2.13', available at: http://bobgellman.com/rg-docs/rg-FIPShistory.pdf [11 February 2015].

Grimmelmann, J. (2015) 'An Offer You Can't Understand', JOTWELL, 15 May.

Hoboken, J.V.J. van (2006) 'Wrikken en wegen over gegevens, Een analyse van de weging van het belang van de burger bij de nieuwe regeling voor de strafrechtelijke gegevensvergaring', Master's Thesis in Law under Supervision of L.F. Asscher, Amsterdam: Universiteit van Amsterdam, April 2006.

Hoboken, J.V.J. van, A. Arnbak and N.A.N.M. van Eijk (2013) 'Obscured by Clouds or How to Address Governmental Access to Cloud Data from Abroad', *Privacy Law Scholars Conference 2013*, available at: http://papers.ssrn.com/sol3/papers.cfm?abstract_id=2276103.

Hoboken, J.V.J. van and I. Rubinstein (2014) 'Privacy and Security in the Cloud: Some Realism about Technical Solutions to Transnational Surveillance in the Post-Snowden Era', *66 Maine Law Review* 488.

Hoofnagle, C. (2013) 'How the Fair Credit Reporting Act Regulates Big Data', *Future of Privacy Forum Workshop on Big Data and Privacy: Making Ends Meet*, available at: (SSRN) http://papers.ssrn.com/sol3/papers.cfm?abstract_id=2432955.

Hoofnagle, C. (2014) 'The Potemkinism of Privacy Pragmatism', *Slate*, 2 September.

Kerr, O. (2009) 'The Case for the Third-Party Doctrine', *107 Michigan Law Review* 561.

Koops, B.J. (2013) 'On Decision Transparency, or How to Enhance Data Protection after the Computational Turn', pp. 196-220 in M. Hildebrandt and K. de Vries (eds.) *Privacy, Due Process and the Computational Turn*, Abingdon: Routledge.

Koops, B.J. (2014) 'The Trouble with European Data Protection Law', *International Data Privacy Law*, Doi: 10.1093/idpl/ipu023.

Kosta, E. (2013) *Consent in European Data Protection Law*, Leiden: Nijhoff Studies in EU Law.

Landau, S. (2015) 'Control the Use of Data to Protect Privacy', *Science* 347, 6221: 504506.

MacNamee, J. (2015) 'EU Commission – Finally – Confirms That Its Promise on Data Protection Will Be Respected', *European Digital Rights*, 22 July.

Martijn, M. (2014) 'Politie en inlichtingendiensten kunnen via een achterdeur bij gegevens van de Belastingdienst', *De Correspondent*, 30 September.

McDowell, D.F., D. Reed Freeman and J.M. Harper (2013) 'Privacy Class Actions: Current Trends and New Frontiers in 2013', *Bloomberg Law* 3, July.

Ministerie van Binnenlandse Zaken (2015) *Concept-wetsvoorstel Wet op de inlichtingen- en veiligheidsdiensten* 20xx; Consultatieversie.

Moerel, E.M.L. and J.E.J. Prins (2015) *Further Processing of Data Based on the Legitimate Interest Ground: The End of Purpose Limitation?*, Tilburg: Tilburg University.

Mundie, C. (2014) 'Privacy Pragmatism', *Foreign Affairs*, March/April 2014.

Nissenbaum, H. (2009) *Privacy in Context, Technology, Policy and the Integrity of Social Life*, Stanford, CA: Stanford University Press.

Prins, C., D. Broeders, H. Griffioen, A.G. Keizer and E. Keymolen (2011) *iGovernment*, report 86, Amsterdam: Amsterdam University Press.

Roessler, B. and D. Mokrosinska (2015) *Social Dimensions of Privacy, Interdisciplinary Perspectives*, Cambridge: Cambridge University Press.

Schwartz, P.M. (2009) 'Pre-Emption and Privacy', *Yale Law Review* 118, 5: 902.

Sloot, B. van der (2013) 'From Data Minimization to Data Minimummization', pp. 273-287 in B. Custers et al. (eds.) *Discrimination and Privacy in the Information Society*, SAPERE 3, Berlin Heidelberg: Springer-Verlag.

Solove, D.J. (2013) 'Privacy Self-Management and the Consent Dilemma', 126 *Harvard Law Review*, 1880.

Solove, D.J. and W. Hartzog (2014) 'The FTC and the New Common Law of Privacy', *114 College Law Review* 583.

Spokeo (2014) *Petition for a Writ of Certiorari Filed*, available at:
http://sblog.s3.amazonaws.com/wp-content/uploads/2014/06/13-1339-
Spokeo-Inc.-v.-Robins-Br.-for-Amici-eBay-Inc.-et-al.-Jun....pdf [May 2014].

Strandburg, K.J. (2008) 'Freedom of Association in a Networked World. First Amendment
Regulation of Relational Surveillance', *49 B.C.L. Review* 741.

Strandburg, K.J. (2011) 'Home, Home on the Web and Other Fourth Amendment
Implications of Technosocial Change' 70', *Maryland Law Review* 101.

Strandburg, K.J. (2014) 'Monitoring, Datafication, and Consent: Legal Approaches to
Privacy in the Big Data Context' in J. Lane et al. (eds.) *Privacy, Big Data and the
Public Good, Frameworks for Engagement*, Cambridge: Cambridge University
Press.

U.S. Department of Health, Education and Welfare (1973) *Secretary's Advisory Committee
on Automated Personal Data Systems, Records, computers, and the Rights of
Citizens*, Washington DC.

Westin, A. (1970) *Privacy and Freedom*, New York: Atheneum.

White House (2014a) *Big Data: Seizing Opportunities Preserving Values*, Executive Office of
the President of the United States.

White House (2014b) *Big Data and Privacy: A Technological Perspective*, Executive Office of
the President of the United States, PCAST.

World Economic Forum (2013) 'Unlocking the Value of Personal Data: From Collection to
Usage, World Economic Forum, Industry Agenda', prepared in collaboration with
The Boston Consulting Group Industry.

NOTES

1 The GDPR proposals were made by the European Commission in January 2012 (European Commission 2012). The European Parliament adopted its position in first reading in March 2014 (European Parliament 2014). The Council finalized its General Approach in Spring 2015 (Council of the European Union 2015). On this basis, the institutions have started their trialogue negotiation process, which they aim to conclude before the end of 2015, in which case the GDPR could be officially adopted in early 2016. The EU data protection supervisor EDPS has issued its own set of detailed recommendations with respect to the proposed GDPR in July 2015 (EDPS 2015).

2 Regulation No xxx/2016, on the protection of individuals with regard to the processing of personal data and on the free movement of such data (General Data Protection Regulation). Consolidated text available at www.emeeting.europarl.europa.eu/committees/agenda/ 201512/LIBE/LIBE%282015%291217_1/sitt-1739884. The GDPR will enter into force two years after its official adoption, in early 2018.

3 With respect to the processing of personal data by state bodies for national security and intelligence, the EU generally does not have any competence. There are a number of EU level instruments with respect to the protection of personal data in the law enforcement context and with respect to specific EU level data processing systems related to immigration and policing. Together with the proposals for a new Regulation replacing the DPD, an EC proposal was made for a new Directive for the protection of personal data in the law enforcement context, providing for more harmonization at the EU level. A discussion of these instruments goes beyond the scope of this article.

4 For a discussion of these laws and the policy and scientific debate leading up to them, see Van Hoboken 2006.

5 National data retention obligations remain in place in a number of European member states, including the UK.

6 This consideration about the core of the right to data protection is somewhat surprising. The fact that these particular measures to prevent loss or destruction of data seem to have been included in the Directive in view of the value of the data for government agencies and not in view of data privacy of individuals concerned seems to have escaped the CJEU's attention.

7 Or, in the words of the Advocate General, what requires "the utmost vigilance [is] the actual collection and retention of the data at issue, as well as the data's impact on the right to privacy [...]". AG Opinion 12 December 2013, CJEU, C-293/12 (*Digital Rights*), par. 59.

8 For a review of endorsement of different versions and sets of Fair Information Practice Principles by the FTC, see Gellman 2015.

9 For a discussion of the increasing occurrence of privacy class action litigation in the , see McDowell et al. 2013.

10   On the question of the social and collective value of privacy, see recently Roessler and
        Mokrosinska (eds.) 2015. Nissenbaum's theory of privacy as contextual integrity also empha-
        sizes the (context-dependent) social, political and moral values inherent in the right to pri-
        vacy (Nissenbaum 2009).

10 BIG DATA AND INFORMATIONAL SELF-DETERMINATION. REGULATIVE APPROACHES IN GERMANY: THE CASE OF POLICE AND INTELLIGENCE AGENCIES

Alexander Roßnagel & Philipp Richter

10.1 INFORMATIONAL SELF-DETERMINATION: THE FOUNDATION OF GERMAN DATA PROTECTION

The right to 'Informational Self-Determination' was concretized by the German Federal Constitutional Court (BVerfGE) in 1983 from the basic liberties in Art. 2 I and 1 I German Constitution (GG) as protection from the risks of modern data processing. Data subjects may generally decide for themselves on the extent of disclosure and the processing of their personal information (BVerfGE 65, 1 [43]). Alongside Freedom of Information and Secrecy of Telecommunications, Informational Self-Determination is the central basic right of the information society (Trute 2003: 153 ff.). It includes protection for the individual as well as objective protection for a democratic society.

Informational Self-Determination on one hand enables the freedom of decisions, including the possibility to act upon these decisions (BVerfGE 65, 1 [42 f.]). On the other hand, Informational Self-Determination makes possible the self-determined development and unfolding of the individual. The individual's personality is constituted by the overall picture of the person acting and communicating in different social roles. The development and unfolding of personality requires individuals to be able to present themselves in these roles and have these presentations reflected back in communication with others. Individual development and unfolding can only succeed if data subjects can control disclosure of their persons. If they cannot keep track of when and under what circumstances such disclosure takes place, they may be severely impeded in their ability to plan and decide in a self-determined manner (BVerfGE 65, 1 [43]). Individuals need to be able to decide what personal information they disclose in what social role. The importance of autonomous decision-making in the disclosure of personal information is protected by Informational Self-Determination.

This individual right is encroached upon by anyone processing personal data against the data subject's will, regardless of whether the processor is a public agency or a private corporation. The data subject is in equal need of protection in both cases, and in both cases disregard for the subject's Informational

Self-Determination is a legally relevant encroachment of this basic right (BVerfGE 84, 192 [195]). However, the legislator may determine under what circumstances and precautions such an encroachment will be allowed in the public interest.

Even if every disregard for Informational Self-Determination is an encroachment on this basic right, encroachment by state institutions and private corporations must be distinguished. Only for the former does the right include a directly defensive function. Private corporations may invoke civil liberties, Freedom of Profession being foremost among them. However, basic rights do not legitimize encroachment on other basic rights. It is rather the legislator's duty to define the scope of competing basic rights in a way that acting upon them will not interfere with the basic rights of others. Insofar as the legislator does not confine Informational Self-Determination in favour of legitimate private interests, private bodies have no right to process the personal data of others (Roßnagel et al. 2001: 46 ff.).

Informational Self-Determination is not only the individual right of the data subject. It is also the foundation of free and democratic communication. A societal and legal order where citizens cannot know who knows what about them on a given occasion would be incompatible with the right to Informational Self-Determination. It would not only impede personal development, but also the public interest, because self-determination is an elementary requirement for a free democratic community built on the ability of its members to act and contribute (BVerfGE 65, 1 [43]; BVerfG 2006, 979). The basic right protects citizens from being intimidated in the practice of other basic rights, which can stem from not knowing who knows what about oneself on a given occasion (BVerfG 2006, 979). Informational Self-Determination thus supports a communication order which enables a self-determined exchange of information and a free democratic forming of the political will.

In this more than individual function, Informational Self-Determination is one element of an 'objective order of values' – a constitutional decision that applies to all areas of law, providing guidelines and impulses for legislation and administration as well as jurisdiction (BVerfGE 39, 1 [41]). Informational Self-Determination, together with other basic rights, is the cornerstone of a free societal order. It is to be observed in the interpretation of all legal norms and fills out the widely formulated norms in civil law.

Informational Self-Determination is thus the precondition for the practice of all other civil liberties. Any practice of such liberties through communication would be endangered without the self-determined exchange of information. Informational Self-Determination is the foundation of a democratic order of communication – an elementary requirement for civil engagement in a free democracy.

10.2   INFORMATIONAL SELF-DETERMINATION VS. INFORMATION PRIVACY

Informational Self-Determination does not establish a proprietary legal position over personal data. As a precondition for a free and democratic society, it is not left to the individual to market his data for a price. Such an understanding would not do justice to the character of personal data as a multi-relational model of reality (Steinmüller 1993: 261 ff). Car maintenance data not only 'belongs' to the car's owner, but also to the service station. An exclusive allocation is not possible, neither to the author nor to the object of the reality model 'car maintenance' (BVerfGE 65, 1 [44]). Rather, Informational Self-Determination calls for an order of information and communication in which everybody is allowed to interact with this model in a specific manner. This order shall not impede but enable communication in a self-determined manner.

Informational Self-Determination is therefore not limited to a 'right to be left alone', as is the protection of 'Privacy' in the US. This is rather the function of basic rights granting withdrawal from society, as Privacy of the Home in Art. 12 GG or Secrecy of Mail and Telecommunications in Art. 10 GG. The basic right to Informational Self-Determination protects everybody acting and communicating *in* society. Societal engagement requires communication leading to an obligation to communicate and disclose personal data in specific situations. Insofar as collective or individual interests of greater importance require, the processing of personal data against the individual's will is possible. Data protection law regulates these situations.

European law does not use the term 'Informational Self-Determination'. Art. 8 I of the European Convention on Human Rights grants a right to "respect for [...] private and family life, [...] home and correspondence". Art. 7 of the European Convention on Human Rights (HRC) has a similar formulation. However, The European Court of Human Rights (ECtHR) sees more in the right to respect for private life than a mere "right to be left alone". In a broad sense, all areas of life which do not concern others belong to private life. In addition, Art. 8 HRC includes a separate right to the protection of personal data.

European data protection law has been heavily influenced by the concept of Informational Self-Determination and its derivative concepts in regulation. Conceptual relations to the jurisdiction of the German Constitutional Court can be found in the jurisdiction of the ECtHR as well as the European Court of Justice. The data protection Directive includes numerous principles derived from the Basic Right to Informational Self-Determination, and drafts for a general data protection regulation continue to maintain them.

10.3   INFORMATIONAL SELF-DETERMINATION AND PUBLIC SECURITY MEASURES

In order to give teeth to the basic right, the Constitutional Court has derived requirements for its protection in a number of rulings (BVerfGE, 65, 1 [44 ff.]; 84, 192 [195]; 100, 313 [358 ff.]; 110, 33 [52 ff.]; 113, 348 [364 ff.]). Specifications in data protection law, especially in the Federal Data Protection Act (BDSG), are often implementations of this normative protection programme. Every processing of personal data is an encroachment on the basic right to Informational Self-Determination (BVerfGE 100, 313 [366]). This also applies to the processing of personal data by private bodies (BVerfGE 84, 192 [195]), which shall be prevented as far as is possible (§ 3a BDSG; Roßnagel 2011: 41 ff.). It is only allowed if the legislator or the data subject have allowed it, regarding both purpose and scope (§ 4 I BDSG).

The processing of personal data must be made transparent to data subjects so that they will be able to assess its legality and enforce their rights (e.g. §§ 4 III, 33 and 34 BDSG). The processing of data must be restricted to the approved purpose and may only be executed so long as it is necessary for achieving this purpose (e.g. §§ 12 ff., 28 BDSG). These principles must be assured by technical and organizational measures (§ 9 BDSG). The data subject is entitled to participation rights and damages (e.g. §§ 6 and 35, 7 and 8 BDSG).

These requirements generally also apply to the processing of personal data for the purpose of public security. As far as telecommunications are concerned, the Secrecy of Telecommunications in Art. 10 I GG takes precedence, but the Constitutional Court has derived similar requirements from it as from Informational Self-Determination (BVerfGE 100, 313 [359]; 110, 33 [53]), so that both basic rights may be seen as interrelated in this context. In a number of rulings over the past 15 years, the Court has specified requirements for the processing of personal data.

Not only is examining personal data an encroachment on basic rights; collecting personal data is one as well. The severity of the encroachment is measured mainly by the information included in the collected data. The encroachment may be deemed more serious if a measure has broad impact, affecting many people who are not targets of surveillance (BVerfGE 120, 274 [323]; BVerfGE 113, 348 [382f.]; BVerfGE 34, 238 [247]; 107, 299 [321]). It may be more serious if there is no inducement or suspicion, leaving the data subject without options to evade surveillance (BVerfGE 100, 313 [376]; 107, 299 [318 ff.]; 109, 279 [353]; 115, 320 [347]). Encroachment may be more serious if the surveillance takes place secretly, leaving citizens no possibility to defend themselves (BVerfGE 107, 299 [321]; 115, 166 [194]; 115, 320 [353]; 118, 168 [197f.]; see also BVerfGE 113, 348 [383f.]; 110, 33 [53]; 120, 274 [323f.]). Breaking the legitimate trust of data subjects may also increase the severity of encroachment (BVerfGE 113, 348 [383]; see also BVerfGE 34, 238 [247]; 107, 299 [321]).

Finally, an encroachment is seen as especially severe if it enables extensive insight into a person's personality, up to and including profiles of behaviour and communication habits (BVerfGE 120, 274 [323f.]).

Encroachments on Informational Self-Determination by state agencies are only allowed if explicitly permitted by law. Requirements for such legal provisions – especially exactness and proportionality, applying to domestic security measures – have been formulated by the Constitutional Court.

Legal provisions must be exact enough so that citizens can adapt to incriminating measures, administrators can find in them guiding and limiting instructions for their execution, and courts can carry out legal supervision (BVerfGE 110, 33 [52 ff.]; 113, 348 [375 ff.]). The exactness of laws is in the first place supposed to prevent decisions on citizens' freedom being put to the sole discretion of public administration (BVerfGE 78, 214 [226]; 110, 33 [54]). The inducement, purpose and boundaries of an encroachment must be determined area-specifically, precisely and clearly in the legal provision permitting it (BVerfGE 100, 313 [359f., 372]; 110, 33 [53]. 113, 348 [375]; 118, 168 [186f.]; 120, 274 [315f.]). By binding surveillance measures to specific inducement and by dictating specific thresholds, the data subject must be able to see on what occasions and under what preconditions behaviour is likely to be surveilled (BVerfGE 113, 348 ([376]).

Generally, the Constitutional Court has accepted the objective of prevention and therefore permits encroachments prior to tangible threats or suspicion. When the legislator is unable to bind preventive encroachment to the threshold of tangible threat or suspicion, he must describe crimes taken as inducement and requirements for facts taken as pointing to future transgressions with enough precision to make the risk of a false prognosis constitutionally acceptable, which is known to be especially high in the early stages of investigation (BVerfGE 110, 33 [56]; 113, 348 [377f.]). The principle of legal exactness also applies to preventive investigations and demands provisional characteristics limiting the scope of possible measures. They must set a standard that enables the anticipation and monitoring of surveillance measures similar to the one demanded by the rule of law for traditional threat prevention and criminal prosecution (BVerfGE 110, 33 [55f.]).

The principle of proportionality is significant, especially the requirement for measures to be objectively reasonable (or adequate). The legislator must shape affairs in a way that prohibits one-sided solutions and balances domestic security and the protection of basic rights (BVerfGE 113, 348 [382]). The protection of basic rights must prevail as much as possible. This means that thresholds for encroachment must be adequately high in relation to the severity of encroachment and significance of the basic right and the level of its exposure (BVerfGE 115, 320 [345]; see also BVerfGE 100, 313 [383f.]; 109, 279 [350 ff.]; 115, 320 [345f.]; 118, 168 [197); 120. 274

[322]). Many surveillance measures are only permitted to deter or prosecute severe crimes, not petty crimes or those of middle severity (e.g. BVerfGE 113, 348 ([387]). In preventing threats, a concrete threat to a highly valued legal objective is necessary, for example the stability of the state or the life, health or freedom of a person (BVerfGE 115, 320). Many surveillance measures are only permitted if concrete evidence or specific circumstances arise, indicating a considerably raised and sufficiently probable level of risk (BVerfGE 115, 320 [361f.], Rn. 137; see also BVerfGE 100, 313 [383f.]; 109, 279 [350 ff.]; 113, 348 [386f.]). Informational Self-Determination does not allow 'shots in the dark' if investigative measures interfere with basic rights (e.g. BVerfGE 115, 320 ([361]).

Protective measures for basic rights must be determined for a measure to be proportional (BVerfGE 65, 1 [44]; BVerfGE 53, 30 (65); 63, 131 [143]; 120. 274 [326]). This requires, for example, special scrutiny before the encroachment takes place, special protection of collected data, or a court order by an independent judge for each individual case (BVerfGE 120, 274 [331]; 113, 348 (391f.); SächsVerfGH, JZ 1996, 957 [964]). Finally, a measure is only proportional if it is as transparent as possible to data subjects, enabling them to request legal protection.

The Constitutional Court in its ruling on data retention has decreed that freedom from total recording and registration is part of the constitutional identity of the Federal Republic of Germany (BVerfGE 125 [260], Rn. 218; concerning constitutional identity see also BVerfG, NJW 2009, 2267 [2272], Rn. 240). Legislation aiming at the comprehensive storage of all data useful to prevent threats and prosecute crimes would be unconstitutional from the outset; taken together, surveillance measures must not impinge on the activities of all citizens by allowing for all citizens' activities to be reconstructed from different sources to preserve its constitutional identity, Germany may even be bound to vote against further surveillance measures in the European and international context (BVerfGE 125 [260] Rn. 218).

10.4   INFORMATIONAL SELF-DETERMINATION AND BIG DATA

While the Constitutional Court has not yet ruled on the processing of personal data in Big Data analytics, the issue is hotly debated in the legal literature on data protection. Big Data here must answer to the protection of Informational Self-Determination implemented in data protection law. Big Data contrasts sharply with the effective data protection principles.

The principle of *purpose binding* means that personal data may only be processed for specific and predetermined purposes. But the very concept of Big Data is to retain data for unspecified purposes and to combine data freely and repeatedly. The principle of the *necessity* of processing personal data for specific purposes will be bypassed if no purpose has been determined in advance. If data is to be analysed for unspecified purposes, it will always be necessary. Legal provisions and individual consent permitting data processing are also meant to limit it to specific purposes. They hereby prohibit the free use of personal data in Big Data analytics. The *transparency* of processing personal data is also hard to implement in Big Data as the data is so large and unstructured; even analysts often cannot comprehend which data has been used in a specific case. The principle of *data reduction and data economy* is flatly contradicted by Big Data.

Big Data enables – as no technology has done before – the prediction of personal characteristics that have not even been disclosed, up to and including a citizen's political views and current emotional states. This conflicts with the *prohibition on personality profiles*. All chances for self-determined control over the flow of data by selection of disclosed information can be undermined. Big Data undercuts every information-asceticism by inference from similar people. Even if individuals have disclosed no personal information, their future behaviour may be inferred from similar persons who do disclose information. The right of the data subject to *correct* false data may also erode since prevailing probabilistic predictions cannot be deemed wrong so long as they are calculated on the basis of correct data.

10.5   APPLICATION OF BIG DATA BY POLICE AND INTELLIGENCE AGENCIES

Big Data promises great potential for security agencies. Its abilities for pattern recognition and prediction could enable predicting terror attacks and crime and thus more effective prevention.

10.5.1   BIG DATA AS DRAGNET INVESTIGATION BY POLICE AND INTELLIGENCE AGENCIES

Big Data offers highly efficient means for the surveillance of individuals, enabling de-anonymization, behaviour-monitoring and identifying individuals from the mass through predetermined characteristics, as in previous dragnet investigations, but in real-time. Using Big Data in dragnet investigations would therefore deepen known legal problems.

While police dragnet investigations have not been in the centre of surveillance discussions since the last ruling on the issue by the Constitutional Court in 2006 (BVerfGE 115, 320), similar measures by intelligence agencies, if under different names, have been in the centre of attention following the revelations of whistle-blower Edward Snowden in 2013. Revelations have disclosed to what extent intelligence agencies around the world, including German domestic and foreign intelligence agencies, have been collecting, exchanging and analysing electronic communications, e.g. in order to find wanted persons or to prevent crime (see e.g.

Greenwald 2014). Big Data plays a significant role here by analysing with search words huge amounts of telecommunications traffic data, internet usage data and content.

10.5.2 BIG DATA FOR PATTERN RECOGNITION AND EXTRACTION OF CHARACTERISTICS

Big Data, however, goes far beyond an efficient dragnet investigation. Big Data analytics are able to recognize new patterns through the statistical analysis of huge amounts of data. For security agencies, this means that new characteristics relevant to dragnet investigations may be found by for example analysing the social contacts or travel profiles of known terrorists for correlative patterns of behaviour or other circumstances. Having found such patterns, it becomes possible to screen the whole populace to detect potential offenders and to further surveillance or defensive measures.

10.5.3 PREDICTIVE POLICING

A specific development of Big Data pattern recognition is contained in so-called 'Predictive Policing'. This trend in law enforcement, with known products such as 'Precobs', reminds us of the movie 'Minority Report', where the police (aided by the 'Precogs') is able to arrest offenders even before they commit crimes. But predictive policing in reality only partly mirrors the movie. In recent approaches that have reached Germany from the US, predictive policing is not used to predict individual offenders (which at the moment is much more clearly the objective of the intelligence agencies). Rather, crime statistics are used to predict locations where crime is likely to happen. Based on these predictions, police can patrol more efficiently and prohibit crime by maintaining a high profile in select areas, only under best circumstances arresting unknown offenders red-handed. Generally, no personal data is processed electronically because police officers select offenders in the high-risk area based on their own know-how and experience.

However, more advanced approaches in the US have begun predicting individual offenders, leading to cautionary visits by the police (Erbentraut 2014). Also in the US, individual predictions on future criminal behaviour have been used in probation and parole decisions (Zetter 2013).

10.6   REGULATIVE APPROACHES TO BIG DATA

There has, to date, only been limited discussion on the regulation of Big Data (e.g. Ohrtmann/Schwiering 2014; Peschel/Rockstroh 2014; Weichert 2013). There is even less discussion of Big Data as a regulative challenge for police and intelligence agencies.

10.6.1 GENERAL DISCUSSION ON BIG DATA

In Germany several different approaches to data protection have been discussed
for Big Data. For example, due to the burden placed on data subjects, it has been
suggested that legal measures shift more responsibility to controllers so that the
data subject's consent is no longer the main legitimation of personal data processing (Mayer-Schönberger and Cukier 2013: 217 ff.; Katko and Babaei-Beigi 2014).
Restrictions on consent have also been suggested for areas where the disclosure of
personal information by one person may have, through statistical inference, negative consequences for other persons (Roßnagel 2013). As the non-discriminative
and transparent processing of data are seen as crucial, especially auditing for data
protection would have to be strengthened and adapted to the specific risks of
Big Data (Roßnagel 2013). Others have suggested that existing provisions on scoring in § 28b BDSG and on automated individual decisions in § 6a BDSG be further
developed to ensure the transparency of scoring processes and limit the use of discriminating characteristics (Weichert 2014). Due to Big Data's statistical approach,
these two provisions may become centralprovisions for future data protection.

Big Data offers very efficient means to de-anonymise data (Roßnagel 2013).
Data can be processed anonymously for a long time and then suddenly become
personal data through Big Data analytics. The subsequent protection of Informational Self-Determination then becomes nearly impossible. Against this background, we need to discuss how adequate preventive protection for anonymous
data might be designed. For example, processors might be held to check for the risk
of de-anonymization of specific anonymous data. For data with a high risk of de-
anonymization, specific provisions might be declared applicable as preventive precautions (Roßnagel et al. 2001: 61).

10.6.2 SPECIFIC DISCUSSION ON BIG DATA IN POLICE AND INTELLIGENCE AGENCIES

There has been scant legal discussion on regulating the use of Big Data by the public security services. However, jurisdiction on surveillance in general and discussions surrounding the NSA scandal provide leads that also apply to, or are related to, Big Data. These can be taken as starting points for regulation, which we discuss below.

10.7 BIG DATA BY POLICE AND INTELLIGENCE AGENCIES DE LEGE LATA

Police and intelligence agencies might fulfil their duties more efficiently if they
were allowed to apply Big Data. Wanted persons could be better recognized,
assessed and followed; Big Data analytics could help to make their profiles more
accurate and complete, or be used to de-anonymise data. Big Data could also help
create situational overviews, identifying connections, extracting formerly

unknown characteristics for developments to be observed, and predicting human behaviour or locations and time periods in which it is significantly more probable for the relevant behaviour to appear.

It stands to be analysed whether the police and intelligence agencies are permitted by law to apply Big Data analytics for these ends – to collect, record and analyse huge amounts of data from different sources. As far as traffic and content data from telecommunications are concerned, both the Secrecy of Telecommunications and Informational Self-Determination must be observed.

10.7.1   POLICE AGENCIES

The police are responsible for threat prevention and criminal prosecution. Police authority to prosecute is covered by the federal code of criminal procedure (StPO), while the authority to prevent threats is covered by the police codes of the Federation and the Länder. The police code of Hessen (HSOG) serves as an example below.

Collecting personal data

The collection of personal data for threat prevention is permitted by § 13 HSOG, if it is necessary to prevent a threat. In German police law, a threat is a situation which, if it develops unhindered, has sufficient probability to turn into damage. The collection of personal data is thereby limited to concrete individual cases. The police may also collect personal data from publicly available sources, for example public profiles in social networks. However, according to § 13 VI HSOG, every collection of data for unspecified and yet unspecifiable purposes is explicitly prohibited. § 15a HSOG requires a *current* threat (an even higher threshold in German police law than a normal threat) to the body, life or freedom of a person before the collection of telecommunications data is permitted. A court order is necessary for each individual case. Collecting personal data in order to store Big Data and to analyse it later for as yet unknown purposes is not permitted for threat prevention.

In criminal prosecution, collecting publicly available data from the internet is generally permitted without a legal provision, but only within the boundaries of a concrete criminal investigation. This data may not be used to purposefully gather personal data for individual profiling (BVerfG, NJW 2008, 822 [836]). The collection of telecommunication contents (§ 100a StPO) and traffic data (§ 100g StPO) is permitted only for individual cases if suspicion of a severe crime exists. Thus provisions for criminal prosecution do not permit the collection of Big Data without inducement.

Recording personal data

Personal data collected to prevent threats must be deleted according to § 27 II HSOG, if they are no longer necessary for this purpose. Data collected by way of § 100a StPO or § 100g StPO must be deleted according to § 101 VIII 1 StPO if they are no longer needed for prosecution or for a court review of the measure. Chance findings for other investigations will not be deleted, but may only be used for these. Retaining personal data for Big Data analytics with yet unspecified purposes is permitted neither for preventing threats nor for criminal prosecution.

Analysing personal data

Analysing recorded personal data with Big Data might be permitted for dragnet investigations. Dragnet investigations (§ 26 HSOG and § 98a StPO) are permitted only if a *concrete* threat (another specific threat threshold) arises to a highly valued legal objective, such as the stability or security of the Federation or a Land, or to the body, life or freedom of a person; generally menacing situations do not suffice (BVerfGE 115, 320 [357]). Even then, precautions must be observed, such as strict purpose binding, erasure of data as soon as this purpose has been fulfilled, and notification of the data subject as soon as this no longer hinders the investigation. The police are not allowed to freely analyse all legally collected and recorded personal data for dragnet investigations.

It remains unclear in what manner the police may determine characteristics for dragnet investigations. Big Data analytics might search for patterns in data records which are not personal data (any longer), uncovering behaviour patterns and human characteristics that may be indirect statistical indicators of criminal behaviour. If only anonymous data would be used, this extraction of characteristics would not fall within the scope of data protection law.

10.7.2 DOMESTIC INTELLIGENCE AGENCY

Domestic intelligence is conducted in Germany by the Federal and Länder Offices for the Protection of the Constitution. The following analysis focuses on the Federal Office.

Collecting personal data

According to § 3 I of the Code for the Federal Office (BVerfSchG), the office is responsible for collecting and analysing information on efforts against the free democratic order, the stability or security of the Federation or a Land, efforts that aim at violence, that endanger the foreign interests of the Federal Republic of Germany, or dangerous or intelligence efforts for foreign powers. According to § 8 I BVerfSchG, the office is permitted to collect information, including personal data, to fulfil this assignment. For this it may use intelligence tactics and measures, according to §§ 8 II and 9 BVerfSchG.

Collecting telecommunications content is only permitted if there is factual evidence for suspicion that a concrete person has committed a specific crime from a catalogue or that the person is a member of an anti-constitutional association according to § 3 of the Act for Restrictions on the Secrecy of Mail and

Telecommunications (G 10). Prohibitions on collection exist for communications by persons with the privilege to refuse giving evidence, such as ministers and defence attorneys (§ 3b I G 10). According to § 8a II Nr. 4 BVerfSchG, telecommunications traffic data may only be collected in individual cases if facts justify the assumption that severe threats have arisen to the legal objectives stated in § 3 BVerfSchG. The provision must be interpreted very narrowly in order to be constitutional and the legal objectives must be endangered by concrete actions. General, diffuse menacing situations do not suffice for the collection of traffic data (Bäcker 2014a: 5f.). The comprehensive collection of telecommunications data for Big Data analytics is not permitted.

Recording personal data

The Federal Office may record personal data according to § 10 BVerSchG if factual evidence for efforts stated in § 3 I BVerSchG are available and the data is necessary for investigation and the assessment of efforts or actions stated in § 3 I BVerfSchG. Telecommunications data may be recorded, according to § 4 I G 10, if a review conducted every six months finds that the data remain necessary for the purposes in § 1 Nr. 1 G 10. The comprehensive recording of data for future Big Data analyses is therefore not permitted. It nevertheless remains questionable whether collected data is effectively being erased due to this provision, since the necessity of retaining the data has not been fixed to the case for which they were collected, and collected data may prove helpful in uncovering other anti-constitutional activities. The severity of encroachment on the Secrecy of Telecommunications calls for a narrow interpretation of necessity. Nevertheless, there is a risk that a broad interpretation of necessity may arise in light of Big Data analytics.

Analysing personal data

§ 10 BVerfSchG applies to the analysis of collected and recorded personal data. Analysis of data is permitted if either factual evidence for anti-constitutional efforts (§ 3 I BVerfSchG) are available or it is necessary to investigate such efforts. The more specific § 4 G 10 applies to the analysis of telecommunications data. According to § 4 II G 10, telecommunications data may only be analysed for the intelligence purposes laid down in § 1 S. 1 G 10 and for criminal prosecution, according to § 4 IV G 10. For these purposes, data might also be used in Big Data analytics to uncover statistical patterns.

10.7.3   FOREIGN INTELLIGENCE

Foreign intelligence is conducted by the Federal Intelligence Service (BND).

Collecting personal data

According to § 1 II of the Federal Intelligence Service Act (BNDG), the BND is permitted to gather all information on foreign countries that is of foreign policy or security relevance to the Federal Republic of Germany. This allows the collection of all data, excluding personal data, of interest for this purpose. As far as personal data is concerned, § 2 through 6 and 8 through 11 BNDG must be observed. According to § 3 BNDG, the BND may use intelligence tactics and measures in collecting data.

For data connected to concrete persons, § 2a BNDG and § 3 G 10 state that the same provisions apply as for the Federal Office for the Protection of the Constitution. For each individual case, data collection must be necessary for the BND to fulfil its assignment. These provisions are not a legal basis for Big Data analysis.

Additionally to what domestic intelligence agencies are allowed to do, the BND may pursue strategic surveillance of international telecommunications without special inducement, according to § 5 G 10. For this, the raw data stream is screened using search words. Big Data might make this search more efficient, e.g. searching in social networks (N-TV 2014). This strategic surveillance is supposed to be limited by two criteria: it shall be limited to telecommunications with specific states or regions and be limited to 20 percent of traffic capacity. The latter, however, is not an actual limit since less than 20 percent of traffic capacity is usually used (Bäcker 2014a: 13f.). The Federal Administrative Court has recently interpreted this limit to mean that the BND may only surveil such wires that add up to a maximum of 20 percent of all traffic capacity (BVerwG, Ruling from 28.5.2014 - 6 A 1.13, Rn. 29). This limiting interpretation, however, could be bypassed by choosing the wires that conduct most of the traffic (Bäcker 2014b). The limit to specific states or regions has also recently been bypassed. Strategic surveillance of domestic communications is not permitted. However, since especially on the internet, domestic communications are conducted via other countries, all communications are being surveilled in a first step; only subsequently are domestic communications being filtered out (Bäcker 2014a: 10 f.). The BND is thus permitted to collect telecommunications data from different sources and sectors of society.

How search words used for strategic surveillance are extracted is not regulated. Big Data analytics could uncover correlations relevant to the search that have not been previously recognized. It remains highly questionable whether the BND is permitted to analyse telecommunications data using Big Data in order to extract search words; strategic surveillance is supposed to be limited by existing search words.

Recording personal data
Generally, personal data collected in an individual investigation may be recorded by the BND if this is necessary to fulfil its assignment according to § 4 BNDG. According to § 4 G 10, telecommunications data must be reviewed instantly and then every 6 months to asses if retaining it remains necessary for intelligence purposes. If not, the data must be erased. The general retention of all collected per-

sonal data for Big Data analyses is therefore not permitted. However, the data need not be necessary for the individual case for which they have been collected, but only generally for intelligence purposes as laid down in § 1 I G 10. Since the BND is assigned to gather information of foreign policy and security relevance, it might be argued that data which currently have no recognizable relation to these objectives would still be necessary because in Big Data analyses they might help recognize patterns, which do have such a relation. Such a broad interpretation would render the principle of necessity ineffective.

According to § 6 I G 10, data collected in strategic surveillance may only be recorded in so far as it is necessary for the purposes laid down in § 5 I G 10. This is being assessed using the search words. Irrelevant data must be erased. But such purpose binding could be bypassed by the pattern-recognition abilities of Big Data analyses, for example by changing or broadening the scope of search words that indicate a terrorist threat. Even data containing no direct hints will make Big Data analyses more effective. This may result in the temptation to record as much data as possible, for indirectly they may help to fulfil the purposes laid down in § 5 I G 10.

Analysing personal data

According to § 4 BNDG, the same strictures apply to analyses of personal data by the BND as for the Federal Office of the Protection of the Constitution. According to §§ 4 and 6 G 10, telecommunications data may only be used for intelligence purposes and in criminal prosecutions. This means that Big Data analyses by the BND are not permitted to comprehensively screen the raw data stream but only the data remaining after an initial review regarding relevance for intelligence purposes.

10.8   APPROACHES TO A CONSTITUTION-COMPATIBLE REGULATION OF BIG DATA BY POLICE AND INTELLIGENCE SERVICES

In order to be able to apply Big Data analytics, the question will be raised whether the provisions outlined in the previous section should not be extended or interpreted broadly. This, in turn, raises the question of whether such extensions are compatible with the right to Informational Self-Determination. A regulation compatible with the constitution would have to start from the jurisdiction outlined in section 10.3. The different possibilities to apply Big Data would also have to be considered: individualized surveillance, situational pattern recognition, and the prediction of human behaviour. Although they are related, they will not be adequately covered by the same legal instruments.

10.8.1   RISKS TO BASIC RIGHTS

Recommendations for regulation must follow from an assessment of risks to basic rights.

Individualized surveillance

Using Big Data to search for an offender, a suspected offender, or individuals or groups causing risks, well-known risks to basic rights are to be expected. By the standards shown in section 10.3, such searches will usually mean a very severe encroachment on Informational Self-Determination. Since Big Data analyses make use of more data from more sources, analyses might yield deeper insights into areas with special basic rights protection, including more comprehensive conclusions concerning the personality of the data subject. This might be lessened if specific characteristics would not be permitted to be used in analysis (see section 10.8.2). Comparing the profiles to individual persons would, as in recent dragnet investigations, be conducted without individual suspicion (see BVerfGE 115, 320 [355]).

However, data subjects would be even less able to assess what behaviour has been extracted as an indicator of threats and would be unable to adapt to surveillance or evade surveillance through compliant behaviour. A Big Data search would moreover have wide scope: it would concern all persons with whom the profile is compared, not only those who show the characteristics. Depending on the spread of the indicators, many people in this last group would become the targets of further surveillance or other encroachments on their liberties (see BVerfGE 115, 320 [357]).

The new challenge for basic rights is that recent principles for the protection of Informational Self-Determination and Secrecy of Telecommunications such as *purpose binding, necessity, data reduction and data economy* are losing their effect as huge amounts of data drawn from all kinds of purpose contexts become necessary for Big Data searches.

Pattern recognition

Big Data analytics reach a new dimension when used to extract new patterns indicating security-relevant situations. This may be done using statistical, aggregated data rendered anonymous, which then does not fall under data protection law. This data may come from any area of life and need not have a causal or obvious connection to security-relevant behaviour. It may also cover behaviour (recently) seen as normal.

Big Data through this kind of pattern recognition has normative effects. Since patterns cover not only security-relevant behaviour but also unremarkable behaviour correlating to security-relevant behaviour, resulting measures may encroach on the freedoms of people acting in full accordance with the law. In order to evade these disadvantages, the data subjects will try to adapt their behaviour to the patterns, as far as they will be known or will be feared to lead to disadvantages. Through this normative effect, Big Data might indirectly but effectively hinder the practice of basic rights. Anonymous Big Data patterns might thus have the same dampening effects on individual personality development, free communication and will forming in society as the Constitutional Court found in its Census Judgement on individualized surveillance (BVerfGE 65, 1 ([43]). And since Big Data analytics can recognize ever newer patterns, it becomes impossible to assess which behaviours might indicate security risks. From this will follow a diffuse feeling of non-conformity and efforts to maintain conforming (unremarkable) behaviour.

Informational Self-Determination in its current shape does not fully suffice to protect citizens against this normative effect of Big Data. Recognition of suspect behaviour patterns can be conducted using anonymous data, for which data protection law does not apply. The data become personal data only when the pattern is applied to individuals. No individual will be surveilled in pattern recognition; all citizens will be surveilled anonymously, and only then will relevant characteristics be extracted to sort people. Big Data analytics' influence on behaviour thus does not require data to be personal. Where data protection law begins to apply – at the moment the pattern is applied to an individual leading to an encroachment of the individual's freedom – data protection law will no longer help. Data protection law generally prohibits the processing of personal data not necessary for legitimate purposes. But by this stage the Big Data analysis will have shown that people with this behaviour pattern are dangerous and that the processing of their personal data is necessary for the fulfilment of police or intelligence work.

Behaviour prediction

The use of Big Data analytics by police and intelligence agencies to predict future individual behaviour would raise fundamental issues with the rule of law. Far-reaching investigations would precede suspicions and threats, and would further expand preventive security. Through such analyses and the measures following from them, fundamental principles such as guilt, responsibility and even human freedom of action would be placed in question. It remains absolutely unclear how data subjects could defend themselves against such Big Data results, how they would be supposed to challenge and disprove them, for they predict *future* behaviour.

But even the prediction of the locations and time periods of security-relevant behaviour causes problems with the rule of law. Indeed, the prognoses only cover dangerous time periods and threatened locations and do not involve personal data. But during patrols, suspicion of criminal behaviour or threat will be transferred to citizens in the location at the time. The correlations extracted by Big Data analytics will probably lead to discriminatory effects. They will probably also bias police and intelligence officers, who will then be unable to treat a data subject impartially.

10.8.2 RECOMMENDATIONS FOR REGULATION

There has to date been no academic discussion on the application of Big Data by police and intelligence agencies. Therefore, it is not possible to present a systematic concept. The following is limited to the individual aspects of a possible legal policy.

Individualized surveillance

Insofar as searches using Big Data are similar to dragnet investigations, one might think of applying to Big Data searches the provisions and requirements following from the jurisdiction on dragnet investigations for Big Data searches, also: They would have to be limited to personal data collected legally and observing purpose binding and there would have to be a connection between the data and the intended insight (BVerfGE 115, 320 [367]; see also § 5 Abs. 2 Satz 1 G 10). Provisions concerning the findings of dragnet investigations – especially purpose binding and erasure of data – would have to be observed. Although this will limit the effectiveness of Big Data analytics, it will safeguard Informational Self-Determination.

Further approaches may be derived from discussion on provisions which do not apply to police and intelligence agencies. According to § 28b Nr. 1 BDSG, scoring results must follow from data shown by a scientifically approved mathematical-statistical method to be relevant for the probability of the particular behaviour. Only data that has considerable impact on the result would be permitted for use in individualized Big Data analyses. While this would forbid some characteristics to be used in dragnet investigations, data from principally all areas of life could still be used.

It appears to be more promising to limit the data permitted to be compared statistically with regard to content/topic from the start. Especially such characteristics should be considered here, which are already counted to be discriminating. The draft of the European Parliament for a General Data Protection Regulation decrees in Art. 20 concrete discriminations disallowed for profiling. This recommendation does not apply to security agencies. While Art. 9 of the draft for a EU Directive on the processing of personal data for crime prevention and prosecution contains no similar restraint, similar restraints are not alien to the security agencies. For example, § 5 II 2 G 10 prohibits search words touching on the core area of private life. It should be discussed for each individual case which other characteristics might be excluded from the authority of the security agencies, without rendering their assignments impossible. It might also be possible to allow using discriminating characteristics by tying their use to additional thresholds.

Given the ability of Big Data analytics to de-anonymise data, data protection law needs to be extended with preventive provisions covering the processing of anonymous data and aliased data. The provisions need to consider that anonymous profiles of persons can become personal data at a single stroke.

Pattern recognition

We must consider a restriction on comparable characteristics for pattern recognition in threat prevention and intelligence work. Through the statistical-correlative approach, principally any behaviour might become suspicious. However, a democratic state abiding by the rule of law must impose restraints on itself and its security agencies concerning knowledge, if it is not to become totalitarian:

> "It would not be compatible with Human Dignity, if the state would make a claim for itself to the right to register and catalogue the human being in all its personality, *even in the anonymity of a purely statistical census*, and by that treat humans as things which may be inventoried in every aspect" (BVerfGE 27, 1 [6], translation and accentuation by the authors).

There must remain an area which is not only anonymous but is unknown in content. Provisions for the extraction of characteristics that would determine which expressions of life may be statistically analysed and which may not will be necessary.

As with protection against total surveillance, influence on behaviour through recognition of security-relevant patterns needs to be limited and encroachments on freedom and equality rights must be avoided. This objective might be reached by reviewing and correcting the patterns before their application, and especially before their publication, in order to avoid encroachments on freedom and equality rights. Measures following from the application of patterns by police and intelligence agencies should only be permitted after additional requirements and preventive reviews have been met, so that behaviour does not automatically lead to negative consequences only because it fits a pattern.

Behaviour prediction

Several German Länder have announced that they want to test predictive policing. Bayern has already begun (Biermann 2015). It is completely unclear, however, on basis of which legal provision this operation is being conducted. To date, there has hardly been any legal academic discussion on behaviour prediction in the security sector. Due to the risks to basic rights outlined in section 10.8.1), specific provisions must be demanded which determine minimum standards for the systems and for use of their findings, such as restraints on characteristics which may not be used due to their discriminative potential, or restraints on measures that are permitted to follow from prognoses. Furthermore police officers must be enabled to treat the results, presented to them by the systems with scepticism.

10.9   CONCLUSION

The basic right to Informational Self-Determination has shown itself to be eligible
for the protection of freedom of decision and freedom of action in a digitalized
world. Freedom of personality, freedom to evolve, and democratic engagement are
only possible if the societal order of communication is based on the principle that
every individual may decide for him or herself about the processing of their own
personal data. However, the protection principles derived from Informational
Self-Determination, however (purpose binding, necessity, data reduction and data
economy, transparency and control) fail in practice with Big Data, since the
Big Data approach undermines the intended restrictions.

The application of Big Data analytics by police and intelligence agencies is only
permitted within the narrow boundaries set forth in effective provisions; processing huge amounts of personal data from different sources is limited by the provision on purpose binding. If Big Data analytics are to be applied, new protection
principles for procedures using personal data must be found. As for situational and
behavioural pattern recognition, Informational Self-Determination on its own
does not suffice to protect freedom of decision and freedom of action against the
normative effects of Big Data analysis. To limit the freedom-restricting powers of
statistics, limits must be determined as to what is worth knowing and what is
worth implementing.

REFERENCES

Bäcker, M. (2014a) *Erhebung, Bevorratung und Übermittlung von Telekommunikationsdaten durch die Nachrichtendienste des Bundes, Stellungnahme zur Anhörung des NSA-Untersuchungsausschusses*, 22 May 2014.

Bäcker, M. (2014b) 'Strategische Telekommunikationsüberwachung auf dem Prüfstand', *Kommunikation & Recht* 556, 9.

Biermann, K. (2015) 'Noch hat niemand bewiesen, dass Data Mining der Polizei hilft', available at: www.zeit.de/digital/datenschutz/2015-03/predictive-policing-software-polizei-precobs [29 March 2015].

Erbentraut, J. (2014) 'Chicago's Controversial New Police Program Prompts Fears of Racial Profiling', *The Huffington Post*, available at: www.huffingtonpost.com/2014/02/25/chicago-police-home-visits-_n_4855319.html [25 February 2014].

Greenwald, G. (2014) *No Place to Hide*, New York: Metropolitan Books/Henry Holt.

Katko P. and A. Babaei-Beigi (2014) 'Accountability statt Einwilligung? Führt Big Data zum Paradigmenwechsel im Datenschutz?', *Multimedia und Recht: MMR: Zeitschrift für Informations-, Telekommunikations- und Medienrecht* 17, 6: 360.

Mayer-Schönberger, V. and K. Cukier (2013) *Big Data – Die Revolution, die unser Leben verändern wird*, München: Redline Verlag.

N-TV (2014) 'In sozialen Netzwerken live dabei – BND plant Echtzeitanalyse', available at: www.n-tv.de/politik/BND-plant-Echtzeitanalyse-article12931546.html [31 May 2014].

Ohrtmann, J. and S. Schwiering (2014) 'Big Data und Datenschutz – Rechtliche Herausforderungen und Lösungsansätze', *Neue Juristische Wochenschrift*: 2984.

Peschel, C. and S. Rockstroh (2014) 'Big Data in der Deutschen Industrie, Chancen und Risiken neuer datenbasierter Dienste', *Multimedia und Recht*: 571.

Roßnagel, A. (2011) 'Das Gebot der Datenvermeidung und -sparsamkeit als Ansatz wirksamen technikbasierten Persönlichkeitsschutzes?', pp. 41 in M. Eifert, W. Hoffmann-Riem (eds.) *Innovation, Recht und öffentliche Kommunikation*, Berlin.

Roßnagel, A. (2013) 'Big Data - Small Privacy? Konzeptionelle Herausforderungen für das Datenschutzrecht', *Zeitschrift für Datenschutz* 3, 11: 562-567.

Roßnagel, A., A. Pfitzmann and H. Garstka (2001) *Modernisierung des Datenschutzrechts*, Berlin: Bundesministerium des Innern.

Steinmüller, W. (1993) *Informationstechnologie und Gesellschaft*, Darmstadt: Wissenschaftliche Buchgesellschaft.

Trute, H. (2003) 'Verfassungsrechtliche Fragen des Datenschutzrechts', pp. 156 in A. Roßnagel (ed.) *Handbuch Datenschutzrecht*, München.

Weichert, T. (2013) 'Big Data und Datenschutz. Chancen und Risiken einer neuen Form der Datenanalyse', *Zeitschrift für Datenschutz* 6: 251-258.

Weichert, T. (2014) 'Scoring in Zeiten von Big Data', *Zeitschrift für Rechtspolitik* 47, 6: 168-171.

Zetter, K. (2013) 'US Cities Employ Precog Algorithm to Predict Murder', Wired.co.uk,
        available at: www.wired.co.uk/news/archive/2013-01/11/precog-algorithm
        [11 January 2013].

Legal Documents

BDSG (*Bundesdatenschutzgesetz*)	Federal Data Protection Act
BNDG (Gesetz über den Bundesnachrichtendienst)	Federal Intelligence Service Act
BVerfSchG (*Bundesverfassungsschutzgesetz*)	Code for the Federal Office
GG (*Grundgesetz*)	Constitution
HSOG	The Police Code of Hessen
StPO	Federal code of criminal procedure

Case Law

BVerfGE 27, 1
BVerfGE 34, 238
BVerfGE 39, 1
BVerfGE 53, 30
BVerfGE 63, 131
BVerfGE 65, 1
BVerfGE 84, 192
BVerfGE 100, 313
BVerfGE 107, 299
BVerfGE 109, 279
BVerfGE 110, 33
BVerfGE 113, 348
BVerfGE 115, 166
BVerfGE 115, 320
BVerfGE 118, 168
BVerfGE 120, 274
BVerfGE 125, 260
BVerfG 2006, 979
BVerfG, NJW 2008, 822
SächsVerfGH, JZ 1996, 957 [964]

ABOUT THE AUTHORS

Robin M. Bayley is President of Linden Consulting Inc., Privacy & Policy Advisors. She holds a Master's Degree in Public Administration from the University of Victoria. She has co-authored several chapters and reports on privacy regulation and methodologies such as privacy impact assessments. She helps organizations subject to Canadian privacy laws identify privacy risks and address them with policies and processes, and has assisted privacy regulators in developing privacy compliance guides and tools for organizations and the public.

Colin J. Bennett is a professor at the University of Victoria, where he has taught in the Department of Political Science since 1987. His research has focused on the comparative analysis of surveillance technologies and privacy protection policies at the domestic and international levels. In addition to numerous scholarly and newspaper articles, he has published six books, including *The Governance of Privacy* (MIT Press 2006) and *The Privacy Advocates: Resisting the Spread of Surveillance* (MIT Press 2008), as well as policy reports on privacy protection for Canadian and international agencies. He is currently researching the capture and use of personal data by political parties in Western democracies.

Rosamunde van Brakel is a researcher and doctoral candidate at Vrije Universiteit Brussel (VUB) who is finalising her PhD in criminology: *Taming the future? A rhizomatic analysis of preemptive surveillance of children and its consequences.* In addition to this she is director of the NGO Privacy Salon and managing coordinator of the annual international conference Computers, Privacy and Data Protection. In recent years she has published articles in the fields of policing, (mass) surveillance, law and technology-based strategies.

Dennis Broeders is a senior research fellow and project coordinator at the Netherlands Scientific Council for Government Policy (WRR) and Professor of Technology and Society at Erasmus University Rotterdam. His research interest broadly focuses on the interaction between technology, policy and society, with a specific interest in cyber security and internet governance as well as surveillance and migration control. He has published articles in various leading international journals in the fields of sociology, political science and criminology. At the Council, he currently heads the project 'Big data, privacy, and security', which resulted in the report *Big Data in a Free and Secure Society* (Big Data in een vrije en veilige samenleving).

Gemma Galdon Clavell is Director of Eticas Research & Consulting, where her work is focused on building socio-technical data architectures that incorporate legal, social and ethical concerns in their conception, production and implementation. She is a policy analyst by training and has worked on projects relating to surveillance and human rights and values, the societal impact of technology, smart cities, privacy, security policy, resilience and policing. She completed her PhD on surveillance, security and urban policy at the Universitat Autònoma de Barcelona, where she also obtained an MSc in Policy Management, and was later appointed Director of the Security Policy Programme at the Universitat Oberta de Catalunya (UOC).

Seda Gürses is a Postdoctoral Research Associate at CITP, Princeton University and an FWO fellow at COSIC, KU Leuven University in Belgium. Her work focuses on privacy and requirements engineering, privacy-enhancing technologies and surveillance. Previously she was a post-doctoral fellow at the Media, Culture and Communications Department at NYU Steinhardt and at the Information Law Institute at NYU Law School, where she was also a member of the Intel Science and Technology Center on Social Computing. She completed her PhD at the Department of Computer Science at KU Leuven and was a member of the Privacy and Identity Management Group at COSIC. She completed her Diploma in Informatics at Humboldt University in Berlin, where she also worked at the Institute of Information Systems.

Paul De Hert is Professor of Law in the Faculty of Law and Criminology at Vrije Universiteit Brussel and holds the chairs in Criminal Law, International and European Criminal Law and Historical introduction to eight major constitutional systems. He is Director of the research group on Fundamental Rights and Constitutionalism (FRC) and a senior member of the research group on Law, Science, Technology & Society (LSTS). Paul De Hert is also an associate professor in Law and Technology at the Tilburg Institute for Law and Technology (TILT). He is also a member of the editorial boards of several national and international scientific journals such as the Inter-American and European Human Rights Journal (Intersentia) and Criminal Law & Philosophy (Springer).

Joris van Hoboken is a Postdoctoral Research Fellow at the Information Law Institute at New York University, and NYU's Department for Media Culture and Communication. He is also a lecturer at CornellTech, a Visiting Scholar at the NYU Stern Center for Business & Human Rights, and an affiliate researcher at the Institute for Information Law (IViR) at the University of Amsterdam. His research addresses law and policy in the fields of digital media, electronic communications and the Internet, with a focus on the fundamental right to privacy and freedom of expression. He holds a PhD from the University of Amsterdam on search engines and freedom of expression (2012), as well as graduate degrees in Law and Theoretical Mathematics. He is Chairman of the Board of Directors of the Dutch digital rights organization Bits of Freedom.

Sander Klous is Professor of Big Data Ecosystems for Business and Society at the University of Amsterdam's (UVA) Faculty of Science. He researches the way in which business and society can responsibly maximise the benefits of insights gained through data analysis. Klous is Managing Director of Big Data Analytics at KPMG and is a member of the global leadership team at Data & Analytics, responsible for the advanced analytics infrastructure. He obtained his doctorate in high-energy physics at the National Institute for Subatomic Physics (NIKHEF), where he worked on various projects at the CERN particle accelerator. His book *We are Big Data* was runner-up in the management book of the year awards in 2015.

Hans Lammerant has studied philosophy and law and is a PhD researcher at the Law, Science, Technology and Society-research group (LSTS) at Vrije Universiteit Brussel (VUB). Currently he's working on the BYTE-project (www.byte-project.eu), which investigates positive and negative externalities of Big Data and is developing a roadmap and community to address these externalities. In his research he focuses on the impact of new developments in data science and statistics on surveillance and privacy, and law in general.

Bart Preneel is a professor at KU Leuven University, where he heads the COSIC research group, a member of the iMinds research centre. He has written more than 400 scientific publications and is an inventor who holds five patents. His main research interests are cryptography, information security and privacy. He is president of the not-for-profit organisation LSEC vzw (Leaders in Security) and a former president of IACR. He has served as a panel member and chair of the European Research Council. He is a fellow of International Association for Cryptologic Research(IACR), a member of the Permanent Stakeholders group of ENISA (European Network and Information Security Agency) and of the Academia Europaea. In 2014 he received the RSA Award for Excellence in the Field of Mathematics.

Philipp Richter has been managing director of the Project Group Constitution Compatible Technology Design (provet) at the University of Kassel since September 2015. He obtained his legal degree in 2009 in Berlin. He subsequently joined provet, starting his research in a project on the legally compatible design of online voting systems, obtaining his doctorate on the same topic in 2012. From 2011 to 2013 he worked on the research project 'Internet Privacy'. Big Data has been at the heart of his research in recent years. He frequently publishes, presents and lectures in the field of legally compatible technology design, data protection and IT law.

Alexander Roßnagel is Professor of Public Law at the University of Kassel, specialising in Environmental and Technology Law. He has been publishing books and journal articles in the fields of information technology design and data protection for many years. He obtained his doctorate in 1981 with a thesis on amendments to the German Constitution. Since 1986 he has been research director of the

Project Group Constitution Compatible Technology Design (provet). In 1991 he presented his habilitation thesis on 'Legally based Technology Impact Assessment'. In 2007 he was the first legal researcher to be appointed a fellow of the German Informatics Society (GI). From 2003 to 2011 he was Vice President of the University of Kassel. He is also Director of the Scientific Centre for Information Technology Design (ITeG) at the University of Kassel.

Erik Schrijvers is a senior research fellow and project coordinator at the Netherlands Scientific Council for Government Policy (WRR). He studied at Utrecht University, taking a degree (*cum laude*) in international relations in 2002 and in philosophy of history in 2003. He received his PhD in 2012 for a dissertation on unelected representative bodies in the Netherlands in the post-war period. At the Council, he has been working on a broad range of topics, publishing reports, edited volumes, and articles on culture and cultural policy, economic inequality, labour migration, and the marketization of public services. In 2015 and 2016, he worked on the report *Big Data in a Free and Secure Society* (Big Data in een vrije en veilige samenleving). Currently, he heads the project 'Middle-classes under pressure'.

Bart van der Sloot specializes in questions revolving around privacy and Big Data. He has worked for the Netherlands Scientific Council for Government Policy (WRR) on a report on the regulation of Big Data in relation to privacy and security (*Big Data in een vrije en veilige samenleving*). Funded by a Top Talent grant from The Netherlands Organization for Scientific Research (NWO), his current research at the Institute for Information Law (University of Amsterdam) analyses the dominant privacy paradigm, which is focused on the individual and their interests. He is general editor of the European Data Protection Law Review and coordinator of the Amsterdam Platform for Privacy Research (APPR), which incorporates around 70 researches from the University of Amsterdam who focus on privacy-related issues in their daily research and teaching.

For Product Safety Concerns and Information please contact our EU
representative GPSR@taylorandfrancis.com
Taylor & Francis Verlag GmbH, Kaufingerstraße 24, 80331 München, Germany